PILGRIMAGE OF THE HEART

PILGRIMAGE
OF THE
HEART

—

A TREASURY OF
EASTERN CHRISTIAN SPIRITUALITY

—

Edited by George A. Maloney, S.J.

1817

Harper & Row, Publishers, San Francisco

Cambridge, Hagerstown, New York, Philadelphia
London, Mexico City, São Paulo, Sydney

FIRST EDITION

Designer: Jim Mennick

Library of Congress Cataloging in Publication Data

Main entry under title:

PILGRIMAGE OF THE HEART.

Bibliography: p.
1. Spiritual life—Addresses, essays, lectures. I. Maloney, George A., 1924-   .
BV4495.P56   1983   248.4'802   82-48933
ISBN 0-06-065413-9

83 84 85 86 87   10 9 8 7 6 5 4 3 2 1

To Barbara and Jack Warburton,
who have integrated beautifully
into their marriage and family life
the Eastern and Western
Christian spirituality

CONTENTS

ACKNOWLEDGMENTS

I wish to thank the following publishers for their kindness in permitting me to include these selections:

Faber & Faber of London for selections from *The Philokalia: The Complete Text,* Vol. 1, tr. and ed. by G. E. H. Palmer, Philip Sherrard, Kallistos Ware, et al. (London, 1979); *Philokalia: Early Fathers from the Philokalia,* tr. by E. Kadloubovsky and G. E. H. Palmer (London, 1954); *Philokalia: Writings from the Philokalia on Prayer of the Heart,* tr. by E. Kadloubovsky and G. E. H. Palmer (London, 1951); *St. John Climacus: The Ladder of Divine Ascent,* tr. by Archimandrite Lazarus Moore (London, 1959); *The Art of Prayer: An Orthodox Anthology,* compiled by Igumen Chariton of Valamo, tr. by E. Kadloubovsky and G. E. H. Palmer (London, 1966).

Wm. B. Eerdmans Publishing Co. for selections from *The Ante-Nicene Fathers,* ed. by A. Roberts and J. Donaldson (Grand Rapids, Mich., n.d.) and *The Nicene and Post Nicene Fathers,* tr. by Philip Schaff and Henry Wace, Second Series (Grand Rapids, Mich.).

Paulist Press for selections from their Classics of Western Spirituality: *Symeon the New Theologian: The Discourses,* tr. by C. J. de Catanzaro (New York, 1980); *Origen: Exhortation to Martyrdom; Prayer; First Principles,* tr. by Rowan A. Greer (New York, 1979).

St. Vladimir's Orthodox Theological Seminary Press for selections from *The Life in Christ* by Nicholas Cabasilas, tr. by C. J. de Catanzaro (Crestwood, N.Y., 1974) and *St. Gregory Palamas and Orthodox Spirituality,* by John Meyendorff, tr. by Adele Fiske (Crestwood, N.Y., 1974).

Cistercian Publications for selections from *Evagrius Ponticus: Praktikos and Chapters on Prayer,* tr. by John Eudes Bamberger, O.C.S.O., Cistercian Studies no. 4 (Spencer, Mass., 1970).

The Society for Promoting Christian Knowledge (S.P.C.K.) for selections for world rights for the two volumes just cited from Paulist

Press's Classics of Western Spirituality: *Symeon the New Theologian: The Discourses* and *Origen: Exhortation to Martyrdom* and for selections from *A Commentary on the Divine Liturgy,* tr. by J. M. Hussey and P. A. McNulty (London, 1960) and St. John Chrysostom, *Six Books on the Priesthood,* tr. by Graham Neville (London, 1964).

The University Press of America for selections from *Dionysius Pseudo-Areopagite: The Ecclesiastical Hierarchy,* tr. by Thomas L. Campbell (Washington, D.C., 1981).

C. Scribner's Sons for selections from *From Glory to Glory: Texts from Gregory of Nyssa's Mystical Writings,* tr. and ed. by Herbert Musurillo, S.J. (New York, 1961).

Sheed & Ward for selections from *A Treasury of Russian Spirituality,* ed. by G. P. Fedotov (New York, 1948).

John XXIII Center for Eastern Christian Studies at Fordham University for selections from *The Byzantine Liturgy of St. John Chrysostom,* tr. and ed. by Russian Center (New York, 1955).

Alleluia Press for selections from *Byzantine Daily Worship,* ed. by Archbishop Joseph Raya and Jose de Vinck (Allendale, N.J., 1969).

Ancient Christian Writers Series for selections from *St. Gregory of Nyssa: The Lord's Prayer; The Beatitudes,* tr. by H. Graef, Vol. 18 (Westminster, Md., 1954); *Origen: Prayer; Exhortation to Martyrdom,* tr. by John J. O'Meara, Vol. 19 (Westminster, Md., 1954).

The Liturgical Press for selections from *The Faith of the Early Fathers,* tr. and ed. by W. A. Jurgens (Collegeville, Minn., 1970).

Personal gratitude is extended to Rita Ruggiero, Delene Brown, and Deacon Gabriel Seamore for their help in preparing the manuscript and to John Loudon, Editorial Manager of Harper & Row San Francisco, for his many helpful suggestions and encouragement.

INTRODUCTION: EASTERN CHRISTIAN SPIRITUALITY

A very encouraging sign of the times in America and Europe today is the thirst for religious experience and the world of the "spirit," especially among the young. Many are looking into ancient religious disciplines for techniques to expand their consciousness beyond the black and white background of a consumerist culture. Others are searching, through physical exercise, music, even drugs, to touch the realm of bliss and peace that will allow them to cope with what they conceive as an otherwise meaningless world.

Such interior searching is not without its dilettantes, those who give up on their own contemporary culture to find refuge in a counterculture of another time and race of people. Such pilgrims into the inner quest often lose their way and have little to offer their contemporary society.

Many Christians of the West have felt a need for a spiritual vision to offset the Augustinian Platonism that has cluttered up Western Christianity with an un-Christian separation of nature and supernature and with a heavy dichotomy between the human body and soul, the world of matter and spirit, the secular and the sacred. Some have turned to ancient spiritual teachings of the Christian East to find a vision of the Christian life quite different from that of the West.

Such a view, from the Eastern Christian world—out of which Christianity first evolved in what is today the Middle and Near East—has its roots in the experiences of the first Christian communities. These experiences matured during the blood baths of the

early Christian martyrs who sought to capture the crown of martyrdom and thus be united with the Lord Jesus; for example, St. Ignatius of Antioch (†115) desired to be ground wheat to make the
bread of Christ's Body. In the golden period of "theologizing" about
the Christian life in the face of heresies that rose up in the fourth
through the sixth centuries, theologians who were also mystics developed for future generations a dynamic view of the spiritual life
that still offers us modern Christians a rich spirituality.

The Eastern Fathers, because they were close in time and experience to the pristine message of the Gospel, had the unique quality
of piercing through spatial and temporal concepts by viewing the
history of salvation, our relationship to God, not from our myopic
point of view, but from the all-encompassing view of God Almighty.
This fourth-dimensional perspective viewed God's extratrinitarian
activity as a unity—unfolding, it is true, in time and space, but one,
because of the love that remained constant. God's infinite love initiated the first act of creation, and the same dynamic divine love
evolves this initial creation into the fullness of his plan as the whole
universe moves under God's divine, uncreated energies of love in
cooperation with human beings into the full amorization of the "new
creation," foretold by St. Paul (2 Cor. 5:17-19).

Meaning of Spirituality

One of the most difficult concepts to define concretely and ade-
quately is that of spirituality.[1] Basically, the term *spirituality* refers to
the particular way in which one conceives and realizes the ideal of
his or her religious existence. In the Christian context, it refers to
the Holy Spirit, who guides the individual into the mystery of Christian faith. The individual—according to his or her own proper
genius, vocation, and charismatic gifts—cooperates with God's trinitarian action in sharing his divine life with his children in Christ
Jesus through his Holy Spirit.

Can we speak of various spiritualities within the same Christian
faith? Much has been written about two Christian spiritualities or
two theologies, that of the East and that of the West. But are there
really two different approaches to God? Are there two spiritualities
that each teaches us something completely different about how to
attain the Christian goal: union with the Divine Trinity? Are these
two spiritualities worlds apart, or are they merely two complemen-

tary visions of one and the same Christian life, each vitally needed, each dependent on the other for its own integral fulfillment?

An Eastern Perspective

Through centuries in which the Christian Churches of the East and West lived in "splendid isolation" from each other, polemic writers of each Church accentuated these differences and in a triumphant arrogance denigrated the other to support their own vision. Both Catholics and Protestants caricatured the Orthodox traditions, while the Orthodox also wrote of the Western Christian spirituality in terms that did not always reflect loving Christian fellowship.

But when we list differences between the Orthodox and the Catholic viewpoints, we could often easily apply to St. Augustine what we apply to St. Gregory Palamas. Nine out of ten times St. Augustine could be labeled an Oriental Christian. There is nothing so specifically Eastern as an icon. Yet would we have to call the twelfth-century Italians who specialized in so many beautiful mosaic icons Orthodox or Eastern Christians? Would we say that the monks on Mount Athos were crypto-Romans because in the eighteenth and nineteenth centuries they painted their icons in a fashion that was very common in Naples? Would we say that an Orthodox was being untrue to his tradition if he had a great desire to receive the Eucharist daily?

Once, on a visit to Mount Athos, I met a monk who handed me the book of Nicodemus of Mount Athos (eighteenth century): *The Invisible Warfare*. The monk said, "If you Westerns want something that is purely Eastern, read this book." But it is well known that this book is practically a translation of Italian Lorenzo Scupoli's *The Spiritual Combat*, which he wrote after the Council of Trent (1545–1563)!

Is there really, therefore, a spirituality that is typically Eastern Christian? The essential elements of the Christian message must be the same in both traditions, East and West. But a faith experience with basically the same teachings coming out of God's revelation in Scripture and tradition and the same sacraments and liturgy within an apostolically united hierarchy will necessarily be handed on in time and space according to varying cultural elements. The culture of the Jewish-Christian world of Antioch and Syria would bring forth a different expression of the Christian life from that evoked by the culture of the eleventh-century Celtic missionaries.

Even in speaking of the Christian East there may be a greater difference between a Russian and an Ethiopian than between a Russian Orthodox and a Roman Catholic. But in general some common features are attributable to all Eastern Christians, due to the common sources of the East, such as the spiritual literature of the early Church Fathers, the spirituality of the desert monks, and the highly liturgical and mystical quality of Eastern Christian spirituality.

There is only one revealed truth. Christians use the same sources of revelation: Scripture and tradition, as expounded by the living magisterium through the workings of the same Holy Spirit down through the centuries. Yet within the ambit of the teaching body in the Church we discover in the theological and spiritual writings of both the Eastern and Western traditions a great deal of individuality. Each cultural group developed its own approach to the spiritual life, its own peculiar points of emphasis.

In an attempt to draw out some of the most salient and distinctive elements in what we could call Eastern Christian spirituality, let us in this chapter travel through the pages of writers who lived in the traditions of the Christian East. Let us keep in mind that the same Holy Spirit is never a respecter of persons or even of given cultures. Or, better, let us remember that cultures are not tightly sealed compartments that cannot allow for acculturation and cross-fertilization with other cultures. Hence we cannot maintain that certain emphases discovered in the spiritual writings of the Eastern Christians, for example, are never to be found among Western writers. We offer these elements as constitutive parts of a consistent view of the Christian life that form a whole religious *Weltanschauung* that we will nominally call Eastern Christian spirituality.

Early Christianity

The first source of Eastern Christian spirituality is, obviously, rooted in early Christianity. That spirituality was a practical science, a way of life in God. The articulation of that science followed practical experience. The earliest Christians were mainly concerned with living the new-found faith in simple obedience to the message of the Gospel. In the midst of paganism, the followers of Christ gave witness to the "good news" that Jesus Christ came to bring us all. We find a stark living-out of the commandments of Christ, especially those of fraternal charity, without any desire to speculate on the *why.* The event that Christ concretized by his incarnation was a vivid experience, not only through the mystical, resurrectional life of Christ living in the souls of his early followers through grace but also through a closeness in time and space to the historical person himself.

Gradually, especially through attempts to explain this living experience "in Christ" to neighboring pagans and Jews or to preserve the revealed truths from heretical teachings, there arose in the early Church not only among Christian philosophers and theologians but a tradition accessible to all Christians, of reflective knowledge concerning the human relationship to God in his or her last end. Christians felt the necessity of living reflectively and consciously their faith. They had no Christian heritage or culture that permeated society at each step and held them in a Christian milieu. They had to create this milieu for themselves. And they began this process of Christian reflection by asking themselves what was the end meaning of their lives.

The Goal of the Spiritual Life

The early Christian firmly seized this fundamental truth. The goal of life was simply *salvation.* The Greek word for salvation, *soteria,* was rich with nuances that are lost to us in our simple translation. For Plato, *soteria* meant security, a state of prosperity, good health, well-being. Human beings have a natural will, a *physicon thelema,* to seek their own happiness or well-being. But the pagan Hellenic philosophers did not agree as to what made up this goal of all human desires. The Epicureans sought their happiness in material and intellectual pleasures. The Platonists sought it in the contemplation of the eternal ideas. Stoics strove to acquire it through the acquisition of virtues and the deadening of inordinate passions.

The Christians knew that happiness was the fulfillment of the total person, according to the potentialities placed in him or her by the Creator. St. Irenaeus († c. 200), Bishop of Lyons, says the glory of God is humanity living fully. St. Paul exhorts the early Christians to prepare in this life for the coming of the Lord: "and may you all be kept safe and blameless, spirit, soul and body, for the coming of our Lord Jesus Christ" (1 Thess. 5:23).

Salvation or total human happiness was effected in God and only by God. Plato and the early pagan philosophers at the time of the proximate dawning of Christianity seemed to sense this, as Festugiere writes: "Perfect happiness for human beings is in the union with the ideas or more correctly, with the One, the good, with God."[2] Still, Plato felt that people could attain this state of complete happiness through their own innate powers. Christians, on the contrary, recognized that this was the goal of humanity, yet that it could be attained only through the grace of God.

In the Old Testament, God is praised as the savior. Human salvation, human happiness on this earth, consists in serving God. The most characteristic trait of the Old Testament and the most related bond to the concept of grace in the New Testament is that of *hesed,* the condescending merciful love of God in his covenant made with humanity. *Hesed* made the Israelite approach God with confidence because *hesed* was based on the eternal word of God that he would not turn away from his chosen people but that he would protect them from all harm and make them prosper.

In the New Testament, this belief is the basic conviction commented on by the early Church Fathers in their writings and in the Eastern liturgies; namely, that the aim of all human existence is to obtain the salvation that has been promised by God, has been worked out for us by God, and is to be found totally in God. It was God through Jesus Christ that effected salvation, which, viewed negatively, was a liberation from sin and from the power of Satan. Still viewed negatively, salvation was a liberation from the fate that had filled the pagans with black, pessimistic fatalism in their inability to cope with the problem of evil and death.

The New Testament revealed to humanity a loving father in heaven who permitted evil in order to draw out greater good in his merciful providence. Salvation was a liberation from the despair of human loneliness by incorporating the individual person into a new society, a community of the people of God, the *koinonia,* that gave individual Christians a social, spiritual life of unity with their neighbors by the bond of charity in Christ. Salvation as conceived by the New Testament, negatively, was liberation from death through the gift of eschatological life; it was freedom from mortality and corruption, achieved by making the Christian enjoy the immortality (*aphtharsia*) of the risen savior who had conquered over death and its sting. Positively, salvation is the possession of God who alone is the *good.* Possessing him, we possess the happiness for which he created us.

Salvation Only Through Christ

Jesus Christ is the fullness of God's life, the *pleroma* of whom we have even in this life received. Christ is in some way the total Christianity. This seems so evident to any Christian that we would not be surprised to find this the central point in the early Christian writings.

St. Peter insists, "For of all the names in the world given to men, this is the only one by which we can be saved" (Acts 4:12). Against heresies such as Docetism, Gnosticism, and the Christological errors of Arianism, Nestorianism, and Monophysitism, the early magisterium mounted a strenuous battle of words to retain the full Christ and the centrality of his actions in and through us to effect our salvation. Correct thinking concerning our salvation was intimately tied up with correct notions on the fundamental truth of Christianity, that of the incarnation and person of Jesus Christ.

Thus imitation of Christ, following St. Paul's constant exhortation "to become imitators of us and of the Lord" (1 Thess. 1:6), became the way of virtues that led to salvation. If Christians were enjoined by their founder to be perfect as their heavenly father was perfect, how more readily would they find the way, the truth, and the life of that perfection that was closed to human eyes, but opened to them in the incarnate person of Jesus Christ? For the first three centuries, the imitation of Christ was the center of Christian living.

In the Holy Spirit

This process of growth in Christ is effected by the Holy Spirit who is the lifegiver, the *zoopoion*, the maker of life. Whatever the Church does by way of sanctifying its members in Christ, it does through the Holy Spirit. "No one can say, 'Jesus is Lord' unless he is under the influence of the Holy Spirit" (1 Cor. 12:3). For the early Christians, *spiritual* meant not only some immaterial quality but also an effect that depended in origin and for continuation on the Holy Spirit. As the Spirit brings men and women to perfection, the spiritual person is the perfect human being. Only a spiritualized person, one in whom the Holy Spirit lives and acts, could discourse about God and give guidance in the spiritual life. From the fourth century onward, following this belief in the illumination of the Holy Spirit in true knowledge about God and his Logos, true theologians would be those who, under the illumination from the Holy Spirit, after a long purification and asceticism as preparation, wrote and discoursed about God.

Martyrdom

The Spirit of the risen savior drove the early Christians into a love of the cross and persecutions for the sake of their master. He had promised them that they would be persecuted for his name's sake, but they were to rejoice and be glad when that happened. Amidst several centuries of persecution by Roman emperors who saw Christians as stumbling blocks to their state-supported religion, early Christians saw actual shedding of their blood for Christ as the most desirable way of ending their pilgrimage on earth. Their daily lives were to be a constant preparation for their readiness to lay down their lives for Christ's name.

Thus the Eastern Christians inherited the exaltation of the cross as a basic theme and a lived experience. Sufferings accepted out of love for one another and especially for the name of Jesus, their Lord, were to be desired in the experience of daily living that death to selfishness which alone can bring a true share in the resurrectional life of Jesus.

Living in such tenuous pilgrimage, the early Christians developed a fervent eschatological hope and expectation of the *parousia* or the second coming of the Lord. Jesus had promised that he would come back again. Christians in the early Church and in the Eastern Churches strove to live detached from the things of this world in order to keep their eyes fixed always on the Lord. "Come, Lord Jesus, *Marana tha*," was their constant cry (Rev. 22:20; 1 Cor. 16:22).

Semitic Emphasis on Life

Throughout the spiritual writings of Eastern Christianity, not only in the Apostolic and Apologetic writers of the first two centuries but in the writings of later Eastern thinkers, we begin to see two tendencies that would continue as two distinct schools of Eastern spirituality. Both in the latter books of the Old Testament and in the New Testament writings, we see the parallelism between *life* and *light*. Much has been written about the characteristics of the Semite mind in the Old and New Testament writings. The Semitic emphasis is placed on the dynamic, the voluntaristic, the existential and psychological.

The Hellenic influence, especially from Platonism and Stoicism, emphasizes *light,* which represents reality as a world of static ideas, abstract and logical. The Christian Platonists, such as Clement of Alexandria, Origen, and Evagrius, developed the spiritual life as a form of Christian Gnosticism. The Christian is the Gnostic who is called to know God, to possess him and to see him. This is not merely intellectualism. It is a spiritual gift, a mystical vision that transcends all materiality. The human soul, once purified from all the worldly stains that prevent it from contemplating God as the Eternal One, becomes a mirror that reflects God. This is the nature of humanity: to reflect God as in the mirror of our human souls.

The Semitic Christianity grew up around Antioch and spread out into two directions: (1) that of St. Irenaeus and the theologians who would follow his holistic and incarnational approach and (2) that of Pseudo-Macarius and the existential transformation of the total human person, body, soul, and spirit, into the experienced indwelling of the Trinity. This spirituality was beyond human reason. Humanity did not see God in visions but, like Moses, heard God in the burning bush. Encountering God as speech to us through his word, human beings are to listen and respond by loving obedience. God is *life,* and he shares this with the humble and pure of heart.

This emphasis on life is seen strongly in the Johannine Gospel. Christ came to give us life that we might have it more abundantly (John 10:10). Jesus had said, "I am the Way, the Truth, and the Life" (John 14:6). Of 133 times in the New Testament that the word *life* is used, St. John uses it 64 times.

The Antiochene School of spirituality in the East accepted this Semitic concept as an essential part of Christ's message. He is life, our true life, our *full* life. Such writers transmit faith, the Gospel, the sacraments under the aspect of life. Faith is the germ of life. To preach the Gospel is to sow the word of life. This new life is given in baptism. It is the total person submerged in death in baptism, but also the total person who is to rise even in this life in a transformation of body, soul, and spirit into Christ's resurrection. Salvation is a process of entering more fully into the new life in Christ.

Intellectualism

Under the influence both of heresies and of Platonism and other non-Christian philosophies that became the main vehicle for the Alexandrian School of spirituality to teach Christianity, the spiritual life gradually moved from the existential, holistic life approach to a more intellectual emphasis. Werner Jaeger, who has focused on early Christianity and the Greek *paideia,* shows that Greek humanism and Hellenic culture provide thought patterns, categories of thought for the early Christian thinkers.[3]

Gradually the message of St. John's Gospel, with its strong accent on Christ as life of our souls, is seen merely as the primitive message, preserved somewhat longer in regions where Christianity had penetrated before Hellenic philosophy had a chance, as in East Syria where through political, doctrinal, and linguistic differences an Aphrahat and an Ephrem developed a Christian spirituality outside of any philosophical system. We will see also how Pseudo-Macarius, a Syrian, continued this Semitic, holistic approach to the Christian life. But under attacks from heretical teachings of Gnosticism, such theologians as St. Irenaeus, Clement of Alexandria, Origen, St. Athanasius, and the Cappadocian Fathers, St. Basil, St. Gregory of Nazianzus, and St. Gregory of Nyssa employed concepts from Platonism and even eclectic Gnosticism to develop a Christian gnosis, an intellectual contemplation, that brought about union with God on the Platonic principle that "like assimilates like."

One danger of such an intellectual emphasis, especially as taught by the Alexandrian School, was to introduce the Platonic dichotomy that severed the sensible world from the world of the intellect. The human being became principally a soul—or more precisely, the higher part of soul, the intellect—while the body was looked on as a drag, a consequence of sin. Humanity's full realization would come in suppressing the material of the body and releasing the spiritual of the intellect to contemplate a reality that existed beyond this present world.

With such an emphasis on intellectual contemplation, a spirituality of flight from encountering this present universe and becoming a leaven to the masses to effect St. Paul's "new creation" could and actually did result throughout the Byzantine world. This we must keep in mind as we see the effect of monasticism, which all too often, even today, tends toward a *Monophysitism,* an excarnation that belittles the humanity of Christ as well as the human and material existential.

Image and Likeness

One basic theme in Eastern Christian spirituality is the image and likeness doctrine leading to the divinization of humanity. This theme is so essential that to present Eastern spirituality without this predominant "theological anthropology" presupposed by all such Eastern Christian writers would be to strip Eastern spirituality of its essential uniqueness. This theme is the basic model or reference point as the early Eastern theologians discussed God in his relationship to humanity, the theory of grace and human nature, a process of continued redemption and sanctification.

Human nature for the Greek Fathers is a whole person—the body with all its senses and passions, the soul with its intellect and will, and the Spirit—all growing in a continued process of union with the triune God that begins in this earthly existence but progresses even in the life to come. The whole scope of the spiritual life and the work of Christ and his Spirit are to make a given, concrete human nature approximate that nature intended by God in his will act of giving existence to it.

Thus nature (*physis*) for the Eastern Fathers is never a universal, abstract concept. It refers always to an ontological, existing being, according to the given potencies and the plan of God with all his graces given to a concrete person in order that he or she might fulfill God's salvific designs in his or her regard and thus attain perfect, *natural* self-realization.

God Is Love

God is love, and he spills out his love in activity in the creation of men and women and the entire material universe, but also in the incarnation of his Divine Son, in his death and resurrection, in his outpouring of his Spirit, in the transformation of the entire cosmos into Christ that will be manifested as a unity only in the final *parousia* when there will be only Christ and Christ will be in all things (Col. 3:11). To exist, love must always be loving, always pouring itself out from its own abundance, always giving of itself. It is thus through God's uncreated energies of love (not created things or actions, but God in his trinitarian, personalistic relationships toward us human beings) that we can respond to his immanent indwelling to accept union with Love himself.

In this oneness of love, we become united with every other human being created and loved by God. The nature of God is such that, while being one, it demands a plurality, a many, as objects of his love, of his giving. In our constant response to this invitation of God's love consists all his greatness and fulfillment. Our loving in return (always presupposing God's grace) divinizes us, brings us into a oneness in love so that God truly lives in us by participation.

St. Irenaeus first, in the second century, developed the teaching of the image and likeness by seeking to find in God's revelation a refutation of Gnosticism that denied both the goodness inherent in God's material creation and the free will in humanity. He found his model in the first creation account in *Genesis:* "God said, Let us make man in our own image, in the likeness of ourselves" (Gen. 1:26).

St. Irenaeus considers human progress in divinization to have two stages. "According to the image" he sees as the potential that every human person always possesses to be called into an actual child of God by grace. This imageness resides in the total human person as made up of body and soul relationships. As a human person is purified by the operation of the Spirit of the risen Christ and dies to selfishness, he or she is able to actualize what is given in baptism as in a sign; namely, a likeness in consciousness is brought about by God's grace and human cooperation. This development of the likeness of Christ within the human person admits of an infinity of growth in this life and in eternity as the person yields progressively more and more in loving submission to Christ. This "likeness" is an ontological relationship between the human person and the risen Christ effected through his Holy Spirit.

Other Greek Fathers followed the framework of St. Irenaeus, but writers such as Clement of Alexandria, Origen, St. Athanasius, the Cappadocian Fathers, and St. Cyril of Alexandria tended to evolve the holistic spirituality of St. Irenaeus and the Antiochene School away from the experiential presence of the Trinity, divinizing the whole person in all body, soul, and spirit relationships toward one of a Logos mysticism.

Logos Mysticism

The great emphasis of the Neo-Platonic Christian writers, led by Origen, evolved around the Logos doctrine. Christ is the Word, the Logos, through whom God speaks to us, and in that speech we have our being. The abyss between the ineffable God and our human, created nothingness is spanned by the Logos. The whole world is created in him (John 1:2), and we can return back to God only through contemplating the inner presence of the divine Logos in all things.

St. Maximus the Confessor (†662), coming at the end of the great period of theologians, fought to clarify a balanced Christology against the many christological heresies that sprang up in the first seven centuries of Christianity. He develops a complete vision of a Logos mysticism. For Maximus, as for St. John the Evangelist, the whole world is interrelated in its harmony according to the differentiated *logoi* or the created existences of individual things according to the mind of God. All things are created through the Logos, through whom the creative will of the Father finds materialized expression.

We become divinized as we cooperate freely to live according to our own full Logos that can be actualized only in a conscious, loving union with Jesus Christ, God's Logos made flesh. We have our total being insofar as we have a loving relationship to Christ, allowing him to fulfill within us that imageness destined to be brought to perfection in our first creation by the potency God has given to us. This imageness or Logos is to be actuated by a lifetime of knowledge and virtue. But *philautia* or self-love destroys this Logos relationship in us. "Love, the divine gift, perfects human nature until it makes it appear in unity and identity by grace with the divine nature," writes St. Maximus.[4]

Orthodox Christology

In the Eastern Christian tradition, the theologian, as Evagrius of the fourth century wrote, is one who prays. And if one prays, he will be a theologian. One cannot speak of Eastern Christian spirituality without speaking of theology, for in the East "to do theology" is to go out in search of God. It is a search that leads inevitably to the discovery of humanity. It is a search that, while employing reason and philosophical concepts, leads to an encounter on the other side of reason. St. Gregory of Nyssa, one of the great Eastern theologians, describes this approach: "Concepts create idols and only wonder lays hold upon something." To do theology is to participate in the living reality of the Christ who by the Spirit offers himself to us every day in the private conversation of prayer, in the coming together of the Christian community daily to offer the Eucharist, in the living Word of the Bible, in each of us individually and in every person whom God calls us to serve and heal by God's healing love within us.

What should have been a continued experience in the spiritual lives of the early Christians became threatened in its reality by heresies that rose up to disfigure God's objective, historical breaking in to the human race through his son, Jesus Christ. Theologians such as St. Irenaeus, Clement of Alexandria, Origen, St. Athanasius, St. Cyril of Alexandria, and the Cappodocian Fathers, St. Basil, St. Gregory of Nazianzus, and St. Gregory of Nyssa saw their mission as one of formulating clearly in human concepts the boundaries, the "definitions" or parameters beyond which one would no longer be truly a Christian embracing God's revealed Word.

Perhaps no other early Christian writer was a greater defender of the divinity and equality of Jesus Christ with the Father against the heretical Arians, who denied the divinity of Jesus Christ, and against the non-Christians, than was St. Athanasius. He clearly saw that if Christ were not totally divine, we would not have yet been redeemed. He shows that Christ is the divine Logos, the image of the Father but a likeness of absolute equality, a perfection mirroring the total being of the Father. The Logos is begotten, "engendered," but not extrinsic nor foreign to the Father. To participate in being is to bespeak a relationship to the divine Logos. The Logos unites all things in a harmony, one with another, and brings them all back to God. He gives to Christian theology the term *homoousios* to describe the equality in essence of the Logos made flesh with the Father.

The Logos incarnate comes to restore humanity to the imageness that we possessed before sin but he adds a new grace, a new incarnational relationship between humans and the Word-made-flesh, the risen Savior. Divinization, or our sharing of God's very own divine life, is now possible, and the life of virtue in imitation of the indwelling Jesus Christ is our proper response.

One of the classics of Christian spiritual writing that offered a model frequently imitated in the writings about the lives of the Saints was written by St. Athanasius on the life of St. Antony, one of the first great hermits of the desert. In his *Vita Antonii,* Athanasius outlines the way of asceticism that every serious Christian should follow in order to live "according to the image." At times in this classic, as well as in other such ascetical treatises of the Eastern writers, we come on passages that seem to indicate that humanity, by merely willing it, can become sanctified, especially by doing heroic, ascetical feats. But Athanasius is emphasizing the role that humanity must play by cooperating with God. Neither he nor his readers nor subsequent writers who imitated him forgot for a moment that God begins the process of our deification and continually directs it.

Totally Divine, Totally Human

The true, orthodox teaching about the incarnate Word—namely, that Jesus Christ is totally divine, totally human—was fought for valiantly by the other great theologians, especially by the Cappadocian Fathers, St. Basil, St. Gregory of Nazianzus, and St. Gregory of Nyssa. These teachers knew that all Christianity would fall if a true Christology were not maintained as found in scripture and passed on in the traditions of the early Church.

St. Cyril of Alexandria (†444), following the theology of St. Athanasius formulated in the Council of Ephesus (431)—which was repeated and clarified by Pope Leo in his Tome sent to the Council Fathers of Chalcedon (451)—the Christology that has become traditional for later Christians. In his divinity, Jesus Christ is God by nature. But the humanity that he assumed was not divine by nature and hence had to be, as ours, raised to divine adoption by participation. During his temporal life, according to St. Cyril, Jesus performed every conscious act out of love for his heavenly Father through the Spirit, and a divinization of his humanity took place that not only incorporated without losing its own identity the image that the Logos was as the only begotten Son of God by nature, but also incorporated Christ, the image according to whom we human beings all have been created.

It is St. Maximus the Confessor (†662), above all other Eastern writers, who models the divinization not only of us human beings but also of the entire created cosmos on the divinization of the humanity of Christ in a "perichoresis" of union without confusion or absorption of the two distinctly different but unseparated natures. Just as in the person Jesus Christ there existed two distinct elements, the divine and human natures united without destroying the distinct identity of the two component elements, so, too, Maximus argued, the created cosmos is composed of distinct elements, yet the whole is also fashioned into a unity. Both as the preexistent divine Logos and as the fullness of existing human nature, Jesus Christ is the bond providing the unity of intelligibility and of cosmic energy (love) that is hidden beneath the surface of the material, disparate appearances of creatures.

Cosmic Diversity in Unity

St. Maximus the Confessor is the main Eastern writer who has high-lighted the repercussions on the cosmos of the incarnation and God's love for his material creation. We humans who stand between heaven and earth, possessing both spirit and matter, must first find self-unity and then perform our God-given task of mediation between the rest of the created cosmos and its creator. The Divine Logos-made-human provides Maximus with the means to effect this unity, first in individual human beings, then through such Christified persons by means of their creative work in a "synergy" of loving oneness with the Trinity, immanently inserted into the material world through the risen Savior in his glorified humanity.

Although his predecessors—St. John the Evangelist, St. Justin, St. Irenaeus, Clement of Alexandria, Origen, St. Athanasius, and St. Gregory of Nyssa—had used the Logos doctrine to explain the incarnational activity of Jesus Christ in the cosmos, no Greek Father had developed it as deeply and systematically as Maximus. This theme became one of the predominant emphases in Eastern Christian spirituality. The Logos of each creature is its principle of harmony that shows us the relationship of a given creature to God's total providence or to the total order of salvation. The whole world is interlocked and interrelated, but the thinking human alone is capable of seeing the harmonious relationship between the *logoi* of all material creatures and the *Logos* of God. He or she alone with God can transform the universe into a harmony.

All things are created through the Logos that is Jesus Christ, the Alpha and the Omega. It is through *praxis,* the purification of the human heart of all self-love (*philautia*), and the acquisition of Christ-like virtues by putting on the mind of Christ, that we are able to contemplate in the created order the inner *logoi* in God's Logos. This idea Maximus called *theoria physica.* The spiritual life is not conceived of as a series of ascetical feats that a Christian must perform before God gives the gift of contemplation. Purification of the heart removes the scales from the spiritual eyes to allow us to contemplate what has always been in the physical world: all things are in Christ and are completing the Body of Christ.

In his *Four Centuries on Charity,* Maximus writes:

> Just as the sun when it rises and lights up the world manifests both itself and the things lit up by it, so the Sun of Justice, rising upon a pure mind,

manifests itself and the essences of all the things that have been and will be brought to pass by it.[5]

True Theology

It is St. Maximus who develops the fullness of the contemplative life that he inherited from Evagrius of the fourth century in his teaching on *theoria theologica*. This teaching he calls true theology, a mystical contemplation of the Holy Trinity in all things. After contemplating the Logos in all created things, the true contemplative Christian is led progressively farther and farther from earthly thoughts into an assimilation into the trinitarian family itself. The principle that guides all theory of contemplation and divinization in the Christian East is that like can be known only by like. True knowledge of the Trinity can be given to us humans only in proportion to our assimilation of the likeness of God.

The teaching on image and likeness in Eastern spirituality reaches its fullness in our restoration to the integrity in which God created human beings and that he wished them to possess. To those who have attained true *theologia* in this life, God reveals himself no longer through creatures or the *logoi* in creatures, but in his own trinitarian life of active love dwelling within the individual Christian. *Praxis* removes the obstacles to a more intimate knowledge of God. *Theoria physica* brings to the contemplative the mind of God immanently present in all created things. But in *theoria theologica* God speaks about himself in a direct self-giving to the Christian, without the medium of created forms.

This speaking is true charity, not an ascetical act of loving kindness shown toward other people, but the presence of God as a community of loving, indwelling persons, transforming the human person also into love. This is the final goal in Eastern Christian spirituality: charity toward God and every creature in the cosmos by the outpouring of the Holy Spirit, who makes it possible for a human Christian to live in such a permanent union with the Trinity.

Humanity, the Transformer of the World

In the spirituality of St. Maximus, which represents the peak in the development of the Christian East, humanity stands at the center of the cosmos. Divinized humanity, in whom God lives and through whom he acts to fulfill the world, is the mediator between the disparate and disjointed world and the unity that has been achieved perfectly in the God-Man's humanity through the incarnation. Man and woman, permeated by God's "uncreated energies of love" that for St. Maximus is primal grace, achieve a unity within themselves that allows them to effect a cosmic unity in the material world around them.

Vladimir Lossky summarizes the doctrine of St. Maximus the Confessor and the common teaching of the Eastern Fathers concerning the transformation of the universe into Christ: "In his way to union with God man in no way leaves creatures aside, but gathers together in his love the whole cosmos disordered by sin, that it may at last be transfigured by grace."[6]

Early Monasticism

What kept such theological articulation of the spiritual life in the Christian East from becoming too abstract and removed from reality was that this theology had its roots in the early monasticism of the Desert Fathers. Toward the end of the fourth century, when the Roman emperors had become Christians and martyrs no longer shed their blood in witness to their faith and love for Christ, a strange phenomenon occurred in Egypt. Prior to Constantine's edict of toleration, the pagan world fought to eliminate the Christian by martyrdom. But now it was the hermits who took up the attack and eliminated the world from their being. The dominant tone was aggression. The darkened prisons where Christians wasted away, the amphitheaters where voracious beasts tore the martyrs apart, were replaced by the immense desert. For these early athletes of Christ, the desert was the twilight zone between the profane world that groaned under the bondage of sin or chaotic disorientation from God and the heavenly Jerusalem of the transfigured world to come. They did not run away from the world in cowardliness or in self-centered spiritual egoism, but, rather, as conscious cocreators, fighters at the most advanced outposts, "men intoxicated with God" (as Pseudo-Macarius calls them), they were eschatological prophets, building a community, a way of life with God that most closely would resemble the life to come in the *eschaton*. Although living in a body in time and space, they pointed to a transfigured, spiritual existence outside of time and space.

We are told by Palladius in his *Lausaic History* that thousands of men and women left the cities to build large communities according to St. Paul's "New Creation," throughout all of Egypt, Syria, and Mesopotamia. But the beginnings and the continued sign of the perfect Christian life in the desert revolved around the eremitical life of a solitary hermit living as did St. Antony, the father of the desert athletes. From the *Life of St. Antony,* we see that their spiritual combat consisted of vigils, fastings, mortifications, and constant prayer.

By entering into themselves, these ascetics sought by God's grace to fructify the seeds of divinity placed in them when God decreed to make them according to his image and likeness. These early desert pilgrims sought chiefly to experience in the deepest recesses with all their heart, mind, and strength the love and presence of the living, loving Trinity. They expressed with their lives the conviction that it was ultimately necessary to go apart from the world and to find God in the solitude of constant prayer and austere penance.

The Incarnate Word was the center of their lives. They yearned with all their heart and soul to be consumed by him. No price was too great to pay. They were mystics, seekers of God, in the truest sense of the word and, therefore, they were willing to surrender all and everything in order to experience greater love and union with God. Into the dry, barren wasteland they went, these mad, passionate lovers of Christ, these Christians intoxicated with God. They hoped and believed that in the deadness of the sterile desert they would be given Life. They entered the desert that they might be transformed into a new creation as their former, false selves were put to death.

Pseudo-Macarius in his second homily describes the realism of the Desert Fathers: "When the Apostle urges the putting off the old man (Eph. 4:22), he refers to the entire man, having new eyes in place of the old, ears replacing ears, hands for hands, feet for feet."[7]

Hesychasm

Hesychasm is a most distinctive Eastern Christian form of spirituality that grew out of the first hermits, who pushed ever deeper into the deserts of Egypt and Syria to attain solitude and *hesychia* (the Greek word for "tranquility"). St. Arsenius was always considered the perfect example of a true *hesychast.* Such a spirituality describes the Christian through grace and his or her own intense asceticism reintegrating one's whole being into a single ego that is then placed completely under the direct influence of God dwelling within the Christian.

Arsenius, as the story is told in the *Lives of the Fathers,* while still at the imperial court of Constantinople, prayed to God in these words: "Lord, lead me along a way of life where I can be saved." A voice said to him, "Arsenius, flee men and you will be saved." The same Arsenius, now a hermit, in this new life made again his same prayer, and he heard a voice that said to him, "Arsenius, flee, keep silence, remain tranquil; these are the roots of impeccability."

Those who aspired to attain this most intimate union with God revealing himself in the depths of their being had first of all to *flee*. Such physical removal from the world was considered as the first condition to attain purity of heart. Exterior and interior silence, in the words of St. Basil, is the beginning of purity of heart. St. John Climacus further defines silence as, first of all, detachment from concern with regard to necessary and unnecessary things; secondly, as assiduous prayer; and thirdly, as the unremitting action of prayer in the heart.[8]

But true silence and solitude was the attainment of inner integration of one's entire being, of all body and soul appetites, to be put under the dominance of God. This interior struggle to live only for God was carried on by a constant vigilance or sobriety (*nepsis*) over one's thoughts. Much of Eastern Christian spiritual writing concerned itself with the psychology of thoughts: how to control the "passionate" thoughts and how to move into a "thoughtful" consciousness of the indwelling Lord.

Evagrian Spirituality

It is impossible to limit the powerful influence of Evagrius of Pontus of the fourth century not only on Eastern Christian spirituality but also on the monastic contemplation of Western Christianity. Evagrius came under three principal influences that helped to fashion his spirituality into what Louis Bouyer calls "an erudite monasticism." The first influence came from the Cappodocian Fathers— Basil, Gregory of Nazianzus, and Gregory of Nyssa—who, like Evagrius, were men shaped by their Hellenic culture and who passed on to Christianity the intellectual heritage of the classical Greek world. The second influence was that of Origen, who gave to Evagrius the thought categories of Platonism with an allegorical interpretation of Scripture. Thirdly, Evagrius was profoundly influenced by the desert spirituality of silence and humility that the hermits before him had developed and on which Evagrius himself thoroughly grounded his own spiritual life as a hermit in the Egyptian desert.

Evagrius was something of a practical, self-taught psychologist with keen insights into the workings of the human psyche. His writings provided valuable guidance for those searching to live the hesychastic life in purity of heart and wordless contemplation. In his work, *Praktikos,* Evagrius declares that the aim of the ascetic life is *apatheia:* health of the soul, purity of heart, right ordering of emotions (passions), a state of passionlessness. This aim must not be confused with indifference, apathy (ennui), or stoicism. Rather, it is the ordering of the deep-seated emotions that brings about a state of interior wholeness and becoming one's true self.

Louis Bouyer offers a helpful insight in the understanding of *apatheia* of Evagrius:

Actually, for Evagrius, *apatheia* is simply the domination of the passions in us that are opposed to charity. It withdraws us from the domination of demons to give us back to that of God. It suppresses nothing of the most natural human feelings, but it purifies them in taking away from them anything that is disordered.[9]

In his two principal works on the spiritual life that had immense influence on Eastern spirituality, *Chapters on Prayer* (which for centuries until modern time was attributed to St. Nilus of Sinai) and *Praktikos,* Evagrius gives a guide for living the "practical" or ascetical life. His goal is to present the spiritual life as contemplation or intimate union with God by living out the Christian dialectic of death and resurrection. Passions or *logismoi* are nonintegrated thoughts that lead, if one yields to their temptations, to further disunity and disintegration.

Evagrius was the first to name the traditional eight capital sins or "passionate" thoughts that are, according to him, at the root of all sin, namely, gluttony, impurity, avarice, sadness, anger, *acedia* (spiritual torpor or boredom), vainglory, and pride. But, more importantly, he gives sensitive and accurate psychological descriptions of how such thoughts develop, and strategies as to how to counteract such temptations.

Demonology

The teaching on demons as found traditionally in Eastern Christian spirituality also comes primarily from the writings of Evagrius. The monks of the Egyptian desert considered the spiritual life to be a combat against demonic forces, the powers of the world that have been unleashed throughout the world and that center especially in attacks against those Christians seeking perfection. The relation between the demons and one's thoughts is very close in the writings of Evagrius. In some places he considers the demons as prompters of the thoughts that lead to sin, while at other times he seems to consider them as the thoughts themselves. What is important for Evagrius is to give monks valuable psychological methods for dealing with the shadow side of the personality. Evagrius personifies and shows succeeding generations how to combat these very real forces in the human personality.

If we substitute the words "superficial ego" with its "projections" for demons, we can see that Evagrius has constructed a brilliant system of spiritual psychology. His principal teaching on the ascetical life is that the human personality, the ego, resists the emergence of the natural self, which would, by human nature as being according to the image and likeness of God himself, be exclusively involved in the contemplation of God but instead is taken up with the demands of the false self in its striving for self-gratification.

Praying in the Void

Evagrius teaches contemplative prayer; he insists that the ideal of Christian perfection cannot be attained by *apatheia* or ascetical practices but that these must be accompanied by a life of prayer. To follow Christ is to pray without thoughts, without distraction. This capacity is a gift from God and cannot be achieved by human effort alone. St. Maximus receives his two stages of contemplation from Evagrius; namely, that of *theoria physica* and *theoria theologica*.

True contemplative prayer consists of an absolutely empty mind. Purification from all limiting concepts (even good and spiritual thoughts) is necessary for the attainment of knowledge in *pure prayer*. All clear and distinct ideas are a form of ignorance and must be eventually rejected if a Christian is to enter into true union with God. Evagrius writes, "Stand guard over your spirit keeping it free of concepts at the time of prayer so that it may remain in its own deep calm." [10]

Thus true prayer for Evagrius is entering into a *void* or an emptying of all thoughts in order that in deepest consciousness the monk can receive from God his own presence in a glorious experience of interior light. This Evagrius calls "pure prayer." This is our ultimate end, to experience God immediately as light without the medium of any sense thought or concept or image. This experience of light transforms the individual in the depths of his or her spirit and brings him into the divinization by sharing in the Trinity's life. For Evagrius, the individual is not essentially a creature composed of body and soul, but an intelligence (*nous*) whose proper activity is religious contemplation. Therefore his attention is not focused on the substitution of love of God for love of self and of the world, but rather on the removal of the mind from things of the world to the contemplation of God. His intellectualism shows evident influences of Origen's Neo-Platonism and was to have much influence on promoting the noninvolvement with the world and the social sphere that has typified so much of spiritual writing in the East.

Spirituality of the Heart

Pseudo-Macarius (a Syrian monk who is known as Macarius and who was thought erroneously by generations of Eastern Christians to have been Macarius the Great of Egypt), who wrote his fifty spiritual homilies in the latter part of the fourth century, is one of the main influences in hesychasm of the heart spirituality. He continues the more Semitic influence with its accent on the total, existential encounter with God in the "heart," found chiefly in the Antiochene School of St. Ignatius of Antioch, St. Polycarp, St. Irenaeus, and St. Antony of the desert and opposed mainly to the Evagrian intellectual school of Platonized Christianity.

God is encountered is a holistic manner within the heart and not in the mind as the ground of one's being. Macarius insists on the total encountering in ever increasing awareness and even "feeling" of that presence of the indwelling Trinity. He describes in his fifteenth homily the mythic use of the word *heart* as the focus where God meets humanity in its concrete existence. The divinizing effect of the Holy Spirit works through grace to lead humans into ever mounting levels of transcendent possibility and realized human development according to our image and likeness that is Jesus Christ:

His (God's) very grace writes in their hearts the laws of the Spirit. They, therefore, should not put all their trusting hope solely in the scriptures written in ink. For, indeed, divine grace writes on the "tables of the heart" [2 Cor. 3:3] the laws of the Spirit and the heavenly mysteries. For the heart directs and governs all the other organs of the body. And when grace pastures the heart, it rules over all the members and the thoughts. For there in the heart and mind abides as well as all the thoughts of the soul and all its hopes. This is how grace penetrates throughout all parts of the body.[11]

Such an affective spirituality sought to integrate body, soul, and spirit in prayer to experience God's indwelling presence in the purified Christian as a transforming light. We will see that this is the beginning of the Taboric light (the light Christ appeared in on Mount Tabor) as the goal of the hesychastic mysticism of St. Symeon the New Theologian (†1022) and the followers of St. Gregory Palamas (†1359). Other accents in this "heart" spirituality placed great emphasis on the transcendence of God, the need for *penthos* or weeping for one's sinfulness, the striving to attain incessant prayer, the theme of the cohabitation of sin and grace, the value of profound humility to attract the mercy and healing of God's love and the stress on the conscious awareness of the indwelling Trinity through grace as uncreated energies of love.

The Jesus Prayer

Out of the desert monks' spirituality of the heart grew what is called in the Christian East the *Jesus Prayer*. This form of prayer had its roots not only in the New Testament but even farther back, in the Old Testament. In the Old Covenant we see a developed personal conviction that the invocation of the name of God brought with it the conscious realization of his presence. "Call on my Name, I will hear" (Zech. 13:9). The New Testament gave to these desert Christians a fuller theology of God's name and the power that emanates from the reverent pronouncing of the name of Jesus. St. Paul writes, "God has given him a name that is above all names so that at the name of Jesus every knee shall bend in heaven, on earth and under the earth" (Phil. 2:9–10). The Gospel stories of the two blind men on the road crying, "Son of David, have mercy on us" (Matt. 9:27) and the humble request of the publican, "Oh God, have mercy on me, a sinner" (Luke 18:13) gave the inspiration for this prayer that combined the transcendence of Jesus Christ as the Son of God with his condescending mercy toward sinful man in the formula that became gradually fixed as the *Jesus Prayer:* "Lord, Jesus Christ, Son of God, have mercy on me, a sinner."

Being centered on the presence of the risen Jesus Lord through the repetition day and night of the name of Jesus went along with an interior movement of putting body, soul, and spirit of the total person under the dominance and healing of the Lord Jesus. Such constant recollection of the indwelling Jesus was aided by using the somatic technique of synchronizing the human breath with the repetition of the name of Jesus. This method was a natural conclusion from the Semitic roots of Christianity that matter is a diaphany or point through which God's loving presence could shine forth to touch and transform the believing, purified Christians into loving children of God.

Penthos

There was no magic in reciting the Jesus Prayer. It was basically a psychosomatic technique that the Desert Fathers saw as a fixation or centering on the basic triple movements necessary in Christian prayer—transcendence, immanence, and humanity's broken sinfulness—that by humble crying out the individual would truly experience death and resurrection with a new level of oneness with the risen Jesus.

One feature of Eastern Christian spirituality ensuring that Christians would not use it in pride and self-delusion was the constant striving to live in an abiding spirit of compunction. Placed side by side with their accent on an awesome reverence for almighty God, Father, Son, and Holy Spirit, the darkness of inner brokenness, a bit of Carl Jung's "collective unconscious," appeared to these desert athletes as the "place" where Jesus would become again in their lives the Divine Physician.

They used the term *penthos* to connote the whole complexus of an abiding sense of our own creaturehood and dependence on God as we live amidst a world infected with sin as an interior force in us and the whole cosmos of tending to turn us away from God. It was *penthos* that taught the early Fathers how to imitate Christ who was before his heavenly Father as "meek and humble of heart." They had to enter into a continued conversion, a *metanoia,* and become as little children, stripped of their own independent spirit before God in order to enter into the Kingdom of God through a personal encounter with God as Trinity.

A famous Father of the Egyptian desert, Pimen, expressed this common thinking of desert spirituality: "Weep for your sins, there is no other way of salvation." These Fathers were completely convinced that this internal weeping kept them in the truth that God was the ultimate in their lives and that they would tend toward sinfulness if God did not come to their constant rescue. This attitude was for them not an introspection into one's sinful past, nor a life of morbid scruples. It was an attempt to experience ontologically, and not merely through an intellectual assent, who they really were before God. It is an interior weeping on seeing the goodness of God shining so strongly within them. The slightest turning away, therefore, from God as from one's true end filled them with great fear, a filial reverential fear of a child of God toward his heavenly Father. They took literally the third beatitude: "Blessed are they who mourn, for they shall be comforted." Those who weep will be comforted by God who will come into such purified souls and reveal his person to them.

Apophatic Spirituality

Perhaps the distinguishing characteristic of Eastern Christian spirituality—or better, of its higher stages of mysticism—is its *apophatic* quality. Evagrius, we have seen, taught a form of formless prayer.[12] Such a mysticism insists that the highest union, the infused union where God speaks to us directly about himself, is not achieved in any conceptual knowledge but in an immediate, experiential knowledge wherein he opens himself to us. God, purely and simply and in his transcendence, reveals himself to us when and how he wishes.

St. Gregory of Nyssa could be called the father of the *apophatic* spirituality. He influenced Evagrius, Pseudo-Dionysius, and so many other theologians of prayer, including St. John of the Cross. In his *Life of Moses,* St. Gregory gives us a full presentation of the soul's journey up the mountain to meet God in the darkness of unknowing. In this work Gregory develops the meaning of darkness. The Greek word *apophatic* describes first a certain darkening of human intellect in approaching God by mere reasoning powers. In this sense it is a negation. But in true *apophatic* spirituality as taught by the Greek Fathers there is also a positive element. The accent is entirely on God doing the revealing, giving the gift of himself and no longer is the emphasis on humanity and personal human activity. God, who is so infinitely perfect and good, the incomprehensible, deigns to allow us to know him in some fashion or other by way of a direct experience in deep faith, hope and love.

The movement to union with God is a continual process from light to shadow to darkness. St. Gregory shows the higher degrees of entering into the darkness of God's incomprehensibility in his *Commentary on the Song of Songs:*

Our initial withdrawal from wrong and erroneous ideas of God is a transition from darkness to light. Next comes a closer awareness of hidden things, and by this the soul is guided through sense phenomena to the world of the invisible. And this awareness is a kind of cloud, which overshadows all appearances, and slowly guides and accustoms the soul to look towards what is hidden. Next the soul makes progress through all these stages and goes on higher, and as she leaves behind all that human nature can attain, she enters within the secret chamber of the divine knowledge, and here she is cut off on all sides by the divine darkness. Now she leaves outside all that can be grasped by sense or by reason, and the only thing left for her contemplation is the invisible and the incomprehensible.[13]

St. Gregory resorts to such paradoxical terms as "luminous darkness," "sober inebriation," and so forth to describe the modality of experiencing God directly and immediately without any conceptual form. The closer one approaches to union with God, the more blinding God appears. It is not a question of the knowledge of God becoming more abstruse but of the nature of God becoming more present. Such a knowledge is given as gift from God to the purified.

For St. Gregory such mysticism is built on the Greek word *epectasis* or the "stretching out" to possess the "Unpossessable." He uses the term St. Paul coins in Phil. 3:13 to describe the soul's continued process of tending toward the infinite as the mystic discovers "that the true satisfaction of desire consists in constantly going on with the quest and never ceasing in the ascent to God, seeing that every fulfillment of desire continually generates a further desire for the Transcendent."[14]

Pseudo-Dionysius

Perhaps no one in the history of Eastern Christian spirituality has had a greater impact on Christian mysticism, both of the East and the West, than the writings attributed falsely to Dionysius the Areopagite. The identity of this writer still remains cloaked in anonymity. Historians are agreed that he is not the convert Dionysius mentioned in the Acts of the Apostles, those apostles who heard St. Paul preach on the Areopagus in Athens. Nor is he the bishop of Athens of the second century nor the bishop-martyr of Paris of the third century. He seems to have been a Syrian of Monophysite (the doctrine that Christ retained only one nature) tendencies of at least the fifth century, highly influenced by the Neoplatonism of Plotinus and his disciple, Proclus.

He is the first to use the term *mystical theology,* in his short work of the same name, which prepared the way for his Western commentators such as Scotus Eriugena, the Victorines, St. Albert, St. Bonaventure, St. Thomas Aquinas, and Meister Eckhart to separate mystical theology from scholastic theology. This important work, however, has to be seen as a part of a whole unity achieved in Pseudo-Dionysius's other works, such as *The Divine Names, The Celestial Hierarchy, The Ecclesiastical Hierarchy,* and *Symbolic Theology* (a work lost but often alluded to in the other works).

What we discover in his vision, handed down for future mystics of both East and West, is a breath-taking ecstatic communion of intelligences, both angelic and human, striving to respond to the call of divine love summoning them to unity in Christ, each according to his or her rank and degree of purity in the universal hierarchy of all creatures in a harmonious interdependence. Through this ordered cosmos, the love of God flows out in a thearchy, a divinely ruled order, in which the love of the creature, produced in it by God, leads the creature back to him. It is the generous love of creatures toward one another that helps them all to return ecstatically to the One.

Hans Urs von Balthasar gives an eloquent description of this mystical vision of Pseudo-Dionysius:

A vision in ecstasy of a sacral universe, pouring forth wave upon wave from out of the unfathomable abyss of inaccessible divinity, spreading abroad in ever lengthening undulations until it touches the shores themselves of Nothingness. . . . A cosmos gyrating in a dance of ceremonial liturgic adoration about the luminous darkness of that innermost mystery, aware of the awesome nearness of this center . . . and of the ever widening distance from that One which is beyond essence and beyond inconceivability. This fascinating vision of the universe, which in its sacral and litugric movement inebriates even while it clears the mind, has a purity about it that is discoverable neither in Alexandrian thought nor in Cappadocian, and much less in anything so austere as that of Egypt or so earth bound as that of Antioch. . . . It is as though in the sudden glare of a lightning bolt there was revealed the existential compenetration of all the kingdoms of the cosmos, their hierarchies, their mutual relationships, the ceaseless movement of ascension and descent from the invisible summit to the base plunged in matter. Never before had the Christian world contemplated a vision of such amplitude situated within the stable majesty of peace.[15]

Pseudo-Dionysius gives three stages of movement toward ecstatic union with the One that would provide St. Bonaventure and others in the West with the three steps in the way of Christian perfection: the purgative, the illuminative, and the unitive. The first movement in the Dionysian *apophatic* theology is that of "abstractive nega-tion," which basically corresponds to the purification way of tradi-tional Christian spirituality.[16] But this approach is not a moral purifi-cation as much as it is an Evagrian denial of any and all conceptual forms of God.

The second stage is the positive aspect of the *apophatic* ap-proach: the attaining of knowledge of the Unknowable by the cloud of unknowing, as Moses did on Mount Sinai. The final stage is ec-static union with God. This stage lies utterly beyond human activity and is the summit of the spirit, invaded and possessed by ecstatic love directly given by God, a pure grace, a pure love that brings about union with God through ecstasy. Pseudo-Dionysius goes be-yond his teachers, St. Gregory of Nyssa and Evagrius, to show that full ecstasy is not merely going out from all things other than the self, but even out of the self also.

Cenobitic Monasticism

Eastern Christian spirituality has been most influenced by monasti-cism, as it has been earlier pointed out. The monastic impact devel-oped into liturgical piety touching the lives of all Eastern Christians as well as into the spiritual writings, homilies, and lives of the saints that would bring the experiential theology of the early Greek Fa-thers into a living application for the ordinary Christians. Eremetism was the initial form of Eastern Christian asceticism and mysticism with the Desert Fathers seeking always more and more solitude and greater purification of the heart.

But such spiritual giants found that they could not separate them-selves from willing disciples who eagerly sought to attach them-selves to such spiritual guides. Spiritual direction was considered as a charism of the Holy Spirit that fraternal love demanded to be given when disciples asked it of the "elders." As more ascetics, both men and women, flocked to the deserts of Egypt, Syria, and Mesopotamia, the number of those attaching themselves to the rec-ognized "Pneumatophors" or bearers of the Holy Spirit increased, and thus communities of monks formed. Positively, advantages were seen in grouping together for divine services, to exchange counsels and teachings, and to instruct one another in Holy Scripture. Negatively, they began to group together in order to avoid some of the dangers of a solipsistic life that led many hermits into a self-centered pride and even into mental aberrations.

St. Pachomius (c. 292-346) is credited with developing the first cenobitic monastery as we understand the term. About the year 320 he established a communal form of monastic life in Tabennisi, north of Thebes in Egypt. Tradition claims that he received the so-called Pachomian Rule from an angel. This rule spread rapidly outside of Egypt. St. Athanasius in his exile to the West in 340-346 brought the rule to the Latins. St. Benedict was greatly influenced by this rule and by that of St. Basil through the writings of St. John Cassian, whom he referred to as the Master and who spent many years living in Egypt and Syria visiting not only the hermits but also the monks who lived in common.

But the true father of Eastern cenobitic monasticism is St. Basil the Great (c. 330-379). His depth of theology and prayer mingled happily with a basic charism of prudence and discretion to shape monastic community living along the lines of the principles found in the New Testament. His *Great Rules* and his *Short Rules,* with some changes, became the basic source of inspiration and legislation for Eastern monasticism. This type of monasticism stressed the common life under obedience to an abbas, or abbot. It was an experience of Church or the Body of Christ in work, prayer, and social living in community, with the accent on charity concretely expressed in living and serving the community by social works.

Sinaite Spirituality

On Mount Sinai in the ancient monastery of St. Catherine, dating back to the fifth century, we find a leading center of monastic spirituality that brings together in a synthesis of both the Evagrian and the Macarian teachings on asceticism and contemplation that would be passed down through the hesychastic Fathers whose writings so often quote the Sinaite teachers such as Nilus, John Climacus, Hesychius, and Philotheus.

With the Sinaite hesychasts comes an important change. In place of Evagrius's "Man is an intellect," they substitute "Man is a heart." Ascetical practices or *praxis* are still ordered, as for Evagrius, toward *apatheia,* the state in which the passions, never extirpated fully, are controlled by the human will so as to give complete freedom to contemplate God in one's heart. Corporal visions are to be discredited, and the presence of God is to be guarded in the heart by *penthos,* the abiding sorrow for one's sins, developed by continual thought of death, judgment, the gift of tears, and complete detachment from all creatures. The classic writing depicting this spirituality of Sinai is the *Ladder of Divine Ascent,* by St. John Climacus.

The new element that Pseudo-Macarius introduced—namely, that of personal warm devotion to Jesus—is now an habitual disposition. Philotheus, following his master Climacus, writes,

> Sweet memory of God, that is, of Jesus, coupled with heartfelt wrath and beneficent contrition, can always annihilate all the fascination of thoughts, the variety of suggestions . . . daringly seeking to devour our souls. Jesus when invoked easily burns up all this. For in no other place can we find salvation except in Jesus Christ. . . . And so every hour and every moment let us zealously guard our heart from thoughts obscuring the mirror of the soul, which should contain, drawn and imprinted on it, only the radiant image of Jesus Christ, who is the wisdom and the power of God the Father.[17]

A Feeling Spirituality

With the stress placed on remembering the name of Jesus among the hesychastic writers who followed the Sinaite spirituality, it was only natural to find spiritual writers, such as Diadochus of Photike of the fifth century and Mark the Hermit, presenting an orthodox teaching on the psychology of individual consciousness in inner attention to the presence of the risen Jesus. Actually Diadochus developed his correct teaching in controversy with the heretical, highly emotional Messalians, a sect that stressed the presence of God only to the degree that an individual person could "feel" that presence of grace.[18]

Diadochus speaks constantly about "remembering God," especially Jesus, but such a "recalling" of God's presence is a means only to a higher goal, to live in a state of constant loving (*agape*). He shows himself a master psychologist as he develops a theological anthropology to present his doctrine of the reintegration of a human person. For him, human nature is simple and undivided prior to the sin of Adam. Following more the Semitic, holistic approach of Pseudo-Macarius, Diadochus moves away from the Evagrian understanding of the human being as *nous,* intellect, to describe *nous* as the intellectual, directing force that is meant to be a unity with the body faculties. In the *nous* is a special interior sense, called in Greek *aisthesis*. This sense is more than our sense of "feeling." By *aisthesis,* Diadochus means consciousness in the fullest sense, including both intellectual and volitional acts. Feeling and understanding are not to be two, separate, essentially different functions. *Aisthesis* makes the integration of all human powers under the intellect possible in order that we can know invisible realities and be attracted to them by a "connaturality." It could be translated as "sense of the heart," much as Blaise Pascal wrote that the heart has its own reason and knowledge.

By remembering the presence of God through the continued repetition of the name of Jesus, the simplicity of the *nous* is brought about and the human becomes an integrated person. In a text that shows the influence of Pseudo-Macarius and would have great influence on the affective use of the Jesus Prayer among succeeding hesychastic writers, Diadochus describes the health of such a whole person:

At first, grace conceals its presence within the soul of the baptized person, waiting to see what option he will choose. If the man turns completely to the Lord, grace manifests its presence in the heart with indescribable sweetness. Then it waits again to observe the movement of the soul. If it does not prevent the arrows of the demon from penetrating to the depths of the soul's interior sense, it is in order to incite it to seek God with a more ardent fervor and with humility. If then the man begins to make progress by keeping the commandments and continually calling upon the Lord Jesus, the fire of divine grace reaches out even to the external senses of the heart, burning out the cockle from this human field. As a result the temptations of the demon are driven back and scarcely ever penetrate beyond the sensible part of the soul.

Finally when a man has put on all the virtues, especially that of perfect poverty, grace illumines his whole being with a still greater sweetness and by its warmth moves it to a most fervent love of God.[19]

Syrian Spirituality

Among the Eastern Christian writers, we find a unique Semitic emphasis among those writers who wrote in Syriac and in general lived in Syria or parts of Persia, thus retaining more of a Semitic than a Hellenic approach to the Christian life. Such writers include those of the fourth century, Aphrahat and St. Ephrem, deacon; the fifth-

century writer; John the Solitary of Apamee; the sixth-century writ-
ers Jacob of Saroug, Philoxenus of Mabboug, and Stephen Bar Sou-
daili; and the seventh-century writers Jacob of Edessa and Dadiso
Qaṭraya. The most important and the greatest mystical writer of all
Eastern Christian writers is also of the seventh century, namely, St.
Isaac the Syrian of Nineveh.

If we could find any common elements among these outstanding
writers, it would be the accent placed on a primitive spirituality, a
holistic approach with great stress given to the ascetical practices of
vigils and solitude. In addition, there is an unusual scientific approach in describing with greater nuance the movements of the soul,
the workings of the "passions," and the various states of prayer.

St. Ephrem especially has bequeathed a corpus of sacred hymns
and metrical homilies that contain some of the most beautiful Christian poetry ever written.[20] He deals with allegorical images drawn
faithfully from the Old and New Testament writings, stressing the
themes of the human-divine espousal between human and God, the
virtue of compunction, and the centrality of Jesus Christ as savior
and healer, along with a continued stress on eschatology, the second coming of Christ, and the transformation of this world into the
heavenly Jerusalem.

St. Isaac of Nineveh

No one in the Eastern Christian tradition wrote more and encour-
aged Christians concerning continual prayer than did St. Isaac of
Nineveh. He wrote much that we have mainly in Syriac and Arabic,
and his many writings show us a doctrine of the highest mysticism
described from his own experience. After a short time living in the
monastery of St. Matthew near Nineveh, he spent many years living
in solitude. He accepted the call to become the bishop of the great
city of Nineveh. He, however, only stayed a few years before he
returned again to his solitary life in the desert. There he entered
into the deepest struggles with his inner self, capable of leading
others along the same paths to the highest union of mystical prayer
with God.

He relies very much on the writings of Evagrius, but goes much
farther as he describes a superior state of continual prayer that he
calls "pure prayer." This state begins when other activities of prayer cease and a person enters into a sort of ecstatic delirium. Remi-

niscent more of Pseudo-Macarius than of Evagrius, Isaac describes the movement into true contemplation in ways that now will become very desirable:

> When your soul is nearing the way out of darkness, then this will be for you a sign: your heart is aflame, burns like fire day and night; and so the whole world seems to you like dust and dung; you even have no desire of food, for the sweetness of new flaming thoughts, constantly arising in your soul. Suddenly fountains of tears open up in you, flowing freely like an inexhaustible stream and mingling with all your activities, with your reading, your prayer or meditation, your eating or drinking or aught else. When you see this in your soul, be of good cheer, for you have crossed the sea.[21]

The prayer to which Isaac encourages the Christian is an interior prayer that transcends all activities of the human person and is sheer gift of God acting directly on the individual. Such pure prayer is for the perfect who have prepared themselves by years of solitude, fasting, spiritual reading, recitation of praises, prayers of compunction, prostrations, and psalmody. But when this gift of contemplation is given, the love of God, in the words of Isaac, is by nature hot, and when it grips a man beyond measure, it throws the soul into ecstasy. A man who feels this love exhibits a remarkable change; his face becomes fiery and joyful, and his body is warmed; fear and shame leave him. The contemplation of his mind allows no kind of interruption in his thought of the celestial; he is aware of no impulse excited by objects, for, even if he does something, he is quite insensible of it, so ravished is his mind in contemplation, and his thought is always as it were conversing with someone.[22]

The Gift of Tears

St. Isaac highlights St. Ephrem's theology of compunction. Evagrius, his teacher, insisted, "Pray first for the gift of tears so that by means of sorrow you may soften your native rudeness."[23] St. John Climacus taught, "Greater than baptism itself is the fountain of tears after baptism."[24] But St. Isaac shows weeping as a specific psychosomatic gift of God that precedes directly the more perfect gift of pure contemplation.

> When you reach the realm of tears, then know that your mind has left the prison of this world, has put its foot on the path of a new age and has begun to smell the scent of near and wondrous air. Tears begin to flow because the birth of the spiritual child is near. . . . But these tears are of a

different order from those which come from time to time. . . . I am not
speaking of this order of tears, but of such as flow unceasing day and night.
The eyes of a man who has reached this degree become like a spring of
water for up to two years and more, after which he comes to the still of
thoughts.[25]

Such tears cleanse the mind to receive the direct illumination of
the Holy Spirit. The battle with the enemy becomes easier and
temptations are quelled and calmed. From the depths of the
"heart" pours a certain ineffable sweetness, reacting on the whole
body and bringing an exulting joy even though parts of the body
may be weak and suffering. This is the state of reintegration.

Liturgical Piety

One of the most predominant features of Eastern Christian spirituality is its liturgical characteristics. Liturgy was considered the "work
of the people," as the Greek word *liturgia* literally means. If individuals fed their piety on the liturgical sources, such piety was always
connected to the "people of God," the gathered Body of Christ who
come together in liturgical prayer to meet the living Savior and
through contact with Christ to enter into the familial life of the
Trinity. Here is living spirituality, experiential but on personal, social, and cosmic levels.[26]

Eastern Christian piety draws through the centuries its life from
its participation in liturgical life. This life refers to much more than
what in the West we call *liturgy*. Liturgy in the East embraces primarily the Divine Liturgy, celebrated with great splendor and joy
each Sunday, along with all the Offices such as Vespers and Matins,
with their beautiful, dogmatic, but highly poetic and lyrical composi-
tions of hymns and prayers composed by the great mystical theologians of the East. It embraces also the reading and preaching of the
Divine Word along with the celebration of all the sacraments. Last-
ly, it includes also the individual prayer in the home by people alone
or by those gathered together as a family or group in prayer. The
sense of the collective, the Church praying, is always present, and
this makes, whatever be the form, for a liturgical piety.

A Variety of Liturgies

Stemming out of the New Testament communities gathered to celebrate the Eucharist of Jesus Christ, early forms of the Eucharist, as
the *Didache* or the *Teaching of the Twelve Apostles* of the first

century, evolved into other liturgies such as the Syrian, that of St. James of Jerusalem, the Nestorian and Persian liturgies, and the Coptic liturgies of great richness and number. Many of these liturgies, especially in the Byzantine Empire, from the sixth century on, evolved into the fixed liturgies that we know today, especially the more familiar liturgies of the Byzantine churches of St. John Chrysostom and St. Basil.

We find in these liturgies the "fixed" and the "alternating" parts. In the fixed parts, the unvariable canons or "anaphoras," we encounter in a beautiful manner the basic dogmas and teachings of Christianity presented in a language of exquisite beauty that captures the triple movement of a body of human beings, representing the whole human race, living out the history of salvific history of estrangement from the awesome transcendent and almighty God, due to human sinfulness. Yet the abyss separating the majesty of God and the lowliness of humanity is spanned by the incarnation of the Word of God become man, who for our sakes dies on the cross but rises in glory to share that glory in this liturgical act with all who gather in his name.

The alternating parts of each divine liturgy as well as the office bring together prayers and hymns composed by the great theologians and poets of the Christian East such as St. John Damascene, St. Andrew of Crete, St. Sergius, Patriarch of Constantinople, Romanos the Melodious, and a host of others whose creative genius has been enshrined in their liturgical works even if their names have not come down to us.

In the alternating parts of the liturgical life of the Eastern Churches, individual Christians are able to enter into a new living and experiencing of the key mysteries of their faith. In the *Triod,* the *Pentecostarion,* and other collections, such Christians find a collection of fundamental doctrines about the death, resurrection, and the outpouring of the Holy Spirit on sinful humanity to divinize them into sharers in the resurrection of the Lord Jesus. Such spiritual doctrines are powerfully presented in symbol and myth drawn from the Old and the New Testament writings. Typical of such fonts that develop a liturgical piety are the following two hymns attributed to St. John Damascene from the canon of the Easter service and a quote from the homily of St. John Chrysostom used in the same service:

We celebrate the death of death, the destruction of hell and the beginning of new life—of eternal life. . . . A Holy Easter has appeared to us today, a new and Holy Easter, a mystical Easter, a sacred Easter! An Easter which is Christ our liberation! An immaculate Easter, the great Easter, the Easter of the faithful; the Easter which opens the doors of paradise and sanctifies all the faithful!

This is the day of the Resurrection, let us be illumined with joy, let us embrace one another and address each other as brothers! Even to those who hate us let us say: Let us forgive one another for the sake of the Resurrection, and let us sing: Christ is risen from the dead. He has triumphed over death by death and has given life to those who were in the tombs.

Devotion to the Mother of God—*Theotokos*

Devotion to Mary, the Mother of God or the *Theotokos,* the birth-giver of God, had been in the Eastern Churches from the beginning, but especially in the Council of Ephesus (431) the Eastern Fathers canonized the title of *Theotokos,* that Mary truly gave birth to a son who was equally God and man. The early Fathers of the Church, under the illumination of the Holy Spirit, contemplated Mary as found in Holy Scripture. They could move freely from Mary to Church to the individual Christian and see the essential similarity because they were true contemplatives who moved in terms of archetypal symbols.

Under the symbols of virginity and maternity, the Fathers held Mary up as a model of Christian integration of total surrender to the Holy Spirit in her virginal consent and of her gifting the world in her active response of giving birth to Christ in human form. The two great sources for this tender and fervent devotion toward Mary among Eastern Christians are found in their liturgical feasts and texts and in their devotion to sacred icons of Mary, always depicted beside her Son.

One of the beautiful hymns composed to honor Mary is sung daily in the Byzantine Liturgy:

It is indeed proper to bless thee, Mother of God, the eternally blessed and completely sinless one and the Mother of Our God. Higher in honor than the Cherubim and incomparably more glorious than the Seraphim, who without harm to thy virginity didst give birth to the Word of God; we thee extol, true Mother of God.

In the Divine Liturgy and in other liturgical functions or services, the Eastern Christian has always been fed with solid scriptural and theological teaching about the Mother of God, expressed in music and poetry that is unrivaled for splendor and richness. Most of the Christian liturgical feasts that are celebrated with devotion in the West to honor Mary grew out of the feasts that developed in the Eastern Churches such as the Nativity of Mary, her presentation in the Temple, Christmas, the Annunciation, and her Assumption or Falling Asleep (Dormition).

Prayers that feed a spirituality particularly devoted to Mary as Mother of God, a feature of piety that down through the centuries kept alive the *anima* or feminine quality in the Christian East, are found, besides the texts in the Divine Liturgy, in the liturgical books called the *Menea,* the *Oktoich Triod, Akathistnik, Euchologion,* and the *Moleben.* The *Moleben* is a short petitional service to Christ, the Virgin Mary, some particular saint, or the angels.

But the most poetic expression of devotion to Mary can be found in the *Akaphist,* a rather long service in Mary's honor that was originally composed on the occasion of the liberation of Constantinople from its enemies in the seventh century. In this service, Mary's whole earthly life is mirrored through the poetry of the author, who dwells on each Marian Gospel scene and, using highly colorful metaphors, addresses the Mother of God with the beginning word, "Rejoice." Each image adds its own beauty to the fast-moving crescendo of epithets. An example of this is the first *ikos* taken from the *Akaphist of Our Lady:*

The Angel, sent by God from heaven to say to the Mother of God: "Rejoice," seeing Thee, O Lord, become Incarnate, trembled as he stood before her; then he greeted her: "Rejoice, Thou through whom joy will shine forth. Rejoice, through whom the curse will be dissolved. Rejoice, through whom freedom from Adam's fall is won. Rejoice, Thou who driest the tears of Eve. Rejoice, Thou, the height surpassing man's comprehension. Rejoice, depth not fathomed even by Angels. Rejoice, for Thou art the throne that supports the King. Rejoice, for Thou bearest Him who bears all creation. Rejoice, O Star, preceding the dawn. Rejoice, womb in which God becomes Man. Rejoice, through whom [all creatures find new Life. Rejoice, through whom] we adore our Creator. Rejoice, Bride yet ever Virgin!"

A Theology of Icons

Anyone wishing to understand Eastern Christian spirituality needs to understand the theology behind the devotion such Christians have had from earliest times toward the painted images called *icons*. What stands behind a deep childlike piety as such Christians, either in their churches or in their homes, reverently kiss the paintings depicting Christ, Mary, the Mother of God, or other saints or angels, is an incarnational theology that grew out of the Christological controversies from the fourth until the sixth centuries. The accepted dogma of the Council of Chalcedon (451) affirmed that God so loved his material creation that his Son, total God, become total man in order to divinize material humanity and the entire material cosmos.

In the eighth and ninth centuries, an anti-icon movement called *iconoclasm* spread throughout the Byzantine world, led by Byzantine emperors who had been influenced by Islamic rationalism. The struggle ended with the reestablishment of the veneration of sacred images by the "Feast of Orthodoxy," which the Orthodox Churches celebrate annually from that date of 842 to honor the Church's restoration of image veneration under the Empress Theodora.

An icon is more than a mere painting of Christ, Mary, or the saints or angels. Certain traditionally approved rules on how to depict subjects of icon painting guide such painters. In an icon of Our Lady, it makes little difference if Mary's hands and body do not have the proportions of other women. The artist seeks to represent, as far as a graphic medium can, the spirituality of the person. The suppliant kneeling before her image is moved by the spirituality expressed in her image and through this rises to her real presence.

An icon, therefore, is first of all a channel of grace, a point of contact made between the praying Christian and the heavenly person represented. Such a blessed icon makes it possible for the Christian praying before it to rise through this visible representation of an invisible person to the spiritual presence of that person. St. John Damascene has written a beautiful treatise on icon devotion in the Eastern Churches. He sums it all up in the words, "What is seen sanctifies our thoughts and so they fly towards the unseen Majesty of God." Basically, devotion to icons is a living out of the Logos mysticism already described that flows out of the basic principle of Christianity, lived out so beautifully in Eastern Christian spirituality, that matter is a diaphany of God who shines through such a material representation with his Word.

A Mystic of Fire and Light

In Christianity, fire and light have long been archetypal symbols of illumination and transformation accredited respectively to the work of the Holy Spirit and to Christ. The Eastern Christian mystic that wrote so eloquently about intimate union with Christ and a feeling relationship with the Holy Spirit is St. Symeon the New Theologian (†1022). One of the greatest mystics of the Christian East, who makes an original synthesis of the two forms of Eastern Christian mysticism already discussed; namely, that of the "heart" spirituality of Pseudo-Macarius and the Semitic School of writers that followed his holistic emphasis and that of the intellectual mysticism of the Alexandrian School of Clement, Origen, and Evagrius.

But here we see something new in the history of Eastern Christianity. Up until Symeon's time, we find no spiritual writer who wrote so candidly of his own personal mystical experiences. The Syrian writers—St. Isaac, St. Ephrem, St. Diadochus, St. Mark the Hermit, Pseudo-Macarius, Evagrius, St. Gregory of Nazianzus, and St. Gregory of Nyssa—all wrote eloquently about the higher states of mystical experiences. But such writers rarely spoke about their own experiences. The closer they approached God in contemplation and uninterrupted union, the more humble and self-abasing they became, and the less inclined to speak about the hidden workings of grace in their souls.

Yet Symeon not only freely speaks about the mystical graces that he received from God (even though at times, in imitation of St. Paul, he uses the third person) but he appeals to his experiences as what is possible for his spiritual disciples. He goes so far, however, as to make his experiences normative for all Christians.

Symeon liked to call himself the "Enthusiastic Zealot," because he was so eager, not only to share intimately his great, mystical graces, but also to teach all who wanted to hear what the Holy Spirit was saying through him in continuity with what he considered to be the common teachings of the early Fathers. He lived in a period of static formalism within the Byzantine Greek Church and felt convinced that the Holy Spirit wanted him to speak and write openly about his mystical experiences to stir Christians to an experiential knowledge of the indwelling Trinity, as opposed to the Greek "scholasticism" that had penetrated Eastern Christian theology and monasticism.

His whole mystical theology begins and ends with the Holy Trinity. Symeon could not comprehend how not only monks but ordinary Christian laity could believe the truth about the indwelling Trinity within them and not live in a conscious awareness of this reality at all times. The whole Christian life for him was a mystical, ever increasing consciousness of the abiding presence of the Trinity, not only within the mystic, but through every atom of the created universe. Here we find a bringing together of the "feeling" of grace of Pseudo-Macarius with the Logos mysticism and intimate union with the indwelling Trinity of St. Maximus the Confessor.

He highlights the apophatic theology of St. Gregory of Nyssa and Pseudo-Dionysius in his approach to such a sublime mystery as the Trinity. In his Hymn 21 of Divine Love he writes,

> The Spirit has been sent by the Son
> not to the unbelieving, nor to the friends of glory,
> . . . nor to those who have studied the works of the Greeks,
> nor to those who are ignorant of our Scriptures, the interior
>   meaning. . . .
> but to those who are poor in spirit and in their way of living,
> to those who are pure of heart and of body,
> to those who speak simply, live more simply
> and whose thinking is simpler still.[27]

A Feeling Light

St. Symeon prepares the way by his double stress on immediate "feeling" awareness in consciousness and the inner light of the triune presence for a transition in Eastern Christian mysticism and theology that would reach its peak of articulation in the doctrine of St. Gregory Palamas on the uncreated energies of love and the perceiving of the Taboric light as a transforming light within the contemplative. Symeon uses constantly such Greek words as *aisthisis* (sensation, awareness), *gnosis* (knowledge), *peira* (experience), *ergon* (in deed or real fact), and *dynamis* (a power), to convey his concept of a growth in conscious awareness that is beyond a mental concept and that affects the whole person.[28]

His basic principle of consciousness is rooted in deep faith, hope, and love and not merely in a sensible emotion, and can be phrased thus: Whoever is known by God, knows he is known and knows that he sees God. St. Symeon believed and experienced in his own life the words of Jesus Christ and taught that other serious Christians even now in this life should experience his same union with the Trinity: "He who loves me will keep my commandments and I will love him and I will manifest myself to him" (John 14:21).

St. Symeon's writings are filled with descriptions of seeing Jesus Christ as an inner light. As Christian contemplatives are delivered from the darkness of sin and allow the divinizing trinitarian love within them to transform them into children of God, Jesus Christ, along with his Spirit and in union with his heavenly Father, is perceived as light. This is no sense or intellectual knowledge but a level of inner consciousness of a union with Jesus Christ that defies any human conceptual description. He is uninterested in making nuanced theological distinctions—for which lack of interest his writings exposed him to inquisitional investigation and finally exile. St. Gregory Palamas would have to develop the mystical theology of this inner light.

Symeon's concern is to wake up Christians to see this inner light. He appeals to his own experience and insists that what happened to him could and should happen to other serious Christians:

> And then I knew that I consciously possessed You within me. From that moment I no longer loved You and the attributes that surround You, by recalling them in memory only, but it was really You, subsistent Love, that I was possessing within, such was from that time on my faith! Yes, the same love, for You really are Love, O God.[29]

Mount Athos Hesychasm

In the thirteenth century a renaissance of the hesychastic spirituality with accent on the continued use of the Jesus Prayer took place on Mount Athos, the peninsula that juts out from northern Greece into the Aegean Sea. From as early as the ninth century until today, Mount Athos has been a sanctuary where hesychasm has always flourished as the basic spirituality of the monks who live there. Nicephorus the Solitary or the Hesychast, an Italian of Byzantine origin, probably came to Mount Athos from Calabria or from Sicily. He wrote a treatise, *On Guarding the Heart,* in which he brings together the chief elements of hesychasm, combining the prayer of Pseudo-Macarius and Evagrius. But he adds a new element, that of stressing the interrelationship between the physical, bodily aspects of the Jesus Prayer along with the psychic effects.

Modern scholars, as Irénée Hausherr, S.J., attribute to him the important treatise that earlier writers, especially the compilers of the *Philokalia,* attributed to St. Symeon the New Theologian, *On the Three Methods of Attention and Prayer.*[30] Perhaps no single document in Eastern Christian spirituality tied the ancient traditions of the Desert Fathers in their vigilant attempts to attain inner awareness and sobriety (*nepsis*) to physiopsychological techniques that seemingly reflected a Muslim influence with its use of the *dhikr* or sacred name of Allah.[31]

St. Gregory of Sinai

It is St. Gregory of Sinai who was most responsible for bringing to Mount Athos and the Slavic world a renaissance of hesychastic spirituality. We are told that, when he arrived on Mount Athos at the end of the thirteenth century, he found only three solitaries on the whole peninsula who knew about and practised hesychasm. In his writings, he insists greatly on the purification of the soul and the fight against the passions, on the necessity of arriving at Evagrius's *apatheia,* the infusion of divine light and supernatural knowledge of the created world with intimate union of the soul with God, as his predecessors, especially St. John Climacus and St. Symeon the New Theologian, had taught. He hands down quite faithfully the ascetical purification of the "heart" of his Sinaite predecessors and builds up the tendency of Symeon to concretize and localize the supernatural experience in the human heart.

From now on we have the fixed formula for the Jesus Prayer: "Lord, Jesus Christ, Son of God, have mercy on me, a sinner," linked with the rhythm of controlled breathing. To attain a spontaneous "prayer of the heart" that would give to monks the ability to "pray always," he specifies in detail the position of the body to be assumed so as to facilitate slow breathing and thus to aid the soul to enter into the heart. Still Gregory insists over and over again on the great danger of self-deception and the necessity of listening to spiritual guides rather than following one's own inclinations. He emphasizes, more than any single element in the material technique of performing the Jesus Prayer, the necessity of accompanying prayer with such virtues as fasting, abstinence, vigil, patience, courage, silence, tears, and humility—all virtues greatly stressed by the early Desert Fathers.

In the fourteenth century, a disciple of St. Gregory of Sinai, Patriarch Callistus, who spent 28 years on Mount Athos before he became Patriarch of Constantinople, and his soul-friend, Ignatius of

Xanthopoulous, wrote down for us in their *Directions to Hesychasts in a Hundred Chapters* the two hesychastic tendencies melded together for all time. The first, as already pointed out, is the intellectual, contemplative tendency of Evagrius, Diadochus, Maximus the Confessor, and the Sinaite Fathers, stressing control of all thoughts through solitude, sobriety, and weeping for sins so that the mind, freed from influence of the passions, can contemplate God within. The other tendency stresses the constant repetition of the Jesus Prayer with its material techniques of breathing, posture, and the Taboric light as an experience visible to the corporal eyes.

It must be stressed that these latter Hesychasts who gave detailed descriptions about psychosomatic techniques to be used in reciting the Jesus Prayer always made such suggestions subservient to the union with God and the presupposed thorough purification through constant control over "passionate" thoughts. Succeeding generations perhaps did not always distinguish and in some cases overmaterialized a method that led to abuses and a general discarding of even the essentials.

St. Gregory Palamas

Hesychasm was not only a school of spirituality but it also became the basic theological anthropology accepted by Eastern Orthodoxy from the fourteenth century until the present time to describe the human relationship with the triune God. St. Gregory Palamas, a monk on Mount Athos in the fourteenth century (†1359), met up with the writings of Barlaam, an Orthodox monk born in Calabria, Italy, and educated in the scholastic methods of the West. That clash between the spirit of the Renaissance and the traditional monastic spirituality that would do much to entrench the two differing positions of Eastern and Western theology and to prevent any serious theological dialogue since that time for the past six centuries.

. This dispute centered on our human knowledge of God. Can God be perceived by human beings? Is there any sure and immediate knowledge other than that derived from sense knowledge? Gregory—in line with his predecessors, the Greek Fathers, especially the Cappadocian Fathers—held firmly to the positive, affirming theology. But against the nominalism of Barlaam, who professed an agnosticism as far as any direct knowledge or communication between God and humanity went, Gregory insisted on a more perfect knowledge, the basis of true Christian mysticism. This knowledge is given us by God and rooted in the mystery of the Incarnation. This is the apophatic knowledge we have about God through a knowledge of "unknowing."

Barlaam found the monks on Mount Athos practicing the hesychastic methods along with the Jesus Prayer and professing to see God in the Taboric light. St. Gregory Palamas insists on the patristic teaching and distinction about the inaccessible essence of God that in no way can ever be known by mere humans and the "uncreated energies" of God that are the personal relations of the triune Persons toward the created world. These energies of God are not accidents or "things" but are truly God, Father, Son, and Holy Spirit, as they communicate directly in self-giving to human persons. The end of these energies is to divinize us into sharers of God's very own nature by grace.

St. Gregory Palamas shows the distinction between God's essence and his energies:

> You do not however consider that God lets Himself be seen in His superessential essence, but according to the deifying gift and according to His energy, according to the grace of adoption, uncreated deification and the direct hypostasized glory.[32]

In his treatise, *The Triads in Defense of the Blessed Hesychasts*, St. Gregory Palamas defends the methods used by the monks who practiced hesychasm. He places such techniques in a subservient relation with the essence of the traditional hesychasm and the entire Christian spiritual life. One of the contributions to Eastern Christian spirituality made by Gregory Palamas is his positive emphasis on the body as a vital part of the whole person, as he stresses that divinizing grace, God's uncreated energies of love, also transforms the body, the senses, the natural intellect, so that the entire, whole person participates even now in this life in the supreme act for which humanity was created, namely, union with God.

The Light of Tabor

The light of Mount Tabor that certain hesychastic mystics claimed to have experienced as a sign of the most intimate union with the indwelling Trinity was for St. Gregory Palamas a natural symbol of the Christian reality of divinization by the immediate interaction of the triune Persons indwelling in the heart of the purified Christian. Both Palamas and St. Symeon the New Theologian taught that such an immersion into the trinitarian life admits of ecstatic moments in which God can be seen as brilliant light within the darkness of humanity.

Eastern Christian mystics insisted that they received a real vision of the Taboric light, dependent on their growth in compunction and humility. But Gregory Palamas would insist also that, even when the vision of such a light were not present, the light-presence of the Trinity still shone in the strong, spiritual awareness of the indwelling Trinity. Such a light to the intellect is a prelude to the full glory that awaits the Christian totally transformed into Christ.

Thus St. Gregory Palamas brings to full articulation the ultimate stages of theology as presented earlier by St. Maximus the Confessor in which the contemplative, purified of all self-love, enters into a living relationship of continued communion with the Holy Trinity. This apophatic knowledge is not by his own knowing, but it is knowledge infused by a mystical union of the indwelling Trinity.

Triumph of Hesychasm

The theological synthesis brought about by St. Gregory Palamas was joined with the practical, directional writings of St. Gregory of Sinai to bring Byzantine spirituality away from a patristic, repetitional spirituality into a mystical realism based on Holy Scripture and the sacraments. One such spiritual writer, a disciple of St. Gregory Palamas, is Nicholas Cabasilas of the latter part of the fourteenth century. As a layman, Cabasilas strove to bring the Palamite theology that provided a foundation for monastic mysticism into a synthesis of Eastern Christian spirituality applicable for all Christians, especially for those not living in monasteries.

In his classic, *Life in Christ,* Cabasilas presents a detailed exposition of the three sacraments that incorporate Christians into the Church and nourish them unto maturity; namely, Baptism, Confirmation, and Eucharist. The themes of divinization and ceaseless prayer of the name of Jesus unfold in the context of the Church and the sacraments as the perfect way to union with God. Christ is presented not only as the head but the heart of the Church. Christians need to receive this living Christ in the Eucharist, the bread of life, the climax of Church and the incorporation into Christ. Cabasilas writes,

By the Bread of life we become members of Christ much more perfectly than by any other sacred rite. For as the bodily members live by the head and the heart, so "he who eats me will live by me," the Saviour says. . . . In conformity with the normal role of heart and head, we are moved by him, and live in relation to him. . . . He communicates life to us, as heart or head do to the members of the body.[33]

Syrian Mysticism

With the subjection by the Muslims of many Christians who spoke Syriac, spiritual writing in that area consisted mainly of a repetition and interpretation of the classic spiritual writers who wrote in Greek or Syriac along with some influence from Muslim writers. The one outstanding Christian writer after the peak of Syrian spiritual writing of St. Isaac of Nineveh is Bar Hebraeus (†1286). He wrote prolifically and was the chief spokesman for the Jacobite Christians, those who embraced the Monophysite teaching of the one nature in Christ, condemned in the Council of Chalcedon (451). But in his latter years he grew weary of theological disputes and turned to the writings of the Christian and Muslim mystics, especially the writings of al-Ghazzali, the twelfth-century Sufi mystic. He strove to live, as much as his style of life would permit, the mystical life as described in his sources, such as the writings of Evagrius, Isaac of Nineveh, Gregory of Nazianzus, Basil, Gregory of Nyssa, John Climacus, Hierotheos, and a Syrian writer called John of Saba or Dalyata.

In his three most well-known works—*Ethikon, The Book of the Dove,* and a *Commentary on the Book of Hierotheos*—Bar Hebraeus brought together a syncretistic teaching that presented the mystical life as an esoteric knowledge that came to the purified Christian as a gift from God that had its own knowledge. He complained that there was no mystical leader in the world at his time, so his intent was to present teachings on the spiritual and mystical life for those serious Christians who wanted to move under the knowledge of the Dove (the Holy Spirit) and yet lacked a good spiritual guide. He brought together into a balanced synthesis the sayings of the Fathers of the Egyptian desert, the chief treasures of Semitic mysticism and asceticism mingled with a love and interpretation of Holy Scripture, and the writings of the mystics of the Greek, Syrian, and even Muslim traditions.

Russian Spirituality

When Prince Vladimir of Kiev (†c. 988) became a Christian and brought his people into the same faith, the theological and spiritual riches of the Byzantine Empire were made available to the Russian or Slav people living in that area known today as the Soviet Union or Russia. The Christian literature and culture of the Byzantine Empire were handed to newly converted Christian Russia in a language, Slavonic, that was known to the native Slavs through the missionary activities of St. Cyril and St. Methodius and their disciples. Not only did they invent the Slavic alphabet (Glagolithic and later Cyrillic), but they also made efforts (that were continued after their deaths) to develop Slavonic translations of the Greek classics of spirituality.

Practically all the Russian literature between the eleventh and fifteenth centuries is translated, coming to Russia from the southern Slavic countries through Slavonic translations. The bases of these early Slavonic translations were the Byzantine hagiographical compilations and ascetical treatises produced between the fifth and seventh centuries. The spiritual literature was overwhelmingly practical and of a didactic character.

Cyprian, Metropolitan of Kiev (†1406), learned of hesychasm from St. Gregory of Sinai's disciples in Bulgaria and brought this spirituality to Russia. He stressed a monasticism of poverty, no possessing of property, and social involvement in sharing spiritual and material alms with the poor. The kenotic ideal of being poor, and of even being a fool for Christ according to the values of the world, played an important role in Russian spirituality. St. Theodosius and St. Antony of the Kievan Pechersky Lavra are regarded as the founders of the cenobitic monasticism, modeled on Palestinian asceticism of physical and inner poverty. By this emphasis they brought the kenotic ideal to Russia.

St. Sergius of Radonezh transported the kenotic ideal of these two to the northern "thebaid"* where monasticism intensified its social activity in creating a northern culture. This culture was modeled on the humble example of St. Sergius, one of the most popular of Russian saints, whose remains are still today venerated at the Troitsky Monastery in Zagorsk, outside of Moscow—one of the few active monasteries still allowed to function in the Soviet Union.

St. Nil Sorsky

Nil Sorsky and Joseph of Volokolamsk stand out as the leading thinkers and spiritual writers in the transitional period of the latter

---

*Thebaid, derived from Thebes, refers to a grouping of monks in the same locale.

part of the fifteenth century when Russian thought, cut off from a lively intercourse with Byzantium, sought to develop its own source of creative spiritual thought. Nil Sorsky had spent some time on Mount Athos, where he had learned Greek and had thoroughly grounded himself in the hesychastic spirituality of the Greek Fathers.[34] Returning to Russia and dissatisfied with the decadent state of monasticism, he sought to develop the *skete** type of *idiorrhythmic* (each monk followed his own schedule) monasticism along the Sora River. There he wrote his *Predanie* and *Ustav,* a rule of *skete* life based on the writings of the Greek Fathers. He gathered around him a group of intellectual monks who engaged in translating and critically amending manuscripts of their many errors.

More than any one single person, Nil Sorsky was responsible for introducing into the northern parts of Russia the birth of hesychastic tradition of interior prayer and a love for solitude and poverty that clashed violently with the social monasticism propounded by Joseph of Volokolamsk (†1515). In contrast to the inner freedom and intellectual self-activity enjoined by Nil Sorsky, Joseph's spirituality favored a rigid, legalistic obedience to the letter of the law and the authority of the final arbiter, who was in his thinking the Tsar of Russia, the Third Rome.[35]

The Transvolgian hermits who perpetuated the hesychastic spirituality of Nil Sorsky were persecuted by the Josephites, and soon the monasticism of Joseph Volokolamsk, which was officially accepted and supported by the princes and tsars of Russia, dominated. The sad part of Russian spirituality is that the sixteenth century insisted that a choice had to be made between the pure evangelical spirituality of Nil Sorsky and the accommodated Christianity of Joseph Volokolamsk. And it chose to follow the aegis of Joseph with his emphasis on external ritualism, monastic possessions, and the Church in submission to the Tsar, the Christian Prince who guided the destinies not only of All-Russia but also of the Third Rome, with its messianic complex to speak for authentic Christianity over the whole world.

Still in small monasteries, *sketes,* and hermitages and in the huts of peasants, there persisted the kenotic type of spirituality that the Russians had inherited from the early Desert Fathers through the spirituality of St. Nil Sorsky and his followers.

Skete refers to a small group of monks living together under the guidance of a holy "elder" or spiritual guide.

Paissy Velichkovsky

The eighteenth century witnessed a transplantation of Western civilization into Russia. Peter the Great opened St. Petersburg as the Russian window to the West, and there poured into Russia ideas that stemmed from European rationalism, deism, materialism, and atheism. The peasants and the cultivated gentry split farther apart. The Orthodox Church preserved the liturgical and devotional life of Eastern Christian spirituality even though Russian theology as taught in the seminaries became textbook scholasticism inherited from Roman or Protestant theological manuals.

The leadership of Paissy Velichkovsky (1722-1794) was a major influence in prompting a renaissance of Eastern Christian spirituality as an antidote to Western rationalism. He was born in Poltava in the Ukraine, and after spending some time on Mount Athos in assimilating the hesychastic spirituality of early Byzantine ascetical writers, he settled in the monastery of Neamt in Moldavia (modern Rumania). He brought back the ancient tradition of the *starets*, the spiritual father type of tradition familiar in Byzantine monasticism. Through his influence such famous *startsi* as those of the monastery of Optino, near Tula in Russia, arose to call back in a prophetic role the Russian Christians to the authentic patristic tradition of Eastern Orthodoxy.

Paissy also set up in his monastery a group of writers and translators who formed an outstanding literary center of spiritual ferment. He translated into Old Slavonic the *Philokalia,* a collection of the early hesychastic fathers by the Greek Athonite monk, Nicodemus, and Bishop Macarius of Corinth, published in Greek in 1782. Through the Greek *Philokalia* and Paissy's Slavonic translation, which he called *Dobrotoliubie* (Love of the Good), this renaissance of hesychastic spirituality spread throughout the entire Greek and Slav worlds, introducing the Orthodox Christians again to the Jesus Prayer but also to a spirituality that offset the German pietism and Western rationalism that had begun to infiltrate into Orthodox spirituality.

St. Tikhon Zadonsk

St. Tikhon Zadonsk (†1783) is representative of a synthetic spirituality that drew heavily from both the early Greek Fathers and also the Western Fathers, who, like St. Augustine, wrote in Latin. He also was influenced by the German pietism of A. Arndt. As bishop he occupied the See of Voronezh for four years but resigned his bishopric to withdraw into the hidden life of a hermit of Zadonsky where he lived the rest of his life. In solitude he constantly read Holy Scripture and the early Fathers, meditating especially on the passion and sufferings of Jesus Christ and the end of the world.

His melancholic nature drew him toward the kenotic spirituality of the suffering Savior. He brought into Russian spirituality a prolific amount of writings but often not too representative of the traditional piety of Eastern Christian spirituality. He introduced the Roman Catholic devotion to the human sufferings of Christ. Trained in the rhetorical school of the Hellenic writers such as St. John Chrysostom, he fused this approach with the Baroque writing and preaching current in the seventeenth and eighteenth centuries among Western Catholics and Protestants.

St. Seraphim of Sarov

St. Seraphim, who died in 1833, is without a doubt one of the most popular of modern Russian saints, both before and after the Revolution during times of persecution in the Soviet Union. His popularity stems from his extraordinary gifts that he personally shared with his spiritual children, but also from his doctrine that what he had experienced in the mystical life is open to all Christians to experience. He loved silence, lived fifteen years in complete seclusion in the forests of Sarov, and was a *starets* or spiritual guide to all who asked his advice.

His sole writing is his *Spiritual Instructions,* which gives the traditional teachings of the ascetical Greek Fathers in the spirituality already brought into Russian piety by Nil Sorsky. His influence is due mainly to a mass of recollections, stories, and teachings that were transmitted by oral tradition through his disciples and admirers, particularly the nuns of Diveyev Convent. St. Seraphim brought to Russian spirituality an element that had become eclipsed due to the heavy accent in Eastern Christian spirituality on asceticism; that is, a continued experience of the Holy Spirit who brings the joy of resurrection to those who consent to live by the cross of love. Joy is the main characteristic that endeared St. Seraphim to the masses of Russians.

St. Seraphim broke away from the accepted monasticism of his day both in his thinking and appearance. He wore peasant garb and challenged prospective followers to a life of struggle against the demonic forces, a life of constant prayer, but also to a transformation into the indwelling life of the Trinity that is manifested by joy toward the broken world. He was rooted in the writings of St. Basil, Pseudo-Macarius, John Climacus, and in the *Philokalia* in Paissy's Slavonic translation. He recaptures the paschal "feeling" of joy of Pseudo-Macarius and St. Symeon the New Theologian through his doctrine of the transformative power of the spirit of love.

St. Theophan the Recluse

One of the most learned writers of Russian spirituality is St. Theophan the Recluse (†1894). He was deeply rooted in Greek literature, which he read fluently in Greek, having lived seven years in the East. After having taught moral theology and philosophy and served as the rector of the ecclesiastical academy of St. Petersburg, he was made bishop of Tambov and later of Vladimir. Then he retired and entered into solitude as a recluse where he dedicated himself to writing. He was an indefatigable writer, composing several books of spirituality and translating into five volumes the *Philokalia* from Paissy's Slavonic translation, which brought these hesychastic writings into the modern Russian languages. He changed the makeup of his version by dropping out some of the accents on psychosomatic techniques concerning the use of the Jesus Prayer and by adding other sections not found in Paissy's version.

The Way of a Pilgrim

Of all Russian spiritual writings, perhaps the one single work that brought the prayer of the heart and the traditional teachings of the Desert Fathers not only into the homes of ordinary Russians but also through modern Western translations into the churches and homes of non-Orthodox Christians, is an anonymous work entitled *The Way of a Pilgrim*.

This is a delightful tale of a Russian peasant who walks on foot through Russia, especially Siberia, while he prays the Jesus Prayer. Nothing is known of the author. The writing is presented as a spiritual autobiography of a Russian peasant of the mid nineteenth century, related in intimate conversations that are easily read and enjoyed for their authentic ring of peasant life before the Russian Revolution. Probably there is a real experience of a pilgrim as a basis of this composition, while some educated person may have worked over the original oral confessions.[36]

This work brought the traditional *Philokalia* teaching of the hesychastic Fathers on the prayer of the heart, centering around the reciting of the Jesus Prayer, to the masses of Russian Christians. No longer was this traditional Eastern type of prayer confined to monks living in monasteries or in solitude; it was presented as a way of life open to ordinary laymen and laywomen. It is a work of teaching designed to give laypeople the way to mystical prayer as embodied in the hesychastic teachings of the *Philokalia*. The pilgrim's *starets* or spiritual guide gives the teaching that would encourage so many Christians who have read this classic of Eastern Christian spirituality to aspire to mystical union with the indwelling Trinity by means of the Jesus Prayer:

"The constant inner prayer of Jesus is an unbroken, perpetual calling upon the Divine Name of Jesus with the lips, the mind and the heart, while picturing His lasting presence in one's imagination and imploring His grace wherever one is, in whatever one does, even while one sleeps. This prayer consists of the following words: 'Lord Jesus Christ, have mercy on me!' Those who use this prayer constantly are so greatly comforted that they are moved to say it at all times, for they can no longer live without it. And the prayer will keep on ringing in their hearts of its own accord. . . . You will learn now to master it by reading this book, which is called the *Philocalia;* it comprises the complete and minute knowledge of incessant inner prayer, as stated by twenty-five Holy Fathers. It is full of great wisdom and is so useful that it is regarded as the first and best guide by all those who seek the contemplative, spiritual life. . . ."

"Is it then loftier and holier than the Bible?" I asked.

"No, it is not, but it sheds light upon the secrets locked up in the Bible which cannot be easily understood by our shallow intelligence. . . . Thus the Holy Scripture is like the resplendent sun, while this book—the Philocalia—may be compared to the piece of glass which permits us to contemplate its lofty magnificence."[37]

John of Cronstadt

One final spiritual leader of Russia who brings a totally new accent to the field of Eastern Christian spirituality is Father John of Cronstadt (†1909). He was a married priest who spent all his priestly ministry in the parish of Cronstadt, a military port of St. Petersburg on an island in the Gulf of Finland. There he served the poor and his parishioners in the context of a pastor, preacher, celebrator of the divine mysteries of the Byzantine Liturgy, and extraordinary healer.

His spirituality is rooted in the power of faithful prayer and confidence in accepting the teachings of Scripture as experienced in the liturgical prayer, especially in the Eucharist. He makes a break from the severe asceticism of the Desert Fathers and all the saints in the annals of Eastern Christianity. Lacking also is a life of prayer built around the hesychastic spirituality of the *Philokalia*. He was not a mystic with a love for solitude, but a married parish priest.

His greatest contributions to the spirituality of Eastern Christianity are his teaching of prayer and its intercessory power to obtain needed conversion and healing and his ability to draw people into the living mysteries of Golgotha and the Resurrection as he and they experienced them in the context of the celebration of the Eucharistic Liturgy. He inaugurated again frequent reception of the Eucharist by permitting general and oral confession of penitents before receiving Holy Communion, an unheard-of custom in the Eastern Churches since the early centuries. He lived in the reality of the invisible world of God's loving power and drew all who heard him preach or witnessed him celebrate the liturgy into a sharing in that living world.

His burning faith and hope ring out in his words taken from his well-known work, *My Life in Christ:*

> The chief thing in prayer for which we must care above all is lively, clear-sighted faith in the Lord: represent Him vividly before yourself and within you—then ask of Jesus Christ in the Holy Ghost whatever you desire and you will obtain it. Ask simply, without the slightest doubt—then your God will be everything to you, accomplishing in an instant great and wonderful acts, as the sign of the cross accomplishes great wonders. Ask for both spiritual and material blessings not only for yourself, but for all believers, for the whole body of the Church, not separating yourself from other believers, but in spiritual union with them, as a member of the one great body of the Church of Christ. . . .
>
> When you are praying, either inwardly only, or both inwardly and outwardly, be firmly convinced that the Lord is there, by you and within you, and hears every word, even if only said to yourself, even when you only pray mentally; speak from your whole heart, without in the least justifying yourself; have faith that the Lord will have mercy upon you—and you will not remain unforgiven. This is true. It is taken from experience.[38]

Modern Times

The twentieth century witnessed a new phenomenon. Greek, Russian, Rumanian, Bulgarian, Serbian and Syrian Byzantine Orthodox, Coptic Christians from Egypt, Syrian Jacobites, and Assyrian Christians emigrated from their native lands where their Eastern Christian faith had a major role in forming the culture of those countries. They took up residence in predominantly non-Orthodox countries in Western Europe, North and South America, and Australia. In these countries in most cases the mother language, in which their mother liturgy was celebrated in times past, soon gave way to the new vernacular.

Theologians and spiritual writers began to translate the classical Eastern Christian theological and ascetical works into these new languages. This has had a great influence on Christians of the Roman Catholic and Protestant Churches, because it opened up to them the riches of the Christian East, which up until this century were known only to scholars.

In the field of spirituality, however, Eastern Christian writers tended to retain the traditional spiritual teachings that they had inherited, especially those that had come down to their fellow Christians through liturgical forms of spirituality. Little has yet been done to transform the rich insights of such ancient founts into new, modern applications—which may also be of exciting richness not only to the Eastern Christians found in the diaspora, as well as to those who have remained in their native countries, but also to Western Christians.

Eastern Christian spirituality at present stands with one foot firmly planted in the Old World while the other seeks a firm footing within the context of the New World. Many Eastern Christians still living in their native lands are hampered by a state order that does not always permit a freedom of growth. However, many also remain locked in static spiritual forms that had much to say in former times for Eastern Christians living in such Christian cultures, but today are not relevant enough to transform those Christians into living witnesses of a power to transform the modern world into a dynamic, living Body of Christ.

This anthology is presented as a representative collection of that Christian spirituality that has come out of that ancient past. We have seen that it has its origins in the Gospel and the spirituality of the men and women who fled into the deserts of Egypt, Syria, and Palestine in the fourth and fifth centuries. But it is far from being a monolithic spirituality, consistently founded on static elements that have been passed from generation to generation, without any change or addition.

Pseudo-Macarius, rooted in a Semitic, Syrian spirituality of the "heart," represents the currents in Eastern Christian spirituality that emphasized the holistic element of incessant prayer of the whole person through body-soul-spirit relationships. This accent highlighted the "feeling" consciousness of the indwelling presence of the Trinity through the operations of the Holy Spirit within the "heart," the deepest level or focus of awareness of an individual human person as he or she encounters God as the ground of human being.

Evagrius represents Neo-Platonism with his intellectualism that stressed the emptying of the mind of all images and thoughts so as to reach the passionless state of oneness with God. The soul "returned" to its true nature as a mirror reflecting the ever-present light of God.

Ascetical practices, rooted in Scripture, but also inspired greatly by the philosophy of humanity as propounded by Stoicism and Neo-Platonism, were always an important element in Eastern Christian spirituality. Little was given by way of describing the delights of mystical union with God. Much was taught about the purification of the entire person so as to render him or her completely open and docile to the movements of God's Spirit. *Apatheia* was the goal of such purification, but such "passionate indifference," to quote Teilhard de Chardin's phrase, which aptly describes the Eastern Fathers' teaching on purification of the heart, was only a means to pray always.

The Fathers developed the psychology of the evolution of the human thought along with the basic "passionate" sins on a body, soul, and spirit level, the eight passionate thoughts. *Philautia*, or self-love, is at the basis of every sin and shows itself in the individual's involvement of attachment to body level of temptations toward food, sex, or avarice for things, or in attachment to psychic levels of the temptations of anger, sadness, and *acedia* (boredom). On the spiritual level of attachment to self, vainglory and pride hold the individual in captivity.

Praxis is the spiritual battle over all negative forces that prevent the Christian from being open to God's Spirit, as well as the struggle to put on the "mind of Christ" by developing the Christian virtues necessary to be a loving person over a self-centered one. This inner warfare necessitated *prosochi*, or an inner attention and vigilance that was very demanding. *Nepsis* was the concept used to describe this sobriety or inner vigilance over the demonic forces from without and from within. Demonology played a great part in the spirituality not only of monks but also of the ordinary laity. It allowed simple Christians to use a concrete symbol to focus attention on an enemy that had to be conquered by God's grace and individual attention and discipline.

A Spirituality of Contemplation

Eastern Christian spirituality is chiefly characterized by its contemplative element. *Theoria*, or contemplation of the inner world of God's uncreated energies of love operating at all times in all events and in all creatures, is open to all human beings, for this ultimately is the end for which God created us: to share in his inner life as an experience of self-giving love of person to person. Absent in the annals of such a Christian spirituality is the Western controversy concerning works and grace and the teaching that separates contemplation into acquired and infused contemplation. The teachers of Eastern Christian contemplation stress continually the reality of God's uncreated love that cannot increase. It can only be unveiled or revealed to us when we have brought a disposition of purification of heart to the world around us in order to see what had been there all the time.

Theoria admits of two levels of intensity: *physica* is the contemplation in material creatures of the Divine Logos in each created thing. The Logos of each creature is its principle of harmony that shows us the relationship of a given creature to God's total providence or to God's order of salvation. Comprehending the inner principle of being in each creature, one can live in God's harmony and return love for love by living in truth and freedom according to God's holy will.

Theoria theologica is the mystical contemplation of the Holy Trinity that stems from contemplating all things in God's Logos. The Logos leads the Christian into the highest union with God, in which the individual is restored to the integrity of the image according to which God had created him, according to God's Logos. God reveals himself no longer through creatures or the *logoi* in creatures but through the trinitarian life of active love dwelling within the individual Christian.

We saw how such a quest for continued, increased consciousness of the risen Savior brought about a "feeling" consciousness developed by concentrating on the indwelling presence of Christ Jesus through continued repetition of the name of Jesus synchronized with one's breath. The stress is on the transcendence of God in the risen, glorified Son of God, humanity's own broken sinfulness, and the immanence of a mystical union with the Holy Trinity. This awareness often brought about an experience of God's indwelling presence as an inner, transforming light of God's uncreated energies, called the Taboric light.

Liturgical Spirituality

These elements of transcendence, human sinfulness and cosmic disharmony, and the intimate immanence of God's trinitarian family and the individual Christian were captured in the Eastern Christian liturgies. Liturgical prayers and rituals kept this positive, transforming view of Christianity ever present throughout the ages for Eastern Christians.

Whenever peoples are oppressed by political leaders or by calamitous natural forces, there is developed a hope in a better, future society, in a forthcoming savior who will bring an end to suffering and initiate a messianic age of peace and prosperity. The Eastern Christian liturgies and their liturgical prayers capture the eschatological longing found in Scripture and the teaching of the Church for a better world to come in the return of the glorious Lord Jesus Christ. Moreover, the personal piety of individuals who suffered greatly from political harassment as well as sufferings from natural forces accentuated the end of the world and the judgment of God on the just and the sinners.

Penthos, or the continued sense of sorrow for sins and fear of ultimate condemnation, permeates liturgical and personal prayer. Yet God is not depicted only in his awesome transcendence and fearsome power to punish but is also represented as a forgiving God whose mercy is above all his works. The cry for divine mercy is an accent that is universal in Eastern Christian prayer.

Cosmic Transformation

Due to the stress on both the transcendence of God and his immanence in all things, on a mysticism of God's presence, intimate and operative in all things, Eastern Christians view the spiritual life as a process of continued growth or better of the unfolding of what was implanted in the Christian soul at Baptism. The feast of the Transfiguration of Jesus Christ, so central in Eastern worship, not only celebrates the glorification of the Lord but also proclaims that God is transforming each individual Christian in a process that is ever so gradual but continuous, from glory to greater glory, from participation in the divine life to greater assimilation into the Trinity.

As the individual Christian experiences this transformation within his or her own personal life, a faith act is exercised in each thought, word, and deed that a similar transfiguration is taking place on the cosmic level of the whole universe. The Pauline vision of Christ drawing the whole universe into the fullness destined for it by his Father's eternal plan, but through the cooperation of human beings, is very much at the center of Eastern Christianity's teaching of work as a prayerful cooperation in love in this "reconciliation" process. Christ risen is inserted into the material world, but the Christian by living faith releases a transforming power within the context of the human situation in which the Christian finds him- or herself in God's providence.

In such a spirituality, matter is moving to spirit but the role of the human person is all-important to transform the material world into the Body of Christ.

All Is Eucharist

Ultimately the Christology, the presence of the Trinity among human beings, the Eastern Christian teaching on the structure of the Church or ecclesiology, the climax of all liturgical prayer and celebration, are centered on the mystery of the Eucharist. Here theology becomes experienced spirituality, dogma becomes living prayer, and the entire universe is already caught up in the microcosmic action of Christ in his Body as he pours out his transforming Spirit of love to bring harmony and a unity of many out of a world of separated and uncommunicating people.

The key to Eastern Christian spirituality is found in the living experience of the Eucharist that forms the background for all other aspects of prayer, asceticism, work, and contemplation. In the Eucharist men and women experience the total person of Jesus Christ, energizing them into a new creation (2 Cor. 5:17). Jesus becomes for Eastern Christians the Bread of Life, uniting him with the Trinity but also bringing them into a new oneness with others who form the Church, the Body of Christ, in loving union with its head, Jesus Christ. The Eucharistic celebration is the sacred place and time when the Church is most realized by the power of the Holy Spirit.

The divinizing power of the Trinity experienced in the Eucharist is to be the power that drives Christians outward toward other communities to be Eucharist, bread broken, to give themselves with Christ and the Father abiding within them with their Spirit of love, empowering them to do what would be impossible for them alone.

Lux ex Oriente

No faith vision can ever be passed on from generation to generation unless it is done through the vehicle of a given culture. The culture that has been the carrier of Eastern Christianity has been not one but many. We speak therefore of a fusion of many diverse cultural factors that form the backdrop for this type of spirituality. Yet there are liturgical and traditional elements that form a common heritage called Eastern Christian spirituality. Certain accents and points of emphasis become consistent in the spiritual writings of this form of Christianity.

The writers of the Christian East divide chiefly into two groups: the Eastern theologians and the ascetical writers. The former almost all lived some of their lives within the Eastern ascetical tradition. Yet their writings form a theological anthropology that was presupposed in the writings of the less speculative, more ascetical writers and in the ordinary piety of the Christian laity.

These accents are different from those pursued by the writers of Western Christianity. It is in this hope that this anthology is presented; namely, that these legitimate approaches to the Christian spiritual life will be able to complement the habitual views of the spiritual life as entertained among Western Christians. Such mutual sharings occurred in earlier times within the Church when there was union between the Western and Eastern Churches. First, by studying the writings of the Eastern Christian spiritual writers of times past, not only can we Christians in the West better understand and appreciate the unique contributions to Christianity made by our Eastern brethren, but such knowledge can pave the way for a mutual encounter and interchange on the level of Christian sharing. This, after all, is the aim of true Christian spirituality: to build the Body of Christ into a greater harmony and unity through love while allowing the Holy Spirit to operate in developing the uniqueness of each member of that one Body.

NOTES*

1. On the complexities of this term, see Jordan Aumann, O.P., "Spirituality in the Catholic Tradition," in Aumann, *Christian Spirituality East and West*, pp. 9–27.
2. A. Festugiere, *Contemplation et vie contemplative chez Platon*, pt. 2, p. 288.
3. Werner Jaeger, *Early Christianity and Greek Paideia*.
4. St. Maximus the Confessor, *Ambigua*, in *PG*, 91:1308.
5. St. Maximus the Confessor, in *ACW*, p. 151.
6. Vladimir Lossky, *The Mystical Theology of the Eastern Church*, p. 111.
7. Pseudo-Macarius, *The Spiritual Homilies*, Homily 2,2, p. 34.
8. St. John Climacus, *The Ladder of Divine Ascent*, step 27, pp. 236–250.
9. Louis Bouyer, *The Spirituality of the New Testament and the Fathers*, p. 386.
10. Evagrius Ponticus, *Chapters on Prayer*, no. 69, p. 66.
11. Pseudo-Macarius, *The Spiritual Homilies*, p. 100.
12. Evagrius Ponticus, *Chapters on Prayer*, no. 66, p. 66.
13. St. Gregory of Nyssa, *Commentary on the Song of Songs*, in PG, 44, 1000 D, quoted from Danielou and Musurillo, p. 247.
14. Ibid., p. 270.
15. Hans Urs von Balthasar, *Kosmische Liturgie* (Freiburg, 1941), p. 5, cited in Elmer O'Brien, S.J., *Varieties of Mystic Experience*, pp. 75–76.
16. J. Vanneste, S.J., *Le Mystère de Dieu: Essai sur la structure rationnelle de la doctrine mystique du Pseudo-Denys l'Areopagite* uses this term to describe the first stage toward ecstatic union with God.
17. St. Philotheus, *Forty Texts on Sobriety*, p. 454, nos. 22–23.
18. On the struggle between Diadochus and this heretical group, see F. Dorr, *Diadochus von Photike und die Messalianer . . .*, p. 50; also, I. Hausherr, S.J., "L'erreur fondamentale et la logique du Messalinisme," pp. 328–360.
19. Diadochus of Photice, *Oeuvres spirituelles: Cent Chapitres Gnostiques*, ch. 85.
20. See J. Kirchmeyer, "Ephrem," in *Dictionnaire de Spiritualité*, vol. 4, section 1, cols. 788–822.
21. St. Isaac the Syrian, *Directions on Spiritual Training*, in Kadloubovsky and Palmer, *Philokalia: Early Fathers*, p. 243.
22. Ibid., p. 258.
23. Evagrius Ponticus, *Chapters on Prayer*, no. 5, p. 56.
24. St. John Climacus, *The Ladder of Divine Ascent*, step 7,6, p. 114.
25. St. Isaac the Syrian, *Directions on Spiritual Training*, in Kadloubovsky and Palmer, *Philokalia: Early Fathers*, p. 251.
26. Rev. Alexander Schmemann, in his *Sacraments and Orthodoxy*, well illustrates this feature of Eastern spirituality.
27. St. Symeon, *Hymns of Divine Love*, Hymn 21, p. 96.
28. On this subject, see: P. Miguel, "La Conscience de la grace selon Symeon le Nouveau Théologian," pp. 314–342; and George A. Maloney, S.J., *The Mystic of Fire and Light*, pp. 60–63.
29. St. Symeon, *Traites Ethiques*, no. 3, 195, p. 404; St. Symeon, *Catecheses*, 2, 269–273, p. 352.
30. I. Hausherr, S.J., "La Methode d'oraison hesychastes," pp. 109–210.
31. J. Gouillard, *Petite Philocalie de la Prière du Couer*, in *Documents Spirituelles*,

---

*Complete references for Notes can be found in the Bibliography.

vol. 5, quotes an anonymous text giving a warning against certain physiological, fake consequences coming from this method, which "relies on Islamic fakes and their methods of dhikr" (pp. 305-306). Cf. also M. L. Gardet, "La mention du nom divin en mystique musulmane" in *Revue Thomiste,* pp. 642-646.

32. St. Gregory Palamas, Triade III, 1, 29, in Palamas, *Les Triades.*

33. Nicholas Cabasilas, *The Life in Christ,* chap. 6, p. 14.

34. For a life of St. Nil Sorsky and his thought, see George A. Maloney, S.J., *Russian Hesychasm.*

35. His chief writings are his *Prosvetitel' (Enlightener* and *Ustav Monastic Rule).* For his life and thought, cf. J. Spidik, S.J., *Joseph de Volokolamsk: Un Chapitre de la spiritualité russe.*

36. This is the view of G. Fedotov in *A Treasury of Russian Spirituality,* p. 281.

37. *The Pilgrim,* translated by Nina A. Toumanova, in Fedotov, *A Treasury of Russian Spirituality,* pp. 287-288.

38. John of Cronstadt, *My Life in Christ,* in Fedotov, *A Treasury of Russian Spirituality,* pp. 353-354.

CHAPTER ONE

MADE LITTLE LESS THAN A GOD

Yet you have made him little less than a god. (Ps. 8:5)

Let us make man in our own image, in the likeness of ourselves. (Gen. 1:26)

A. Made According to God's Image

1. Image and Likeness

Now the soul and the spirit are certainly a part of the man but certainly not the man; for the perfect man consists in the commingling and the union of the soul receiving the spirit of the Father and the admixture of that fleshly nature, which was molded after the image of God. . . . But when the spirit here blended with the soul is united to God's handiwork (*plasma*) the man is rendered spiritual and perfect because of the outpouring of the Spirit, and this is he who was made in the image and likeness of God. But if the Spirit be wanting to the soul, he who is such is indeed of an animal nature, and, being left carnal, shall be an imperfect being, possessing indeed the image of God in his formation (*in plasmato*), but not receiving the similitude through the Spirit, and thus is this being imperfect. . . . Neither is the soul itself, considered apart by itself, the man; but it is the soul of a man, and part of a man. Neither is the spirit a man, for it is called the spirit, and not a man, but the commingling and union of all these constitutes the perfect man. . . . For this cause he (Paul) declares that those are "the perfect" who present unto the Lord the three component parts without offense. Those then are the perfect who have had the Spirit of God remaining in them, and have preserved their souls and bodies blameless, holding fast the faith of God, that is that faith which is directed toward God and maintaining righteous dealings with respect to their neighbors. (St. Irenaeus)[1]

For the image of God is His Word, the genuine Son of Mind, the Divine Word, the archetypal light of light; and the image of the Word is the true man, the mind which is in man, who is therefore said to have been made "in the image and likeness of God," assimilated to the Divine Word in the affections of the soul and therefore rational. (Clement of Alexandria)[2]

And God said, "Let us make man in our own image and after our likeness," and then He adds the words: "So God created man in His own image, in the image of God created He him; male and female created He them and He blessed them." Now the expression, "in the image of God created He him," without any mention of the word "likeness," conveys no other meaning than this, that man received the dignity of God's image at his first creation; but that the perfection of his likeness has been reserved for the consummation, namely, that he might acquire it for himself by the exercise of his own diligence in the imitation of God, the possibility of attaining to perfection being granted him at the beginning through the dignity of the divine image, and the perfect realization of the divine likeness being reached in the end by the fulfillment of the (necessary) works. (Origen)[3]

Being God, God gives them (men) a share in His own Image, our Lord Jesus Christ, and makes them after His own image and after His likeness; so that by such grace perceiving the Image, that is, the Word of the Father, they may be able through Him to get an idea of the Father, and knowing their Maker, live the happy and truly blessed life. (St. Athanasius)[4]

For, as when the likeness painted on a panel has been effaced by stains from without, he whose likeness it is must needs come once more to enable the portrait to be renewed on the same wood; for, for the sake of his picture, even the mere wood on which it is painted is not thrown away, but the outline is renewed upon it; in the same way also the most Holy Son of the Father, being the image of the Father, came to our region to renew man once made in His likeness and find him as one lost. (St. Athanasius)[5]

"Man is a great thing, and pitiful man is something honorable," (Prov. 20:6) who has his honor in his natural constitution. For, what other things on earth have been made according to the image of the Creator? To which of the animals that live on the land, or in the water, or in the air, has the rule and power over all things been given? He has fallen a little below the dignity of the angels because of his union with the earthly body. . . . But still, the power of understanding and recognizing their own Creator and Maker also belongs to men. "And he breathed into his nostrils" (Gen. 2:7), that is to say, He placed in man some share of His own grace, in order that he might recognize likeness through likeness. Nevertheless, being in such great honor because he was created in the image of the Creator, he is honored above the heavens, above the sun, above the choirs of stars. For, which of the heavenly bodies was said to be an image of the most high God? What sort of an image of his Creator does the sun preserve? . . . They possess only inanimate and material bodies that are clearly discernible, but in which nowhere is there a mind, no voluntary motions, no free will. (St. Basil)[6]

What is this mystery that is around me? I had a share in the image; I did not keep it. He (Christ) partakes of my flesh that he may both save the image and make the flesh immortal. He communicates a second union far more marvelous than the first, inasmuch as then He imparted the better nature, whereas now He Himself partakes of the worse. This is more godlike than the former action, this is loftier in the eyes of all men of understanding. (St. Gregory of Nazianzus)[7]

The Godhead is mind and word; for "in the beginning was the Word" (John 1:1) and the followers of Paul "have the mind of Christ" which "speaks in them" (1 Cor. 2:16; 2 Cor. 13:3); but humanity too is not far removed from these; you see in yourself word and understanding (logos, nous), an imitation of the very Mind and Word. Again, God is love and the font of love; for this the great John declares that "love is of God," and "God is love" (1 John 4:7–8); the Fashioner of our nature has made this to be our feature too; for "hereby," He says, "shall all men know that you are my disciples, if you love one another." Thus, if this be absent, the whole stamp of the likeness is transformed. The Deity beholds and hears all things and searches all things out; you too have the power of apprehension of things by means of sight and hearing and the understanding that inquires into things and searches them out. (St. Gregory of Nyssa)[8]

2. Body

In the same way as the Divinity of the word Incarnate is common to soul and body . . . so, in spiritual men, is the grace of the Spirit transmitted to the body by the soul as intermediary, and this gives it to experience divine things and allows it to feel the same passion as the soul. . . . Then the body is not driven any more by bodily and material passions . . . but turns on itself, rejects all relation with evil things, and itself inspires its own sanctification and an inalienable deification. (St. Gregory Palamas)[9]

The spiritual joy that comes from the spirit into the body is not at all broken by communion with the body, but transforms the body and makes it spiritual, for then it rejects all the evil appetites of the flesh, and does not drag the body down any more but rises up with it so that the whole man becomes "Spirit" according to what is written: "he who is born of the Spirit is Spirit" (John 3:6,8). (St. Gregory Palamas)[10]

That heavenly fire of the Godhead which Christians receive interiorly in their hearts now in this life, that same fire which now interiorly directs their hearts, bursts forth upon the dissolution of the body. It again pulls together the members of the body and brings about a resurrection of the dismembered body . . . for that interior fire, inhabiting our hearts, then emerges and brings about the resurrection of the bodies. (Pseudo-Macarius)[11]

B. Moving into the Likeness of Christ

All men are made in God's image; but to be in His likeness is granted only to those who through great love have brought their own freedom into subjection to God. For only when we do not belong to ourselves do we become like Him who through love has reconciled us to Himself. No one achieves this unless he persuades his soul not to be distracted by the false glitter of this life. (St. Diadochus of Photike)[12]

Free will is the power of a deiform soul to direct itself by deliberate choice toward whatever it decides. Let us make sure that our soul directs itself deliberately only toward what is good, so that we always consume our remembrance of evil with good thoughts. (St. Diadochus of Photike)[13]

He who has been restored "according to the image and likeness," that is, Jesus Christ, has equally received the ability to see "according to nature." As a consequence, he walks always with becoming dignity as in broad daylight; he sees all things as they are in their very nature. (St. Symeon the New Theologian)[14]

The Creator devised as it were a second root of our race, to bring us back to our former incorruptibility, in order that, just as the image of the first man, the man from the earth, engraved on us the necessity of dying and involved us in the meshes of corruption, so, conversely, the second beginning, the one after Him, that is, Christ, and the likeness to him through the Spirit, would stamp us with indestructibility, and just as disobedience subjected us to punishment in the former, so in the latter compliance and complete obedience might make us partakers of the blessings from heaven and the Father. . . .

It would be absurd to think that Adam, who was earthborn and a man, could send hurtling into the whole race, like some inheritance, the power of the curse that was leveled at him, while Emmanuel, who is from above, from heaven, God by nature, did not give on His part a rich participation in His own life to those who might elect to share His kinship through faith. (St. Cyril of Alexandria)[15]

Now the removal of what is foreign is a return to what is connatural and fitting; and this we can only achieve by becoming what we once were in the beginning when we were created. Yet to achieve this likeness to God is not within our power nor within any human capacity. It is a gift of God's bounty, for He directly bestowed this divine likeness on our human nature at its creation. By our human efforts we can merely clear away the accumulated filth of sin and thus allow the hidden beauty of the soul to shine forth. (St. Gregory of Nyssa)[16]

C. Divinization: Participators in God's Own Nature

1. Divinization

For this is why the Word of God is man, and this is why the Son of God became the Son of man, that man might possess the Word, receive adoption and become the son of God. In no other way could we receive incorruptibility and immortality, unless incorruptibility and immortality had first become what we are, in order that what is corruptible might be absorbed by incorruptibility and what is mortal by immortality, that so we might receive the adoption of sons. (St. Irenaeus)[17]

It follows that He, being the deifying and enlightening power of the Father, in which all things are deified and quickened, is not alien in essence from the Father, but co-essential. For by partaking of Him, we partake of the Father; because the Word is the Father's own. Whence, if He was Himself too from participation, and not from the Father, His essential Godhead and Image, He would not deify, being deified Himself. (St. Athanasius)[18]

The Son of God became the Son of Man in order that the sons of men, the sons of Adam, might be made sons of God. The Word, who was begotten of the Father in heaven in an ineffable, inexplicable, incomprehensible and eternal manner, came to this earth to be born in time of the Virgin Mary, Mother of God, in order that they who were born of earth might be born again of God, in heaven. . . . He has bestowed upon us the first-fruits of the Holy Spirit, so that we may all become sons of God in imitation of the Son of God. Thus He, the true and natural Son of God, bears us all in Himself, so that we may all bear in ourselves the only God. (St. Athanasius)[19]

For one who is a man becomes a son of God by being joined to Christ by spiritual generation;—a man puts off himself and puts on the divine nature. . . . A man becomes a son of God, receiving what he has not and laying aside what he has. (St. Gregory of Nyssa)[20]

He (Christ) has ever been the Only begotten by nature . . . but He is the First-born for our sakes, so that because He is called the First-born of all created things, whatever resembles Him may be saved through Him. (St. Cyril of Alexandria)[21]

But, O what intoxication of light, O what movements of fire!
O, what swirlings of the flame in me, miserable one that I am,
coming from You and Your glory!
The glory I know it and I say it is Your Holy Spirit,
who has the same nature with You and the same honor, O Word,
He is of the same race, of the same glory,
of the same essence, He alone with Your Father
and with You, O Christ, O God of the universe!
I fall down in adoration before You.
I thank You that You have made me worthy to know
as much as it is the power of Your divinity.
I thank You that You, even when I was sitting in darkness,
revealed Yourself to me, You enlightened me,
You granted me to see the light of Your countenance
that is unbearable to all . . .
You appeared as light, illuminating me completely from Your total light.
And I became light in the night, I who was found in the midst
    of darkness.
Neither the darkness extinguished Your light completely,
nor did the light dissipate the visible darkness,

but they were together, yet completely separated,
without confusion, far from each other, surely, but not at all mixed,
except in the same spot where they filled everything, so it seems
    to me. . . .
Listen, now. I am telling you the awesome mysteries of a double God
    who came to me as to a double man.
He took upon Himself my flesh and He gave me His Spirit
and I became also god by divine grace, a son of God but by adoption.
O what dignity, what glory! (St. Symeon the New Theologian)[22]

Man, who among beings counts for nothing, who is dust, grass, vanity, who was adopted to be a son of the God of the universe, becomes the friend of this Being of such excellence and grandeur; this is a mystery that we can neither see nor understand nor comprehend. What thanks should man give for so great a favor? What word, what thought, what lifting up of mind in order to exalt the superabundance of this grace? Man surpasses his own very nature. From a mortal being he becomes immortal, from a perishable being he becomes imperishable. From ephemeral he becomes eternal. In a word, from man he becomes god. In fact, rendered worthy to become a son of God, he will have in himself the dignity of the Father, enriched by all the inheritance of the goods of the Father. O munificence of the Lord, so bountiful. . . . How great are the gifts of such ineffable treasures! (St. Gregory of Nyssa)[23]

Theosis (Divinization) is the elevation to what is better, but not the reduction of our nature to something less, nor is it an essential change of our human nature. A divine plan, it is the willing condescension of tremendous dimension by God, which He did for the salvation of others. That which is of God is that which has been lifted up to a greater glory, without its own nature being changed. (St. Athanasius of Mount Sinai)[24]

2. Fatherhood

If he has any sense, he would obviously not dare to call God by the name of Father since he does not see the same things in himself as he sees in God. For it is physically impossible that He who is good by essence should be the Father of an evil will, nor the Holy One of him whose life is impure. No more can He who is changeless be the Father of a man who is turning from one side to the other, nor can the Father of life have as His son someone whom sin has subjected to death. He who is wholly pure cannot be the Father of those who have disgraced themselves by unseemly passions, nor He who pours out benefits of him who is self-seeking. In short, He who is seen to be pure goodness cannot be Father of those who are wholly involved in some evil. If therefore on examining himself a man finds that he still needs to be purified because his conscience is full of vile stains and sores, he cannot insinuate himself into the family of God until he has been purged from all these evil things. The unjust and impure cannot say Father to the just and pure, since this would mean calling God Father of his own wickedness, which would be nothing but pride and mockery. For the word Father indicates the cause of what exists through Him. (St. Gregory of Nyssa)[25]

If therefore the Lord teaches us in His prayer to call God Father, it seems to me that He is doing nothing else but to set the most sublime life before us as our law. For Truth does not teach us to deceive, to say we are what we are not and to use a name to which we have no right. But if we call our Father Him who is incorruptible and just and good, we must prove by our life that the kinship is real. . . . How ardent must be our zeal so that our conscience may achieve such purity as to have the courage to say "Father" to God? For if you make such prayer with your lips while you are keen on money and occupied with the deceits of the world, while you are seeking fame among men or are enslaved by sensual passions—what, do you think, will He say to it who sees your life and knows what your prayer really is? (St. Gregory of Nyssa)[26]

3. Children of God

Nor is it by the mere fact of loving that they confirm their sonship, by cleaving to God and loving Him as their Father, but also by becoming like Him through love. They are filled with love, but "God is love" (I John 4:16), and they live for love. It is those on whom this noble passion is nourished who truly live, just as all things are dead for those in whom it is absent. Therefore, because they are sons, they honour the Father by their actions. By being themselves alive they proclaim the living God by whom they have been begotten.

By the "newness of life" (Rom. 6:4) in which they, in accordance with Paul's word, are walking, they put their trust in Him and "glorify the Father who is in heaven" (Matt. 5:16). Thus they are ineffably generated by His loving-kindness. As is fitting, "He is not God of the dead, but of the living" (Matt. 22:32), because with them He finds His proper glory. Accordingly He also said to the wicked, "If I am God, where is My glory?" (Mal. 1:6). (Nicholas Cabasilas)[27]

For He alone is both the Only-begotten and the First-born; Only begotten as God; First-born insofar as He became through the salvific union a man among us and among many brothers. By this we also in Him and through Him according to nature and grace have been made sons of God. According to nature insofar as we are one in Him (through the same human nature); by participation and according to grace through Himself in the Spirit. (St. Cyril of Alexandria)[28]

Thus, through Himself He may transmit to the entire human race the glory of sonship by adoption. . . . So He has appeared as man before the Father on our behalf that He might restore us to the Father's presence who had been cut off from it by the ancient transgression. He has sat there as Son in order that we, who are like sons, might be designated sons of God through Him. The fact that Christ who sits there is in all things like us, in that He appeared as man . . . somehow confers on us the grace of this dignity. (St. Cyril of Alexandria)[29]

D. God Is Uncreated Energies

1. Essence and Energies

If it were possible to contemplate the divine nature itself in itself and find out what is proper to it and what is foreign through what appears, we would be in no need at all of words or other signs for the comprehension of what is sought. But because it is higher than the understanding of the things sought, and we reason parting from certain signs about things that evade our memory, it is of all necessity that we be conducted by the energies to the research of the divine nature. (St. Basil)[30]

Since man can participate in God and since the super-essential essence of God is absolutely unparticipable, there is a certain something between the participable essence and the participants, which permits them to participate in God. And if you suppress that which is between the unparticipable God and the participants . . . oh, what a void!—you separate us from God by destroying the bond and establishing a great uncrossable abyss between God on the one hand and creation and the governing of creatures on the other. We must then seek another God who possesses not only His own proper end within Himself, His own proper energy and His own proper

Godhead, but one who is a good God—for thus it will no longer suffice for Him to exist only for the contemplation of Himself—, not only perfect, but surpassing all fullness; thus, in effect, when, in His goodness, He will wish to do good, He will be able to do it; He will be not only immobile, but He will put Himself into motion, He will thus be present for all with His manifestations and His creative and providential energies; in one word, we must seek a God in whom we can have a share in one way or another, so that by participating in Him, each one of us may receive, in the manner proper to him and according to the analogy of participation, being, life and deification. (St. Gregory Palamas)[32]

You do not, however, consider that God lets Himself be seen in His superessential essence, but according to the deifying gift and according to His energy, according to the grace of adoption, uncreated deification and the direct hypostasized glory. (St. Gregory Palamas)[31]

2. Grace

Sometimes it is the object given gratuitously which is called grace, but sometimes it is the very act of giving; at other times neither of these senses apply to the word "grace," which designates the beauty, the beautiful appearance, the ornament and the glory of each nature, and in this sense we speak of the grace of words and of conversation. . . . Hence there is a grace of nature different from deifying grace. (St. Gregory Palamas)[33]

There is a created grace and another grace uncreated . . . but since the gift which the saints receive and by which they are deified is not other than God Himself, how can you say that that is a created grace? (St. Gregory Palamas)[34]

Grace . . . is the energy or procession of the one nature; the divinity insofar as it is ineffably distinct from the essence and communicates itself to created beings, deifying them. (St. Gregory Palamas)[35]

To him who has been baptized into Christ grace has been mysteriously given already. But it acts in proportion to his fulfillment of commandments. Although this grace never ceases to help us in secret, it lies in our power to do or not to do good according to our own will. (St. Mark the Ascetic)[36]

As we have said, from the instant we are baptized, grace is hidden in the depths of the intellect, concealing its presence even from the perception of the intellect itself. When someone begins, however, to love God with full resolve, then in a mysterious way, by means of intellectual perception, grace communicates something of its riches to his soul. Then, if he really wants to hold fast to this discovery, he joyfully starts longing to be rid of all his temporal goods, so as to acquire the field in which he has found the hidden treasure of life (cf. Matt. 13:44). This is because, when someone rids himself of all worldly riches, he discovers the place where the grace of God is hidden. For as the soul advances, divine grace more and more reveals itself to the intellect. During this process, however, the Lord allows the soul to be pestered increasingly by demons. (St. Diadochus of Photike)[37]

Take the example of a fire outside a bronze vessel. When you put wood under it, see, it becomes very hot. . . . But if anyone should become careless and not throw fire under it, the fire begins to become less hot and nearly dies out. So also grace, the heavenly fire, is also within you. So also if you pray and give your thoughts to the love of Christ, see how you have thrown under yourself the wood and your thoughts become fire and are immersed completely in the desire for God. (Pseudo-Macarius)[38]

Some have imagined that both grace and sin, that is, the spirit of truth and the spirit of error, are hidden at the same time in the intellect of the baptized. As a result, they say, one of these two spirits urges the intellect to good, the other to evil. But from Holy Scripture and through the intellect's own insight I have come to understand things differently. Before holy baptism, grace encourages the soul toward good from the outside, while Satan lurks in its depths, trying to block all the intellect's ways of approach to the divine. But from the moment that we are reborn through baptism, the demon is outside, grace is within. Thus, whereas before baptism error ruled the soul, after baptism truth rules it. Nevertheless, even after baptism Satan still acts on the soul, often, indeed, to a greater degree than before. This is not because he is present in the soul together with grace; on the contrary, it is because he uses the body's humors to befog the intellect with the delight of mindless pleasures. God allows him to do this, so that a man, after passing through a trial of storm and fire, may come in the end to the full enjoyment of divine blessings. For it is written: "We went through fire and water, and Thou hast brought us out into a place where the soul is refreshed" (Ps. 66:12). (St. Diadochus of Photike)[39]

Divine grace confers on us two gifts through the baptism of regeneration, one being infinitely superior to the other. The first gift is given to us at once, when grace renews us in the actual waters of baptism and cleanses all the lineaments of our soul, that is, the image of God in us, by washing away every stain of sin. The second, our likeness to God, requires our co-operation. When the intellect begins to perceive the Holy Spirit with full consciousness, we should realize that grace is beginning to paint the divine likeness over the divine image in us. Artists first draw the outline of a man in mono-chrome, and then add one color after another, until little by little they capture the likeness of the subject down to the smallest details. In the same way the grace of God starts by remaking the divine image in man into what it was when he was first created. But when it sees us longing with all our heart for the beauty of the divine likeness and humbly standing naked in its "atelier," then by making one virtue after another come into flower and exalting the beauty of the soul "from glory to glory" (2 Cor. 3:18), it depicts the divine likeness on the soul. . . . Something similar happens to those who are being repainted by God's grace in the divine likeness: when the luminosity of love is added, then it is evident that the image has been fully transformed into the beauty of the likeness. Love alone among the virtues can confer dispassion on the soul, "for love is the fulfilling of the law" (Rom. 13:10). In this way our inner man is renewed day by day through the experience of love, and in the perfection of love it finds its own fulfillment. (St. Diadochus of Photike)[40]

St. Makarios of Egypt says (*First Treatise on Guarding of the Heart*, ch. 12) that the grace which comes to man "does not bind his will by force of necessity, nor does it make him unchangeably good willy-nilly. On the contrary, the power of God which exists in the man gives way before his free will, in order to reveal whether the man's will is in accordance with grace or not." From this moment the union of freedom with grace begins. At first grace stands out-side, and acts from the outside. Then it enters within and begins to take possession of parts of the spirit: but it only does this when man by his own desire opens the door for it, or opens his mouth to receive it. Grace is ready to help, if man desires. By himself man cannot do or establish within himself that which is good, but he longs and strives for it. Because of this longing, grace consolidates within him the good for which he yearns. And so it goes on, until man acquires final mastery over himself, and thus is able to fulfill that which is good and pleasing to God. (St. Theophan the Recluse)[41]

According to the zeal and efforts of the man who gives himself to God, grace will enter and penetrate him increasingly with its power, sanctifying him and making him its own. But one cannot and should not stop at this stage. This is still only a seed, a starting point. It is necessary that this light of life should go further, and permeating the entire substance of the soul and body should in this way sanctify them, claiming them for itself; uprooting the alien and unnatural passionateness which now dominates us, it should raise the soul and body to their pure and natural state. The light should not remain enclosed within itself but should spread over our whole being with all its powers.

But since these powers are all infected with what is unnatural, the pure spirit of grace, coming into the heart, is unable to enter directly and immediately into them, being barred out by their impurity.

Therefore we must establish some channel between the spirit of grace living within us and our own powers, so that the spirit may flow into them and heal them, just as dressings heal the sore places to which they are applied.

These, then, are the activities and exercises which are the means of healing our powers and bringing them back to their lost purity and wholeness: fasting, labor, vigil, solitude, withdrawal from the world, control of the senses, reading of the scriptures and the Holy Fathers, attendance at church, frequent confession and communion. (St. Theophan the Recluse)[42]

CHAPTER TWO

FAR EAST OF EDEN: PARADISE LOST

> Yahweh, do not punish me in your rage,
> or reprove me in the heat of anger.
> Your arrows have pierced deep,
> your hand has pressed down on me;
> no soundness in my flesh now you are angry,
> no health in my bones, because of my sin.
>
> My guilt is overwhelming me,
> it is too heavy a burden;
> my wounds stink and are festering,
> the result of my folly;
> bowed down, bent double overcome,
> I go mourning all the day.
>
> . . . And now my fall is upon me,
> there is no relief from my pains;
> yes, I admit my guilt,
> I am sorry for having sinned. (Ps. 38:1–6, 17–18)

A. Sin: Missing the Mark

1. Death

(Death speaks:)
I am He who has conquered all the wise men;
and lo! in the corners they are heaped for me in hell.
Come, enter, son of Joseph, and see terrible things;
the limbs of the giants,
the mighty corpse of Samson,
and the skeleton of the stubborn Goliath;
Og, moreover, the son of the giants,
who made for himself a bed of iron
and lay thereon,
from whence I hurled him and cast him down;
that cedar I laid low to the gate of hell.

I by myself alone have conquered multitudes,
and one may single-handed seek to conquer me.
Prophets and priests and men of renown
have I carried off;
I have conquered kings in their armies,
and mighty men in their hunts,
and righteous men in their excellencies.
Streams of corpses are hurled by me into hell,
and though they pour into her
she is athirst.
Though one be near or though he be far off,
the end brings him to the gate of hell. . . .

Death ended his speech of derision;
and the voice of our Lord sounded into Hell,
and He cried aloud and burst the graves one by one.
Tremblings took hold on Death;
Hell that never of old had been lighted up,
into it there flashed splendors,
from the Watchers who entered in
and brought out the dead to meet Him,
who was dead and gives life to all.
The dead came forth,
and the living were ashamed,
they who thought that they had conquered
the Life-Giver of all. (St. Ephrem the Syrian)[43]

Someone said with perfect truth that fear of death afflicts a man, whose conscience condemns him; but a man who bears good testimony in himself desires death as much as he desires life. (St. Isaac the Syrian)[44]

The remembrance of death is a daily death; and the remembrance of our departure is an hourly sighing or groaning. (St. John Climacus)[45]

As of all foods bread is the most essential, so the thoughts of death are the most necessary of all works. The remembrance of death amongst those in the midst of society gives birth to distress and frivolity, and even more—to despondency. But amongst those who are free from noise it produces the putting aside of cares, and constant prayer and guarding of the mind. But these same virtues both produce the remembrance of death and are also produced by it. (St. John Climacus)[46]

A true sign of those who are mindful of death in the depth of their being is a voluntary detachment from every creature and complete renunciation of their own will. (St. John Climacus)[47]

Insensibility of heart dulls the mind, and abundance of food dries the fountains of tears. Thirst and vigil afflict the heart and when the heart is afflicted the waters flow. The things we have said will seem cruel to epicures and incredible to the indolent; but a man of action will readily test them, and he who has found them out by experience will smile at them. But he who is still seeking will become more gloomy. (St. John Climacus)[48]

And I cannot be silent about the story of Hesychius the Horebite. He passed his life in complete negligence, without paying the least attention to his soul. Then he became extremely ill, and for an hour he left his body. And when he came to himself he begged us all to leave him immediately. And he built up the door of his cell, and he stayed in it for twelve years without ever uttering a word to anyone, and without eating anything but bread and water. And, always remaining motionless, he was so wrapt in spirit in what he had seen in his ecstasy that he never changed his place but was always as if out of his mind, and silently shed hot tears. But when he was about to die, we broke open the door and went in and after many questions this alone was all we heard from him: "Forgive me! No one who has acquired the remembrance of death will ever be able to sin." We were amazed to see that one who had before been so negligent was so suddenly transfigured by this blessed change and transformation. . . . So by his true and praiseworthy repentance the Lord showed us that even after long negligence He accepts those who desire to amend. (St. John Climacus)[49]

The upright and righteous and good and wise fear not nor tremble at death, because of the great hope that is before them. And they at every time are mindful of death, their exodus, and of the last day in which the children of Adam shall be judged. They know that by the sentence of judgement death has held sway, because Adam transgressed the commandment; as the Apostle said:— Death ruled from Adam unto Moses even over those who sinned not, so that also upon all the children of Adam it passed (Rom. 5:14, 12), even as it passed upon Adam. (Aphrahat)[50]

2. Sin

God gave the command to do good and to avoid sin, but opposing powers make us tend toward evil, and it becomes difficult to do this good. These sinful powers are not innate to man's nature, but they are brought in from outside. (Nilus)[51]

For after man in disobedience died the grievous death of the soul and he received curse upon curse: "Thistles and thorns shall the ground bring forth for you" (Gen. 3:18), and again: "You will cultivate the earth and it shall not yield henceforth unto you its fruits" (Gen. 4:12), thorns and thistles sprouted and grew up in the earth of his heart.

His enemies took away his glory through deceit and clothed him with shame. His light was taken away and he was clothed in darkness. They killed his soul and they scattered and divided his thoughts. And they dragged down from on high his mind and Israel became the man who is slave to the true Pharaoh. And he set over him his supervisors and taskmasters, to do his evil works and to complete the construction of mortar and brick.

And these spirits led him away from his heavenly wisdom and led him down to the material and earthly and muddy evil works and to words and desires and thoughts that are vain. Having fallen from his proper height, man found himself in a kingdom of hatred toward mankind and there bitter rulers forced him to construct for them the wicked cities of sins.

But if man groans then does he receive the beginning of deliverance. And he is delivered in the month of new flowers (Exod. 13:4) in the springtime when the ground of the soul is able to shoot forth the beautiful and flowering branches of justification. The bitter winter storms of the ignorance of darkness have passed as also the great blindness that was born of sordid deeds and sins. (Pseudo-Macarius)[52]

Just as the whole body suffers and not merely one part alone so also the entire soul was subjected to the passions of evil and sin. The prince of evil thus clothed the whole soul, which is the chief member and part of man, with his own wickedness, that is, with sin. And so the entire body fell a victim to passion and corruption. (Pseudo-Macarius)[53]

There are many things of all kinds which receive the name of evil. Some of these are troublesome to all men in general, while some of them are troublesome to some only; but there is nothing like wickedness of the soul and disease of the will.

Some things are bad in themselves, such as the destructive influences of stars and disorders of seasons, barrenness of countries, rendings of the earth, earthquakes and pestilences, as well as poverty and disease, ill-treatment, imprisonment, and scourgings. But for man they are not at all evil. Such things harm him but outwardly and affect no more than his body and his possessions. The body is not the man to the extent that when it is sick he himself should be diseased. . . .

If, however, true humanity consists of having will and reason, which no other beings here have in common with man, it is this which gives rise to virtue and wickedness alike. As for misfortune or prosperity, disease or health, living in distress or in enjoyment, the former would apply to those who have turned aside from the right way, while the other would belong to those who persist in the path of duty. . . .

If, therefore, we need to learn what things cause pain to the true man by being a perversion of nature, we must take the opposite of God's laws. That which is truly evil opposes God's will. By being evil it is an object of hatred for him who cares for the good, and those who hate it wish that good may not come about when it is absent and suffer pain when it is present. By its presence evil causes the good pain, whether it is with them (as long as they have not taken leave of reason!) or with others for whom they pray. It is the good for which they pray for all men, by hastening to the divine loving-kindness and by desiring to see God's glory shining everywhere.

Thus sin alone is grievous to those who live in Christ, because it is evil while their character is virtuous, because it is contrary to God's laws, to whose will they strive to be united, and also, because for those who live in accordance with right reason it is most unsuitable to be vainly afflicted by anything else since they can derive the most useful fruits from pain. . . . In the case of evil of soul, suffering is the remedy. It averts future evil, causes present evil to cease, and is able to release us from punishment for past misdeeds. It was for this reason, I think, that the ability to suffer pain was given to our nature at the beginning, since it is not capable of helping us for anything else.

Now we do not venture to commit sin for no reason, but for the sake of gaining some reward of pleasure we barter away enjoyment of the good health of the soul. It is not for their own sake that we choose the ruin of the soul and the burning up of the mind! Once we know these things and repent of our sinful deeds we are distressed over them and despise the pleasure derived from them. We cast out the passion by means of its opposite, and show this by rejecting what we have accepted and by accepting what we have rejected. At the same time our suffering becomes the penalty which we pay for the sins which we have committed, and having been cleansed by it we need no further chastisement. (Nicholas Cabasilas)[54]

B. Satan

Devils

Our adversary is skillful. He that contends against us is crafty. Against the brave and the renowned does he prepare himself, that they may be weakened. For the feeble are his own, nor does he fight with the captivity that are made captive to him. He that has wings flees from him and the darts that he hurls at him do not reach him. They that are spiritual see him when he assails, and his panoply has no power upon their bodies. All the children of light are without fear of him, because the darkness flies from before the light. The children of the Good fear not the Evil, for He has given him to be trampled by their feet. When he makes himself like darkness unto them, they become light. And when he creeps upon them like a serpent, they become salt, whereof he cannot eat. If he makes himself like the asp unto them, then they become like babes. If he comes in upon them in the lust of food, they, like our Redeemer, conquer him by fasting. And if he wishes to contend with them by the lust of the eyes, they lift up their eyes to the height of heaven. If he wishes by enticements to overcome them, they do not afford him a hearing. If he wishes to strive openly with them, lo! they are clothed in panoply and stand up against him. If he wishes to come in against them by sleep, they are wakeful and vigilant and sing psalms and pray. If he allures them by possessions, they give them to the poor. If he comes in as sweetness against them, they taste it not, knowing that he is bitter. If he inflames them with the desire of Eve, they dwell alone, and not with the daughters of Eve. (Aphrahat)[55]

When the devils see that you are really fervent in your prayer they suggest certain matters to your mind, giving you the impression that there are pressing concerns demanding attention. In a little while they stir up your memory of these matters and move your mind to search into them. Then when it meets with failure it becomes saddened and loses heart. (10)

The devil so passionately envies the man who prays that he employs every device to frustrate that purpose. Thus he does not cease to stir up thoughts of various affairs by means of the memory. He stirs up all the passions by means of the flesh. In this way he hopes to offer some obstacle to that excellent course pursued in prayer on the journey toward God. (46)

Why do the demons wish to commit acts of gluttony, impurity, avarice, wrath, resentment and the other evil passions in us? Here is the reason: that the spirit in this way should become dull and consequently rendered unfit to pray. For when man's irrational passions are thriving he is not free to pray and to seek the word of God. (50)

When the destructive demon is unable to stir up your memory at the time of prayer, then he does some violence to the bodily equilibrium so as to cause a certain strange phantasm to rise in the spirit and to assume a particular shape there. Then the man who is accustomed to stop short at concepts is readily brought low. In this manner then the spirit, which by its nature is driven ahead in its search for immaterial knowledge and for that which is beyond all form, goes astray. It mistakes the smoke for the light. (68)

Train yourself like a skilled athlete. You must learn not to become anxious even if you should see some sudden apparition, or some sword pointed at you, or a beam of light leaping toward your face. Even though you should see some hideous and bloody figure, still stand firm, and in nowise give way to the fear that clutches at your heart. When you thus bear witness to your faith you will face your enemies with ready confidence. (92)

See to it that the evil demons do not lead you astray by means of some vision. Rather be wise: turn to prayer and call upon God to enlighten you if the thought comes from him, and if it does not, ask him to drive away from you the deceptive one quickly. Then take courage, for the dog will not hold his ground. With you praying to God with such ardor he shall be at once driven far off under the invisible lashings laid on by the unseen power of God. (94)

Strive to cultivate a deep humility and the malice of the demons shall not touch your soul. Then the plague shall not approach your dwelling for "he has given his angels the command to watch over you" and to drive away from you, invisibly, every force that is hostile. (96)

Crashing sounds and roars and voices and beatings all of these, coming from the devils, are heard by the man who pursues the practice of pure prayer. Yet he does not lose courage nor his presence of mind. He calls out to God: "I shall fear no evils for you are with me." And he adds other similar prayers. (97)

If the demons threaten you, appearing suddenly from the atmosphere and frightening you greatly and shattering your spirit or mauling your flesh like wild beasts, do not give way to panic because of them. Do not so much as trouble yourself over their threats. They frighten you so as to test your mettle. They wish to see if you will take them seriously or if you ignore them through contempt and whether you communicate in prayer with the omnipotent God, the Creator and Provider of all. (99)

By night the demons demand the spiritual master for themselves to harass him. By day they surround him with pressures from men—with calumnies and with dangers. (139) (Evagrius)[56]

Does Satan know all the thoughts and plans of man? If one man is with another person and knows things concerning him, and if you, twenty years old, know things concerning your neighbor, can Satan, who has been with you from your birth, not know your thoughts? . . . Still we do not say that he, before he tempts, knows what man will intend to do. For the tempter tempts, but he does not know whether man will obey him or not until man gives up his will as a slave.

Neither again do we maintain that the devil knows all the thoughts of man's heart and its desires. Like a tree, it has many branches and limbs. So the soul has certain branches of thoughts and plans and Satan grasps some of them. There are other thoughts and intentions that are not grasped by Satan. (Pseudo-Macarius)[57]

Spiritual knowledge teaches us that there are two kinds of evil spirits: some are more subtle, others more material in nature. The more subtle demons attack the soul, while the others hold the flesh captive through their lascivious enticements. Thus there is a complete contrast between the demons that attack the soul and those that attack the body, even though they have the same propensity to inflict harm on mankind. When grace does not dwell in a man, they lurk like serpents in the depths of the heart, never allowing the soul to aspire toward God. But when grace is hidden in the intellect, they then move like dark clouds through the different parts of the heart, taking the form of sinful passions or of all kinds of day-dreams, thus distracting the intellect from the remembrance of God and cutting it off from grace. (St. Diadochus of Photike)[58]

The demons fill our mind with images, or rather clothe themselves in images for our benefit and impinge on us (introduce a
suggestion) according to the ruling passion habitually acting in the
soul. For generally they make use of passionate habits to multiply in
us passionate fantasies and even in sleep they fill our dreams with
varied imaginings. Moreover, the demons of lust sometimes turn into
pigs, sometimes into donkeys, or into frenzied and fiery stallions. . . .
The demons of anger turn sometimes into pagans, sometimes into
lions; the demons of cowardice into Ishmaelites; the demons of in-
constancy into Idumaeans; the demons of drunkenness and gluttony
into Saracens; the demons of greed sometimes into wolves, sometimes into tigers; the demons of deceit sometimes into snakes, or
into vipers, or into foxes; the demons of shamelessness into dogs;
the demons of laziness into cats. . . . Our fantasy changes the images of demons in a threefold manner corresponding to the tripartite nature of the soul, presenting them in the form of birds, wild
beasts and domestic animals, in accordance with the three powers
of the soul: the desiring, the excitable and the thinking. For the
three princes of the passions rise up against these three powers,
and assuming the image akin to whatever passion qualifies the soul,
assault it in this disguise. (St. Gregory of Sinai)[59]

C. Loss of Divine Life

If, however, thou wilt not believe in Him and wilt flee from His
hands, the cause of imperfection shall be in thee who didst not obey,
but not in Him who called thee. . . . The skill of God, therefore, is
not defective, for He has power of the stones to raise up children for
Abraham; but the man, who does not obtain it, is the cause to
himself of his own imperfection. The light does not fail because
some persons have become blind. The light remains ever the same.
It is those who are blinded that are involved in darkness through
their own fault. The light does not enslave anyone by necessity; nor
does God exercise compulsion upon anyone unwilling to accept the
exercise of His skill. Those persons, therefore, who have aposta-
tized from the light given by the Father and transgressed the law of
liberty have done so through their own fault since they have been
created free agents and possessed of power over themselves. (St.
Irenaeus)[60]

So turning away and forgetting that she (the human soul) was in
the image of the good God, she no longer, by the power which is in

her, sees God the Word after whose likeness she is made; but having departed from herself, images and feigns what is not. For hiding, by the complications of bodily lusts, the mirror which, as it were, is in her, by which alone she had the power of seeing the Image of the Father, she no longer sees what a soul ought to behold, but is carried about by everything and only sees the things which come under the senses. (St. Athanasius)[61]

D. Passions

1. Victory over the Passions

There is only one way to begin; and that is by taming passions. These cannot be brought under control in the soul except by guarding the heart and by attention. Those, therefore, who pass through all these stages in due order, each in its own time, can, when the heart is cleansed from passions, devote themselves entirely and wholly to psalmody, and to fighting against thoughts; and they can look up toward heaven with their physical eyes or contemplate it with the spiritual eyes of the soul, praying aright in purity and truth. (St. Theophan the Recluse)[62]

If you wish to gain victory over the passions, enter within yourself through prayer and God's help; then descend into the depths of your heart and there track down these three powerful giants: forgetfulness, laziness, and ignorance. It is these three that uphold the ranks of our spiritual adversaries: supported by these three, all the other passions, returning to the heart, act, live, and gain strength in self-indulgent and uninstructed souls, but if by means of great attention and persistence of mind, and with help from above, you find those evil giants that are unbeknown to many, you will easily drive them away with the weapons of righteousness—with the remembrance of what is good, with the eagerness that spurs the soul to salvation, and with knowledge from heaven. (St. Mark the Hermit)[63]

But you must realize that this kindling cannot take place in you while the passions are still strong and vigorous, even though they may not in fact be indulged. Passions are the dampness in the fuel of your being, and damp wood does not burn. There is nothing else to be done except to bring in dry wood from outside and light this, allowing the flames from it to dry out the damp wood, until this in its turn is dry enough to begin slowly to catch alight. And so little by little the burning of the dry wood will disperse the dampness and will spread, until all the wood is enveloped in flames.

All the powers of the soul and activities of the body are the fuel of our being, but so long as man does not pay heed to himself these are all saturated and rendered ineffective by the soggy dampness of his passions. Until the passions are driven out, they obstinately resist spiritual fire. Passions penetrate into both the soul and the body, and overpower even man's spirit itself, his consciousness and freedom; and in this manner they come to dominate him entirely. As they are in league with devils, through them the devils also dominate man, although he falsely imagines that he is his own master.

But while your spirit has been re-established in its rightful freedom, the soul and body are still under the sway of passions and suffer violence from them. You have now to arm yourself against your passions and to conquer them. Drive them out of your soul and body. This struggle against the passions is unavoidable, for they will not willingly yield up their illegal possession of your being. (St. Theophan the Recluse)[64]

Passions have different names; but they are divided into those of the body and those of the soul. Bodily passions are subdivided into sorrowful and sinful; the sorrowful are again subdivided into those of suffering and those of punishment. Passions of the soul are divided into excitable, slothful and mental.

The mental are subdivided into those of imagination and those of reason. All of them are either voluntary, through misuse, or involuntary, through necessity. The latter are so-called nonshameful passions which the holy fathers described as due to surroundings and natural characteristics (dispositions).

Some passions are of the body; others are passions of the soul; some are passions of lust, others passions of the excitable part, yet others are passions of thought. Of the latter some are passions of the mind and others of reasoning. All of them combine with one another in various ways and affect one another—and thus change.

Passions of the excitable part are: anger, bitterness, quarrelsome, hot temper, insolence, haughtiness, boastfulness and the like. Passions of desire are: graspingness, debauchery, intemperance, insatiability, voluptuousness, love of money, self-love—the most evil passion of all. The bodily passions are: fornication, adultery, impurity, unseemliness, gluttony, laziness, absentmindedness, attachment to the world, attachment to life and the like. Passions of speech and tongue are: unbelief, blasphemy, deceit, craftiness, curiosity, duplic-

ity, slander, calumny, blame, disparagement, talkativeness, pre-
tense, lying, ribaldry, invective, flattery, mockery, pushing oneself
forward, servility, being puffed up, perjury, idle talk, etc.

Passions of the mind are: conceit, self-exaltation, self-praise, argumentativeness, rashness, self-satisfaction, contrariness, disobedience, dreaminess, fabrications, love of showing off, love of fame,
pride—the first and last of all evils. Passions of thought are: wandering, heedlessness, captivity and slavery, darkening of thoughts,
blindness, evasions (of work), suggestions, identifications, inclinations, distortions, rejections and the like. In a word, all evil thoughts,
feelings and dispositions, contrary to our nature, are divided according to the three powers of the soul, just as all the good ones, consistent with our nature, are similarly divided. (St. Gregory of Sinai)[65]

It is imperative to say as much as possible about *prelest* (passionate thoughts) since for many it is difficult to recognize and almost
incomprehensible owing to the multitude and variety of its snares
and pitfalls. It is said that *prelest* appears or rather comes upon us in
two forms—in the form of fantasies and in the form of outer influences, although its sole cause and origin is always pride. The first is
the origin of the second, and the second is sometimes the origin of
yet a third—frenzy. The origin of the illusory contemplation of fantasies is opinion (pretending to know all) which produces a false
representation of the Deity in one fantastic form or another; this is
followed by *prelest* (passionate thoughts), leading one into error
through dreams and engendering blasphemy, which further plants
fears in the soul both in sleeping and waking. For puffing oneself up
is followed by *prelest* (passionate fantasies), after *prelest* comes blasphemy, after blasphemy fear, after fear trembling, and after trembling frenzy (being out of one's mind). Such is the first form of
prelest, that which comes from fantasies.

The second kind of *prelest,* in the form of outer influences, is as
follows: it has its origin in lust born of natural desire. This lust gives
birth to irrepressibility of unspeakable impurities. Firing all one's
being and darkening the mind by identification with imagined idols,
its burning intoxication drives the mind to frenzy and madness.

In this state the seduced man takes it on himself to prophesy,
gives false prognostications, asserts that he sees certain saints and
repeats words supposedly said to him, for, intoxicated by the frenzy
of passion, his nature is changed and he appears like one possessed.
Laymen, misled by the spirit of *prelest,* call such men "psycharii";

they are to be found sitting by the shrines of saints, and are supposed to be inspired, influenced and tortured by them, and announce revelation received from them. But such men should simply be called possessed, seduced and fallen into error, rather than prophets of the present and the future. The demon of obscenity, having confused their mind with the fire of lust, drives them insane, presenting to them dream images of certain saints, making them hear their words and see their faces. But it happens also that the demons themselves appear and trouble them with fears. Subjecting them to the yoke of Belial, the demons drive them like faithful slaves to act sinfully, against their will, meaning later to lead them to hell. (St. Gregory of Sinai)[67]

Lakes of fire are those passionate souls in which, as in some fetid hogs, the stench of passions feeds the unsleeping worm of intemperance, the irresistible lusts of the flesh. It feeds also the snakes, toads and leeches of evil lusts, loathsome and pernicious thoughts and demons. Such a state is even now a promise of hell's torment. (St. Gregory of Sinai)[67]

2. Despondency

All other passions affect only one part of the soul—either the excitable, or the desiring, or else the thinking, as for instance, forgetfulness and ignorance. But despondency, embracing all the powers of the soul, straightway, at a single breath, brings almost all the passions into motion and therefore presses more heavily than all other passions. Good, therefore, are the words of the Lord that give the remedy against it, "In your patience possess ye your souls" (Luke 21:19). (St. Maximus the Confessor)[68]

Let us not be perturbed if we are in darkness. I mean that special darkness in which the soul languishes at times and is, as it were, among the waves; and whether a man reads the Scriptures, or practices his rule, in whatever he does darkness follows upon darkness.

He leaves his work, and very often is even unable to go near it. That hour is full of despair and fear; hope in God and the comfort of faith in Him are completely lost by the soul, and the whole of it is filled with doubt and fear.

But God does not abandon the soul to such a state for long, and soon makes a way to escape (1 Cor. 10:13).

But I will tell you, and give you this advice: if you have no strength to master yourself and to prostrate yourself in prayer, then wrap your head in your cloak and sleep, until this hour of darkness is over, but do not leave your cell.

People subjected to this temptation are mostly those who wish to lead a life of the mind, and who, on their way, seek the comfort of faith. Therefore at this hour what torments and wearies them most is the wavering of their mind. This wavering is often followed by impious thoughts, and a man is sometimes seized by doubt of the resurrection, and other things of which it is better not to speak.

Those occupied by physical work are entirely free of these temptations. They are assailed by another kind of despondency, familiar to every one, which in its mode of action differs from these and similar temptations.

Blessed is a man who endures it without going out of his door. However, this struggle is not ended in an hour; and grace does not return suddenly to dwell in the soul, but gradually. One thing alternates with another; at times temptation comes, at others comfort. (St. Isaac the Syrian)[69]

3. Pride

Pride is denial of God, an invention of the devil, the despising of man, the mother of condemnation, the offspring of praise, a sign of sterility, flight from divine assistance, the precursor of madness, the herald of falls, a foothold for satanic possession, source of anger, door of hypocrisy, the support of demons, the guardian of sins, the patron of unsympathy, the rejection of compassion, a bitter inquisitor, an inhuman judge, an opponent of God, a root of blasphemy. (St. John Climacus)[70]

God resists the proud. Who then can have mercy on them? Every proud-hearted man is unclean before God. Who then can cleanse such a person? (St. John Climacus)[71]

It is shameful to be proud of the adornments of others, but utter madness to fancy one deserves God's gifts. Be exalted only by such merits as you had before birth. But what you got after your birth, as also birth itself, God gave you. Only those virtues which you have obtained without cooperation of the mind belong to you, because your mind was given you by God. Only such victories as you have won without the cooperation of the body have been accomplished by your efforts, because the body is not yours but a work of God. (St. John Climacus)[72]

The proud man is pomegranate, rotten inside, while outwardly radiant with beauty. (St. John Climacus)[73]

CHAPTER THREE

LOGOS MADE FLESH

He is the image of the unseen God
and the first born of all creation,
for in him were created
all things in heaven and on earth:
everything visible and everything invisible,
Thrones, Dominations, Sovereignties, Powers
all things were created through him and for him.
Before anything was created, he existed,
and he holds all things in unity.
Now the Church is his body,
he is its head. (Col. 1:15-18)

A. An Orthodox Christology

1. Jesus Christ: True God and True Man

Let us take pattern, my beloved, from our Savior, who though He was rich, made Himself poor; and though He was lofty, humbled His Majesty; and though His dwelling place was in heaven, yet rode on a colt and so entered Jerusalem; and though He is God and Son of God, He took upon Him the likeness of a servant; and though He was for others rest from all weariness, yet was Himself tired with the weariness of the journey; though He was the fountain that quenches thirst, yet Himself thirsted and asked for water; though He was abundance and satisfied our hunger, yet He Himself hungered when He went forth to wilderness to be tempted; though He was a watcher that slumbers not, He yet slumbered and slept in the ship in the midst of the sea; and though He was ministered to in the Tabernacle of His Father, yet let Himself be served by the hands of men; though He was the healer of all sick men, yet nails were fastened into His hands; though His mouth brought forth things that were good, yet they gave Him gall to eat; though He injured no man and harmed none, yet He was beaten with stripes and endured shame; and though He was Savior of all mortals, He delivered Himself to the death of the cross. (Aphrahat)[74]

Glory to that Voice which became Body,
and to the Word of the High One
Which became Flesh!
Hear Him also,
O ears, and see Him, O eyes,
and feel Him, O hands,
and eat Him, O mouth!
You members and senses give praise unto Him,
that came and quickened the whole body!
Mary bore the silent Babe,
while in Him were hidden all tongues!
Joseph bore Him,
and in Him was hidden a nature
more ancient than aught that is old!
The High One became as a little child,
and in Him was hidden a treasure of wisdom
sufficing for all!
Though Most High,
yet He sucked the milk of Mary,
and of His goodness all creatures suck!
He is the Breast of Life;
the dead suck from His life and revive.
Without the breath of the air
no man lives,
without the Might of the Son
no man subsists.
On His living breath
that quickens all,
depend the spirits
that are above and that are beneath.
When he sucked the milk of Mary,
He was sucking all with Life.
While He was lying on His Mother's bosom,
in His bosom were all creatures lying.
He was silent as a Babe,
and yet He was making His creatures execute
all His commands.
For without the First-born
no man can approach unto the Essence
to which He is equal.
The thirty years He was on the earth,

Who was ordering all creatures,
Who was receiving all the offerings of praise
from those above and those below.
He was wholly in the depths
and wholly in the highest!
He was wholly with all things
and wholly with each.
While His body was forming within the womb,
His power was fashioning all members!
While the Conception of the Son was fashioning in the womb,
He Himself was fashioning babes in the womb.
Yet not as His body was weak in the womb,
was His power weak in the womb!
So too not as His body was feeble by the Cross,
was His power weak in the Cross.
For when on the Cross He quickened the dead,
His body quickened them,
yea, rather His Will,
just as when He was dwelling wholly hanging upon the Cross,
His power was yet making all creatures move! (St. Ephrem the Syrian)[75]

Let us, therefore, my beloved brethren, be eager to find Christ and see Him as He is, in His beauty and attractiveness. We see many men who are moved by the desire of transitory things to endure many toils and labors. They will travel great distance and even disregard wife and children and every other glory and enjoyment and prefer nothing to their purpose in order that they may secure the attainment of their goal . . . shall we not deliver our souls and bodies to death for the sake of the King of kings and Lord of lords (1 Tim. 6:15), the Creator and Sovereign of all things? Whither shall we flee from His face? (Ps. 139:7) . . . Since then, brethren, we cannot withstand the Lord or flee from His face, come, let us give ourselves as slaves to Him, our Lord and God, who for our sakes "took on Himself the form of a slave" and died for us. Come, let us be humbled under His mighty hand (1 Pet. 5:6), which makes eternal life to spring forth for all, and imparts it abundantly through the Spirit to those who seek it. (St. Symeon the New Theologian)[76]

O new commingling! O strange conjunction! The self-existent comes into being; the uncreated is created, that which cannot be contained is contained, by the intervention of an intellectual soul, mediating between the Deity and the corporeity of the flesh. And He who gives riches becomes poor, for He assumes the poverty of my flesh, that I may assume the richness of His Godhead. He that is full empties Himself, for He empties Himself of His glory for a short while, that I have a share in His fullness. What are the riches of His goodness? What is this mystery that is around me? I had a share in the image; I did not keep it. He partakes of my flesh that He may save the image and make the flesh immortal. He communicates a second communion far more marvelous than the first, inasmuch as then He imparted the better nature, whereas now Himself partakes of the worse. This is more godlike than the former action, this is loftier in the eyes of all men of understanding. (St. Gregory Nazianzus)[77]

Listen, my soul: God has come to us; Our Lord has visited us. For my sake He was born of the Virgin Mary, He who is born of the Father before all time. For my sake He was wrapped in swaddling clothes, He who covers heaven with the clouds and vests Himself with robes of light. For my sake He was placed in the lowly manger, He whose throne is the heavens and whose feet rest upon earth. For my sake He was fed with His mother's milk, He who feeds all creatures. For my sake He was held in His mother's arms, He who is borne by the Cherubim and holds all creatures in His embrace. For my sake He was circumcized according to the Law, He who is maker of the Law. For my sake, He who is unseen became visible and lived among men, He who is my God. My God became one like me, like a man; the Word became flesh, and my Lord, the Lord of Glory, took for my sake the form of a servant and lived upon earth and walked upon earth, He who is the King of Heaven. He labored, worked miracles, conversed with men, was like a servant, He who is the Lord of all. He was hungry and thirsty, He who provides food and drink for all creatures. He wept, He who wipes away all tears. He suffered and mourned, He who is the consoler of all men. He consorted with sinners, He who alone is just and holy. He who is omnipotent toiled and had nowhere to lay His head, He who lives in light inaccessible. He was poor, He who gives riches to all men. He wandered from town to town and from place to place, He who is omnipresent and fills all space. And thus for thirty-three years and more He lived and labored upon earth for my sake—I who am His servant. (St. Tychon of Zadonsk)[78]

2. Christ the Mediator

Christ is the mediator through whom all those good things which God has bestowed upon us, or rather which he is continually bestowing upon us, are given. It was not good enough for him to play his part as mediator once only, in obtaining for us all for which he interceded; he intercedes for us continually, not as ambassadors do, by words and pleas, but actively. How does he do this? He unites us to himself, and makes us each, according to our individual merit and purity, sharers through him in those graces which are his own.

Just as the sight of the eye comes from light, and those who are deprived of light cannot see, so continual union with Christ is necessary to the soul, if it is to live fully and enjoy the tranquillity. As the eye cannot see without light, so the soul cannot have true life and peace without Christ, for he alone reconciles us to God and is the Author of that peace without which we would still be God's enemies, without hope of sharing in the benefits which come from him.

So, if any man has not been united to Christ at the beginning (by Baptism), or, having been thus united, has not remained in union, he counts as God's enemy, and must therefore be excluded from his riches.

What reconciled God to humankind? Simply this, that he saw his beloved son become man. Likewise, he is reconciled personally to every man who wears the stamp of the Only Begotten, and bears his Body, and shows himself to be one spirit with him. Without these things, each of us remains the old man, hateful to God, and having nothing in common with him. (Nicholas Cabasilas)[79]

3. Christ the Recapitulator

For in what way could we be partakers of the adoption of sons, unless we had received from Him through the Son that fellowship which refers to Himself, unless His Word, having been made flesh, had entered into communion with us? Wherefore also He passed through every stage of life, restoring to all communion with God. . . . But what He did appear, that He also was: God recapitulated in Himself the ancient formation of man, that He might kill sin, deprive death of its power and vivify man; and therefore His works are true. (St. Irenaeus)[80]

For, as when the likeness painted on a panel has been effaced by stains from without, he whose likeness it is must needs come once more to enable the portrait to be renewed on the same wood; for, for the sake of his picture, even the mere wood on which it is painted is not thrown away, but the outline is renewed upon it; in the same way also the most Holy Son of the Father, being the image of the Father, came to our region to renew man once made in His likeness and find him as one lost. (St. Athanasius)[81]

By whom was man to be recalled to the grace of his original state? To whom belonged the restoration of the fallen one, the recovery of the lost, the leading back of the wandered by the hand? To whom else than entirely to Him who is the Lord of his nature? For Him only who at the first had given the life was it possible, or fitting, to recover it when lost. This is what we are taught and learn from the Revelation of the truth, that God in the beginning made man and saved Him when he had fallen. (St. Gregory of Nyssa)[82]

B. The Church: The Body of Christ

Men, women and children, profoundly divided as to race, nation, language, manner of life, work, knowledge, honor, fortune . . . the Church recreates all of them in the Spirit. To all equally she communicates a divine aspect. All receive from her a unique nature which cannot be broken asunder, a nature which no longer permits one to take into consideration the many and profound differences which are their lot. In that way all are raised up and united in a manner which is truly Catholic. In her none is in the least degree separated from the community, all are grounded, so to speak, in one another by the simple and indivisible power of faith . . . Christ, too, is all in all, He who contains all in Himself according to the unique, infinite and all-wise power of His goodness—as a center upon which all lines converge—that the creatures of the one God may not live as strangers or enemies one with another, having no place in common, where they may display their love and their peace. (St. Maximus the Confessor)[83]

I cannot grieve God by keeping silent what He ordered to be spoken and confessed. For if, according to the divine Apostle, it is He Himself who has set in the Church, first apostles, secondly prophets, thirdly doctors, it is clear that he has spoken through them. By all of Holy Scripture, by the Old and the New Testament, by the holy doctors and synods we are taught. (St. Maximus the Confessor)[84]

And yet He has made the Church His body, and He builds it with love through the increase of the faithful, until we shall all be united in one perfect Man, unto the measure of the age of the fullness of Christ (Eph. 4:13). If then the Church is Christ's body, Christ is the Head of the body, forming the countenance of the Church with His own features. Perhaps it is this that the friends of the Bridegroom saw when they were given heart: in her they see more clearly that which is invisible. It is like men who are unable to look upon the sun, yet they can see it by its reflection in the water. So the friends of the Bridegroom see the Sun of Justice by looking upon the face of the Church as though it were a pure mirror, and thus He can be seen by His reflection. (St. Gregory of Nyssa)[85]

In Christ, that which is uncreated, eternal, existing before the ages, is completely inexpressible and incomprehensible to all created intellects. Yet that which was revealed in the flesh can to a certain extent be grasped by human understanding. It is toward this element in Christ that the Church, our teacher, looks, and of this does she speak, inasmuch as this can be made intelligible to those who listen to her. What I am chiefly referring to here is the mystery of salvation, by which God was revealed to us in the flesh. . . . And after He had reunited to Himself by the sacrifice of first-fruits the mortal substance of the flesh He had received from an immaculate Virgin, He continued to sanctify our common humanity by His own immortality. This He does through these who are united with Him according to their share in the mystery, by nourishing His own Body the Church, and by harmoniously fitting to it all the various limbs that grow by faith in Him. (St. Gregory of Nyssa)[86]

We are called the body of Christ, according to the words of the Apostle "You are the body of Christ, and members in particular" (I Cor. 12:27) not because by losing our own bodies we become His body, nor because He personally passes into us or is particularized into members; but because, like the flesh of Christ, our flesh also is freed from the corruption of sin. For as Christ by nature was without sin as a man, both in flesh and soul, so we too who believe in Him and have put Him on in the Spirit may, by exerting our will, be in Him without sin. (St. Maximus the Confessor)[87]

C. Sacramental Encounters with Christ

1. Sacraments

Two things, then, commend us to God, and in them lies all the salvation of men. The first is that we be initiated into the most sacred Mysteries, the second, that we train the will for virtue. Human endeavor can have no other function than that of preserving what has been given so as not to waste the treasure: consequently, the power of the Mysteries alone bestows on us all these blessings. Of the various rites each has its own effect; participation of the Spirit and of His gifts depends on the most Holy chrism. Therefore, while one may not be able to demonstrate the spiritual gift at the very time that the sacred rite takes place, but only much later, we should not be ignorant of the cause and origin of the power. The illumination of Baptism is introduced into the souls of those who have been initiated as soon as they have been washed, yet it is not at the time evident to all. For some of the virtuous it appears after a time and through much sweat and toil when they have cleansed the eye of the soul by the love of Christ. (Nicholas Cabasilas)[88]

These, then, are the reasons why the true life passes to us through the Savior's death. This is the way in which we draw this life into our souls—by being initiated into the Mysteries (Sacraments), being washed and anointed and partaking of the holy table. When we do these things, Christ comes to us and dwells in us. He is united to us and grows into one with us. He stifles sin in us and infuses into us His own life and merit and makes us to share in His victory. O how great is His goodness! He crowns those who have been washed and those who partake of His banquet He proclaims victors.

How shall we explain that victory and its crown, the fruit of toil and sweat, which come from the baptismal washing, the chrismation and the banquet? For though we neither struggle nor suffer when we celebrate these rites, we yet sing the praise of that struggle and celebrate that victory and venerate the trophy and display fervent and unutterable love for that Champion. As for those wounds and bruises and that death, we make them our own and apply them to ourselves by whatever means we may, and become one flesh with Him—with Him who was put to death and rose again. Wherefore we fittingly enjoy the benefits which come from that death and those struggles. . . .

Now, then, we depart from this water without sin. Because of the chrism we partake of His graces, and because of the banquet we live with the same life He does. In the world to come we shall be gods with God, fellow heirs with Him of the same riches, reigning with Him in the same kingdom—that is, unless we of our own free will blind ourselves in this life and rend as under the royal garment. This alone we contribute to this life—that we submit to His gifts, retain His graces, and do not reject the crown which God by many toils and labors has prepared for us.

This is the life in Christ which the Mysteries confer, but to which, apparently, human effort also has a contribution to make. He, then, who would speak thereof must first deal with each of the Mysteries. After that it is fitting to consider the activity which is in accordance with virtue. (Nicholas Cabasilas)[89]

2. Baptism: Initiation Rite

HYMN OF THE BAPTIZED

1. Your garments glisten, my brethren, as snow;—and fair is your shining in the likeness of Angels!

2. In the likeness of Angels, you have come up, beloved;—from Jordan's river, in the armor of the Holy Ghost.

3. The bridal chamber that fails not, my brethren, you have received;—and the glory of Adam's house today you have put on.

4. The judgment that came of the fruit, was Adam's condemnation;—but for you victory has arisen this day.

5. Your vesture is shining, and goodly your crowns;—which the Firstborn has bound for you, by the priest's hand this day.

6. Woe in Paradise, did Adam receive;—but you have received glory this day.

7. The armor of victory, you put on, my beloved;—in the hour when the priest invoked the Holy Ghost.

8. The Angels rejoice, men here below exault;—in your feast, my brethren, wherein is no foulness.

9. The good things of Heaven, my brethren, you have received;— beware of the Evil One, lest he despoil you.

10. The day when He dawned, the Heavenly King;—opens for you His door, and bids you enter Eden.

11. Crowns that fade not away, are set on your heads;—hymns of praise hourly, let your mouths sing.

12. Adam by means of the fruit God cast forth in sorrow;—but you He makes glad in the bridechamber of joy.

13. Who would not rejoice in your bridechamber, my brethren?— for the Father with His Son and the Spirit rejoice in you.

14. Unto you shall the Father be a wall of strength;—and the Son a Redeemer and the Spirit a guard.

15. Martyrs by their blood, glorify their crowns;—but you our Redeemer by His Blood glorifies.

16. Watchers and Angels, joy over the repentant;—they shall joy over you, my brethren, that unto them you are made like.

17. The fruit which Adam tasted not in Paradise;—this day in your mouths has been placed with joy.

18. Our Redeemer figured, His Body by the tree;—whereof Adam tasted not, because he had sinned.

19. The Evil One made war, and subdued Adam's house;—through your baptism, my brethren, lo! he is subdued this day.

20. Great is the victory, but today you have won;—if so be you neglect not, you shall not perish, my brethren.

21. Glory to them that are robed, glory to Adam's house!—in the birth that is from the water, let them rejoice and be blessed!

22. Praise to Him who has robed His Churches in glory!—glory to Him who has magnified the race of Adam's house. (St. Ephrem the Syrian)[90]

You are receiving not a perishable but a spiritual shield. Henceforth you are planted in the invisible Paradise. You receive a new name, which you did not have before. Heretofore you were a catechumen, but now you will be called a believer. You are transplanted henceforth among the spiritual olive trees, being grafted from the wild into the good olive-tree, from sins into righteousness, from pollutions into purity. You are made partaker of the Holy Vine. Well then, if you abide in the Vine, you grow as a fruitful branch; but if you abide not, you will be consumed by the fire. Let us therefore bear fruit worthily. God forbid that in us should be done what befell that barren fig-tree, that Jesus come not even now and curse us for our barrenness. But may all be able to use that other saying, "But I am like a fruitful olive-tree in the house of God; I have trusted in the mercy of God forever" (Ps. 52:10), an olive-tree not to be perceived by sense, but by the mind, and full of light. As then it is His part to plant and to water, so it is yours to receive and guard it. Despise not the grace because it is freely given, but receive and treasure it devoutly. (St. Cyril of Jerusalem)[91]

If any man receive not Baptism, he has not salvation; except only Martyrs, who even without the water receive the kingdom. For when the Savior, in redeeming the world by His Cross, was pierced in the side, He shed forth blood and water; that men, living in times of peace, might be baptized in water, and, in times of persecution, in their own blood. For martyrdom also the Savior is wont to call a baptism, saying, "Can you drink the cup which I drink, and be baptized with the baptism that I am baptized with?" (Matt. 21:31). (St. Cyril of Jerusalem)[92]

To be baptized, then, is to be born according to Christ and to receive our very being and nature, having previously been nothing. This we can learn from many sources. First, from the very order itself: it is the first of all the Mysteries (Sacraments) into which we are initiated, and before the others this Mystery introduces Christians into the new life. Secondly, we may learn this from the very names which we call it. And thirdly, from the ceremonies which we employ and the words which we sing. . . .

Properly, then, "birth" appears to signify nothing else than this. "New birth" and "new creation" mean nothing else than that those who are born and created have been born previously and have lost their original form, but now return to it by a second birth. It is as when the material of a statue has lost its shape and a sculptor restores and refashions the image, since it is a form and shape effected in us by Baptism. It engraves an image and imparts a form to our souls by conforming them to the death and resurrection of the Savior. It is thus also called a "seal," since it conforms us to the image of the King and to His blessed form. Since the form clothes the material and puts an end to its formlessness we also call the Mystery "clothing" and "baptism" ("dipping"). (Nicholas Cabasilas)[93]

The symbolical teaching, therefore, reveals that the man baptized according to sacred rites imitates by his triple immersion in the water, insofar as divine imitation is granted to men, the supremely divine death of the life-giving Jesus who spent three days and three nights in the tomb, and in whom according to the mystical and secret tradition of the Scriptures the prince of this world found nothing.

Next they put garments as white as light on the initiated, and because of his manly and godlike insensibility to what is opposed, on account of his constant inclination to the One, the disorderly is set in order, the formless takes on form, and the man is radiant with a life full of light. The most perfective anointing with oil makes the one initiated with the supremely divine Spirit. However, the spiritual commerce which makes perfect and of the sweet odor I leave to those deemed worthy of sacred and deifying communion with the divine Spirit according to the spirit to recognize spiritually since it is most ineffable. At the conclusion of everything, the bishop calls the initiated to the most holy Eucharist, and grants him communion in the perfective Mysteries. (Dionysius Pseudo-Areopagite)[94]

We call it the Gift, the Grace, Baptism, Unction, Illumination, the Clothing of Immortality, the Laver of Regeneration, the Seal and everything that is honorable. We call it the Gift, because it given to us in return for nothing on our part; Grace, because it is conferred even on debtors; Baptism, because sin is buried with it in the water, Unction, as Priestly and Royal, for such were they who were anointed; Illumination, because of its splendor; Clothing, because it hides our shame; the Laver, because it washes us; the Seal because it preserves us, and is moreover the indication of Dominion. In it the heavens rejoice; it is glorified by the Angels, because of its kindred splendor. It is the image of the heavenly bliss. We long indeed to sing out its praises, but we cannot worthily do so. (St. Gregory Nazianzus)[95]

3. Priesthood

However, under the direction of the order of the godly bishops, the illuminating order of priests conducts those being initiated to the divine visions of the mysteries, and it celebrates its own mysteries along with this. By doing this, it shows forth the divine works under the most sacred symbols and brings it about that those who approach as viewers become participators in the holy mysteries. It sends to the bishop those who aspire to the understanding of the sacred ceremonies they have viewed. (Dionysius Pseudo-Areopagite)[96]

"But the power belongs to the priests," they say. I know it too, for it is true. But not simply to priests as such, but to those who serve in the priestly ministry of the Gospel (Rom. 15:16) in a spirit of humility and who live a blameless life. Such priests first present themselves to the Lord (Rom. 6:16) and offer themselves as a "perfect, holy and well pleasing sacrifice," as their own pure act of worship (Rom. 12:1; James 1:27) in the temple of their own bodies (1 Cor. 6:19), inwardly and spiritually. They are accepted and appear on the altar that is on high (Heb. 9:24), offered by Christ the High Priest as a perfect sacrifice, changed and transformed by the power of the Holy Spirit. They have been transformed into Christ, who died for us and rose in the glory of His Godhead. In perfect humility they repent night and day; they mourn and pray with tears not only for themselves, but also for the flock that has been entrusted to them . . . in the world. To such it belongs to bind and to loose (Matt. 16:19; 18:18), to perform priestly acts and to teach, and not to men who have received their appointment and ordination from men only. As he says, "One does not take the honor upon himself, but he is called by God" (Heb. 5:4). He did not say, "He who has received appointment from men," but "He who was predestined by God and foreordained for this." Those who come from men and through men are thieves and robbers, as the Lord said: "I am the door. All who have come" and who come now, "not through Me, but climb in some other way, are thieves and robbers" (John 10:7-8a). (St. Symeon the New Theologian)[97]

The priest must be armed with weapons of steel—intense earnestness and constant sobriety of life—and he must keep watch in every direction, in case anyone should find a naked and unguarded spot and strike him a mortal blow. For everyone stands round him ready to wound him and strike him down, not only his enemies and foes, but many of those who pretend to love him. We must, therefore, choose souls as hardy as God's grace once proved the bodies of the saints in the Babylonian furnace. The fuel of fire is not brushwood, pitch and tow, but something far worse than that. It is no material fire to which they are exposed, but the all-devouring flame of malice envelop them, rising up all round, and attacking them and searching their life more thoroughly than the fire did the bodies of those young men. . . . For as long as the priest's life is well regulated in every particular point, their intrigues cannot hurt him. But if he should overlook some small detail, as is likely for a human being on his journey across the devious ocean of this life, all the rest of his good deeds are of no avail to enable him to escape the words of his accusers. That small offense casts a shadow over all the rest of his life. Everyone wants to judge the priest, not as one clothed in flesh, not as one possessing a human nature, but as an angel, exempt from the frailty of others. (St. John Chrysostom)[98]

What a great personage a priest is! He is in constant converse with God, and God constantly replies to his speech, as whatever the ceremonies of the Church may be, whatever his prayers, he is speaking to God, and whatever the ceremonies of the Church may be and whatever his prayers, the Lord answers him. How, under these circumstances, when assaulted by passions, can the priest forget that such passions are base, impure, especially for him, and that it is impossible to let them enter into his heart, which Jesus Christ alone ought to fill entirely?

A priest is an angel and not a man, everything worldly ought to be left far away behind him. O Lord, "let Thy priests be clothed with justice"; let them always remember the greatness of their calling and do not let them be entangled in the nets of the world and the Devil; let them be saved from "the cares of this world and the deceitfulness of riches, and the lusts after other things" entering into their hearts.

As light and heat are inseparable from the sun, so holiness, instruction, love and compassion for all ought to be inseparable from the person of a priest; for Whose dignity does he bear?—Christ's. Of Whom does he so often communicate? Christ—God Himself, of His Body and Blood. Therefore a priest should be the same in the spiritual world in the midst of his flock, as the sun is in nature: a light for all, life-giving warmth, the soul of all.

A priest ought to endeavor by every means to maintain within himself courage, boldness, daring, in spite of the bodiless enemy, who continually sows in him his illusive fear, his foolish dread; otherwise he cannot be a reprover of human vices, nor a true celebrant of the sacraments. Daring is a great gift of God and a great treasure of the soul! Courage or boldness plays an important part in earthly warfare, for it simply works wonders; but in the spiritual warfare it does far more. (John Cronstadt)[99]

The celebration of the Divine Liturgy requires an elevated soul, or a man with an elevated soul, not bound by any worldly passions, desires and attachments to earthly delights; whose heart is wholly embraced by the flame of the Holy Ghost, by ardent love for God and mankind, for every human soul, and, above all, for the Christian soul, so that with a sincere heart he may ever rise to God in prayer: "I am come to cast fire on the earth: and what will I, but that it be kindled?" This fire was sent down from heaven upon the Apostles in the form of tongues of fire.

This fire is also necessary for us, for our frozen hearts, in order to warm, soften, to melt them again and again, continually to cleanse them, in order to enlighten and renew them. Where is there to be found such a worthy priest who, like the Seraphim, would burn before the Lord with love, praise, and gratitude for His marvels of mercy and wisdom manifested unto us and within us? I am the greatest of sinners in unworthily celebrating this most heavenly Sacrament, for I have ever an impure heart, bound by desires and attachments to earthly delights.

Lord, Thou seest the depths of our hearts; but "Thou shalt sprinkle me with hyssop, and I shall be made whiter than snow." "It is not wonderful if Thou hast mercy upon the pure; and it is not a great thing if Thou savest the righteous, but show the wonders of Thy mercy upon me, a sinner!" (John Cronstadt)[100]

Priest of God! Believe with your whole heart, believe always in the grace given to you from God, to pray for God's people. Let not this gift of God be in vain in you, for by it you can save many souls. The Lord speedily hears your heartfelt prayer for His people, and is easily inclined to have mercy upon them, as He had at Moses', Aaron's, Samuel's, and the Apostles' prayers. Avail yourself of every opportunity for prayer—in church, when you celebrate Divine service or a sacrament, in private houses, at the ministering of the sacraments, during prayers and thanksgivings; everywhere and at all times think of the salvation of God's people, and you shall also obtain great grace of God for yourself.

When you pray with tears and love for the Lord's sheep, and your thoughts praise you to yourself, then say to them: It is not I who prayed for them "with unspeakable groanings"; and the Spirit bound me, too, at that time, in the sweet bonds of His love and of heartfelt devotion. That this is true is evident from the fact that the sweetness of prayer and love can very soon forsake me. (John Cronstadt)[101]

CHAPTER FOUR

THE HOLY SPIRIT
OF THE RISEN LORD

These are the very things that God has revealed to us
through the Spirit, for the Spirit reaches the depths of everything, even the depths of God. And after all, the depths
of a man can only be known by his own spirit, not by any
other man, and in the same way the depths of God can only
be known by the Spirit of God. Now instead of the spirit of
the world, we have received the Spirit that comes from God,
to teach us to understand the gifts that he has given us.
Therefore we teach, not in the way in which philosophy is
taught, but in the way that the Spirit teaches us. . . . A spiritual man, on the other hand, is able to judge the value of
everything, and his own value is not to be judged by other
men. As scripture says: Who can know the mind of the
Lord, so who can teach him? But we are those who have the
mind of Christ. (1 Cor. 2:10, 16)

A. Understanding Scripture

The beginning of the path of life is always to be instructing one's
mind in the words of God and to spend one's life in poverty. Filling
oneself with the one helps to gain perfection in the other. If you fill
yourself with study of the Words of God, this helps toward progress
in poverty; and progress in non-acquisitiveness gives you leisure to
make progress in study of the Words of God. So the two combine to
help the speedy building of the whole edifice of virtues. (St. Isaac
the Syrian)[102]

To drive away the wrong tendencies previously acquired by the
soul, nothing is more helpful than immersing oneself in love of studying the Divine Scriptures and understanding the depths of thoughts
they contain. When thoughts become immersed in the delight of
fathoming the hidden wisdom of the words, a man leaves the world

behind and forgets all that is therein, in proportion to the enlightenment he draws from the words. But even when the mind floats only
on the surface of the waters of the Divine Scriptures and cannot
penetrate to the very depths of the thoughts contained therein,
even then the very fact that he is occupied with zeal to understand
the Scriptures is enough firmly to pinion his thoughts in ideas of the
miraculous alone, and to prevent them from seeking after the material and the carnal. (St. Isaac the Syrian)[103]

In everything you meet with in the Scriptures, strive to find the
purpose of the word, to penetrate into the depth of the thought of
the saints and to understand it more exactly. Those whose life is
guided by Divine grace toward enlightenment always feel as though
some inner ray of light travels over the written lines and allows the
mind to discern from the bare words what is said with great thought
for the instruction of the soul. (St. Isaac the Syrian)[104]

Until a man has received the Comforter, he has need of the
Divine Scriptures to imprint the memory of good in his thought, to
keep his striving for good constantly renewed by continual reading,
and to preserve his soul from the subtleties of sinful ways; for he has
not yet acquired the power of the Spirit, which repels errors and
captures soul-saving memories. When the power of the Spirit has
penetrated the power of the soul acting in a man, then, in place of
the law of the Scriptures, the commandments of the Spirit take root
in the heart and a man is secretly taught by the Spirit and needs no
help from sensory matter. For, so long as it is from matter that the
heart has its teaching, error and forgetfulness straightway follow the
lesson; but when teaching comes from the Spirit, its memory is kept
inviolate. (St. Isaac the Syrian)[105]

Do not approach the words of the mysteries, contained in the
Divine Scriptures, without prayer and asking God's help, but say:
"Grant me, O Lord, to be open to receive the power contained in
them." Regard prayer as the key to the true meaning of what is said
in the Divine Scriptures. (St. Isaac the Syrian)[106]

We think that the way that seems to us right for understanding
the Scriptures and seeking their meaning is such that we are taught
what sort of understanding we should have of it by no less than
Scripture itself. We have found in Proverbs some such instruction
for the examination of divine Scripture given by Solomon. He says,
"For your part describe them to yourself threefold in admonition
and knowledge, that you may answer words of truth to those who

question you" (Prov. 22:20-21). Therefore, a person ought to describe threefold in his soul the meaning of divine letters, that is, so that the simple may be edified by, so to speak, the body of the Scriptures; for that is what we call the ordinary and narrative meaning.

But if any have begun to make some progress and can contemplate something more fully, they should be edified by the soul of Scripture. And those who are perfect are like those concerning whom the Apostle says, "Yet among the perfect we do impart wisdom, although it is not a wisdom of this world or of the rulers of this world, who are doomed to pass away. But we impart a secret and hidden wisdom of God, which God decreed before the ages for our glorification" (1 Cor. 2:6-7). Such people should be edified by that spiritual law (Rom. 7:14) which has a shadow of the good things to come (Heb. 10:1), edified as by the spirit of Scripture. Thus, just as a human being is said to be made up of body, soul, and spirit, so also is sacred Scripture, which has been granted by God's gracious dispensation for man's salvation. (Origen)[107]

So also God, the King, has sent to men the Divine Scriptures as letters, pointing out to them that they are to call out to God and, believing, they are to ask and receive a heavenly gift from the Godhead's very own being. For it is written: "That we should be made participators of the divine nature" (2 Pet. 1:4). But if a man does not approach and beg and receive, it will profit him nothing for having read the Scriptures. But rather he is subject to death because he did not wish to receive from the Heavenly King the gift of life, without which it is impossible to obtain immortal life, which is Christ. (Pseudo-Macarius)[108]

B. The Work of the Holy Spirit

1. The Nature of the Holy Spirit

It is then in the Spirit that the Logos glorifies Creation and deifies it and adopts and conducts it to the Father. But He who unites Creation to the Logos would not make part of the created world just as He who confers filiation upon creatures would not be a stranger to being a Son. If such would be the case, one must search for another Spirit because in the first Spirit man is united to the Logos. This, however, is absurd. The Spirit does not make part of created things, but is proper to the divinity of the Father and it is in Him that the Logos deifies the creatures. (St. Athanasius)[109]

The Son condescends to the imperfect, but the Holy Spirit is the seal of the perfect. (St. Athanasius)[110]

For all things that are of the Father are of the Son also; therefore those things which are given from the Son in the Spirit are gifts of the Father. And when the Spirit is in us, the Word also, who gives the Spirit, is in us, and in the Word is the Father. (St. Athanasius)[111]

For He (the Holy Spirit) is the Maker of all these, filling all with His essence, containing all things, filling the world in His essence, yet incapable of being comprehended in His power by the world; good, upright, princely by nature not by adoption; sanctifying, not sanctified; measuring, not measured; shared, not sharing; filling, not filled; containing, not contained; inherited, glorified, reckoned with the Father and the Son; held out as a threat; the finger of God; fire like God; to manifest, as I take it, His consubstantiality; the Creator-Spirit who by Baptism and by resurrection creates anew; the Spirit that knows all things, that teaches, that blows where and to what extent He wishes; that guides, talks, sends forth, separates, is angry or tempted; that reveals, illumines, quickens or rather is the very Light and Life; that makes temples, that deifies; that perfects so as even to anticipate Baptism, yet after Baptism to be sought as a separate gift; that does all things that God does . . . and making all things clear and plain; of independent power, unchangeable, almighty, all-seeing, penetrating all spirits that are intelligent, pure, most subtle. (St. Gregory of Nazianzus)[112]

When therefore rational beings obtain first their existence from God the Father, then their rational nature from the Word, and thirdly their holiness from the Holy Spirit, they are made capable of receiving Christ in His capacity of Righteousness, because they have now been sanctified through the Holy Spirit; and those who have merited the attainment of this degree of progress through the sanctification of the Holy Spirit obtain just as surely the gift of wisdom through the power of the working of the Spirit of God. . . . That those who were made by God may be present unceasingly and inseparably with Him who is, it is the work of wisdom to instruct and educate them and lead them to perfection, by the strengthening and the increasing sanctification of the Holy Spirit, through which sanctification alone they can attain to God. (Origen)[113]

Therefore, inasmuch as the Holy Spirit perfects rational beings, completing their excellence, He is analogous to form. For he, who no longer "lives after the flesh" (Rom. 8:12), but, being "led by the Spirit of God" (Rom. 8:14), is called a Son of God, being "conformed to the image of the Son of God" (Rom. 8:29), is described as spiritual. (St. Basil)[114]

As the power of seeing is in the healthy eye, so is the operation of the Spirit in the purified soul. Wherefore also Paul prays for the Ephesians that they may have their "eyes enlightened" by "the Spirit of Wisdom" (Eph. 1:17-18). (St. Basil)[115]

For it is impossible to behold the Image of the invisible God except by the enlightenment of the Spirit and impracticable for him to fix his gaze on the Image to dissever the light from the Image, because the cause of vision is of necessity seen at the same time as the visible objects. Thus fitly and consistently do we behold the "brightness of the glory" of God by means of the illumination of the Spirit and by means of the "Express Image" we are led up to Him of whom He is the Express Image and Seal, graven to the like. (St. Basil)[116]

But if the grace, conferred by the Holy Spirit, is something separated from His essence, why did not blessed Moses say clearly that the Creator, after having given existence to the first man, breathed into him grace? And why did not Christ say: "Receive the grace through the instrumentality of the Holy Spirit"? Moses said "the breath of life" for the divine nature is a true life because it is in it that we live and move and have our being. The Savior says: "The Holy Spirit" and it is this Spirit who introduces Him and makes Him inhabit our souls. Through Him and in Him, He leads our nature back to its primitive state, that is to say, refashions us to His own proper likeness through sanctification. . . . The Spirit is the perfect and natural image of the Son. Having been formed according to this Spirit through sanctification, we put on the form of God. It is this that the Apostle (Paul) tells us: "My children for whom I am in labor until Christ be formed in you." Christ is formed in us through the Holy Spirit who refashions us according to God. . . . The Holy Spirit is then God who remakes in us the image of God, not through any instrumental grace, but in giving Himself as a participation of the divine nature to those who are worthy. (St. Cyril of Alexandria)[117]

Surely the Holy Spirit does not paint the divine essence in us like a scene-painter with Himself something other than it. It is not in this way that He brings us to God's likeness. Rather, being Himself God and proceeding from God, He is Himself impressed invisibly in the hearts of those who receive Him, like a seal in wax. Through communion and likeness to Himself He paints our nature completely to the archetypal beauty and makes man once again to God's image. How, then, will He be a creature, He through whom our nature is reshaped to God, inasmuch as it is made partaker of God. (St. Cyril of Alexandria)[118]

You see that those who do not possess the Spirit as one who acts and speaks in them are among the unfaithful. For Christ does not lie since He has not committed sin and there was found no deceit in His mouth (1 Pet. 2:22). If He Himself says that He gives the Spirit to those who believe in Him, surely those who do not have the Spirit are not faithful at heart. (St. Symeon the New Theologian)[119]

The adoption through regeneration is due to the Holy Spirit who makes us become gods by disposition and grace who makes us called heirs of God and co-heirs with Christ . . . whereby we see God and Christ Himself living in us according to His divinity and moving around in a conscious manner within us. (St. Symeon the New Theologian)[120]

In fact, all knowledge and all discernment, every word of wisdom and every word of a more mystical knowledge and also the power of miracles and the gift of prophecy, different languages and their interpretation, the protection and ruling of cities and of peoples, the discernment of future goods and the acquisition of the Kingdom of Heaven, the divine adoption and the very fact of putting on Christ, of knowing the mysteries of Christ, of knowing the mysteries of God's economy of salvation in our regard, in a word, all that unbelievers fail to know and that we, after having received the grace of faith, can know, think and say, all this comes uniquely from the teaching of the Spirit. (St. Symeon the New Theologian)[121]

It is in this state (mystical marriage with Christ) that the Christian is enflamed by the Spirit and becomes completely fire in his soul. He communicates also to His body His own radiance in the manner of material fire which communicates to fire its own nature and the soul becomes for the body that which God has become for the soul. (St. Symeon the New Theologian)[122]

> You will not comprehend Him
> unless He will be revealed to you through the Holy Spirit.
> For the Spirit teaches everything, shining in an ineffable light,
> and He will show you in an intellectual way
> all the intelligible realities

as much as you can see,
as much as is accessible to me
according to the measure of the purity of your soul.
And you will become like to God,
in imitating exactly His words of not only temperance and courage,
but also His love for men,
also in bearing with patience trials
and in loving your enemies.
. . . Then the Creator . . . will send the Divine Spirit.
I am not speaking of another soul such as you have;
but of the Spirit, I mean, who comes from God,
who breathes where He abides,
who will take His abode substantially in you
and will illumine and cast His light and recreate you completely
who will make you incorruptible,
you who are corruptible.
He will make new again the antiquated house,
and the house of your soul, I mean.
And with it He will render totally incorruptible your complete body.
He will make you god by grace, similar to your Model.
O marvel! O mystery unknown to all,
who are prisoners of their passions. . . .
I mean, to those not given to a pure heart,
to those not seeking a fervent heart to receive the Holy Spirit,
to those not believing that God gives the Divine Spirit
to those who truly seek Him.
For disbelief disperses and chases away the Divine Spirit. . . .
If they are not born of God completely, in such a way
that they are living but have not received the Spirit,
their eyes have not been opened.
They do not see the divine light.
. . . Like a piscine of Baptism the Holy Spirit, divine and all luminous,
embraces all those who are worthy, all whom He finds inside—
how shall I explain, how express worthily these effects?
. . . Being God, the Divine Spirit refashions completely those whom
He receives within Himself.
He makes them completely anew.
He renews them in an amazing manner.
So likewise the Divine Spirit, incorruptible, gives incorruptibility.
Being immortal, He gives immortality.
Because He is light that never sets,
He transforms all of them into light
in whom He comes down and dwells.
And because He is life, He bestows life to all.

As He is of the same nature as Christ, being of the same essence
as well as the same in glory,
and being united with Him, He forms them absolutely similar to Christ.
. . . He is our Benefactor
and He wishes that all of us become what He himself is.
. . . Therefore, as you wisely understand this,
hasten to receive the Spirit, who comes from God and is divine,
in order . . . to become heirs of the Heavenly Kingdom for ever.
(St. Symeon the New Theologian)[123]

However, everyone should push himself to beg the Lord to make
him worthy to receive and find the heavenly treasure of the Spirit in
order to be able easily and promptly to fulfill all the commandments
of the Lord, without blame and with perfection, which before he
could not successfully do, no matter how much he tried. . . . But
the person, who has found the Lord, the true treasure, by seeking
the Spirit, by faith and great patience, brings forth the fruits of the
Spirit. . . . All righteousness and the commands of the Lord which
the Spirit orders he does by himself, purely and perfectly and without blame. . . . So also it is with those who are rich in the Holy
Spirit. They truly possess the fellowship of the Spirit within themselves. And when they speak words of truth or deliver any spiritual
conference and wish to edify persons, they speak out of the same
wealth and treasure which indwells within them and out of this they
edify persons who listen to their spiritual discourses. And they do
not fear lest they run short since they possess within themselves the
heavenly treasure of goodness from which they draw to feed those
who hunger for spiritual food. (Pseudo-Macarius)[124]

Only the Holy Spirit can purify the intellect, for unless a greater
power comes and overthrows the despoiler, what he has taken captive will never be set free (Luke 11:21–22). In every way, therefore, and especially through peace of soul, we must make ourselves
a dwelling-place for the Holy Spirit. Then we shall have the lamp of
spiritual knowledge burning always within us; and when it is shining
constantly in the inner shrine of the soul, not only will the intellect
perceive all the dark and bitter attacks of the demons, but these
attacks will be greatly weakened when exposed for what they are
by that glorious and holy light. That is why the Apostle says: "Do
not quench the Spirit" (1 Thess. 5:19), meaning: "Do not grieve the
goodness of the Holy Spirit by wicked actions or wicked thoughts,
lest you be deprived of this protecting light." The Spirit, since He is

eternal and life-creating, cannot be quenched; but if He is grieved—
that is if He withdraws—He leaves the intellect without the light of
spiritual knowledge, dark and full of gloom.

The loving and Holy Spirit of God teaches us that the perceptive
faculty natural to our soul is single; indeed, even the five bodily
senses differ from each other only because of the body's varying
needs. But this single faculty of perception is split because of the
dislocation which, as a result of Adam's disobedience, takes place in
the intellect through the modes in which the soul now operates . . .
we shall be able to unite the earthly appetite of the soul to its
spiritual and intellectual aspiration, through the communion of the
Holy Spirit who brings this about within us. For unless His divinity
actively illumines the inner shrine of our heart, we shall not be able
to taste God's goodness with the perceptive faculty undivided, that
is, with unified aspiration. (St. Diadochus of Photike)[125]

2. Sweetness

If we fervently desire holiness, the Holy Spirit at the outset gives
the soul a full and conscious taste of God's sweetness, so that
the intellect will know exactly of what the final reward of the spiritual life consists. But later He often conceals this precious and life-
creating gift. He does so that, even if we acquire all the other
virtues, we should still regard ourselves as nothing because we have
not acquired divine love in a lasting form. . . . The soul suffers all
the more because it still preserves the memory of divine love; yet,
since it is below the highest level of the spiritual life, it cannot
experience this love actively. It is therefore necessary to work upon
the soul forcefully for a while, so that we may come to taste divine
love fully and consciously; for no one can acquire the perfection of
love while still in the flesh except those saints who suffer to the
point of martyrdom, and confess their faith despite all persecution.
Whoever has reached this state is completely transformed, and does
not easily feel desire even for material sustenance. . . . Those who
have advanced to perfection are able to taste this love continually,
but no one can experience it completely until "what is mortal in us
is swallowed up by life" (2 Cor. 5:4). (St. Diadochus of Photike)[126]

It would be nearer to the essence of the matter to say: who will
explain the sweetness of honey to those who have not tasted it? It is
incomparably harder to explain to those, who have not tasted it,
that sweetness which is Divine and that transubstantial spring of

living joy, which ever flows from true and pure prayer of the heart, of which Jesus, God and Man says: "But whosoever drinks of the water that I shall give him shall never thirst; but the water that I shall give him shall be in him a well of water springing up into everlasting life" (John 4:14). . . . This spiritual sweetness is at the same time essential radiance and light, inconceivable beauty, the last desire of desires, knowledge of God and mysterious deification, which remains inexpressible even after some expression of it, unknowable in part even after some knowledge of it, incomprehensible in part even after some comprehension of it. . . . And St. Basil the Great says: "Utterly inexpressible and indescribable is Divine beauty blazing like lightning; neither word can express nor ear receive it. If we name the brightness of dawn, or the clearness of moonlight, or the brilliance of sunshine, none of it is worthy to be compared with the glory of true light, and is farther removed therefrom than the deepest night and the most terrible darkness from the clear light of midday. When this beauty, invisible to physical eyes and accessible only to soul and thought, illumined some saint, wounding him with unbearable yearning desire, then, disgusted by earthly life he cried: "Woe is me, that I sojourn in Mesech, that I dwell in the tents of Kedar!" (Ps. 120:5). . . . Oppressed by this life, as by a prison, how irresistible was the striving towards God of those whose soul was touched by Divine yearning. Owing to their insatiable desire to contemplate Divine beauty, they prayed that the sight of God's beauty should last for all eternity. (The Monks Callistus and Ignatius)[127]

You say that you are afraid of falling in love with spiritual sweetness. But you surely cannot think of doing any such thing. It is not for its sweetness that prayer is practiced, but because it is our duty to serve God in this way, although sweetness goes of necessity with true service. The most important thing in prayer is to stand before God in reverence and fear, with the mind in the heart; for this sobers and disperses every folly and plants contrition before God in the heart. These feelings of fear and sorrow in the sight of God, the broken and contrite heart, are the principal features of true inner prayer, and the test of every prayer, by which we can tell whether or not our prayer is performed as it should be. If they are present, prayer is in order. When they are absent, prayer is not in its true course and must be brought back to its proper condition. If we lack this sense of sorrow and contrition, then sweetness and warmth may breed self-conceit; and that is spiritual pride, and will lead to pernicious illusion. Then the sweetness and warmth will vanish, leaving only their memory, but the soul will still imagine that it has them. Of this you should be afraid, and so you must increasingly kindle in your heart the fear of God, lowliness, and contrite prostration before Him, walking always in His presence. This is the heart of the matter. (St. Theophan the Recluse)[128]

C. Guidance of the Holy Spirit

1. Discernment

Discernment in beginners is true knowledge of themselves; in intermediate souls it is a spiritual sense that faultlessly distinguishes what is truly good from what is of nature and opposed to it; and in the perfect it is the knowledge which they possess by divine illumination, and which can enlighten with its lamp what is dark in others. Or perhaps, generally speaking, discernment is, and is recognized as the assured understanding of the divine will on all occasions, in every place and in all matters; and it is only found in those who are pure in heart, and in body and in mouth. (St. John Climacus)[129]

Here is an excellent alphabet for all:

A.	Obedience	M.	Hard work
B.	Fasting	N.	Humiliation
C.	Sackcloth	O.	Contrition
D.	Ashes	P.	Forgetfulness of wrongs
E.	Tears	Q.	Brotherly love
F.	Confession	R.	Meekness
G.	Silence	S.	Simple and unquestioning faith
H.	Humility	T.	Freedom from worldly cares
I.	Vigil	U.	Hateless hatred of parents
J.	Courage	V.	Detachment
K.	Cold	X.	Innocent simplicity
L.	Toil	Z.	Voluntary abasement

A good scheme for the advanced, and evidence of their progress is: absence of vainglory, freedom from anger, good hope, silence, discernment, firm remembrance of the judgment, compassion, hospitality, moderation in reproof, passionless prayer, disregard of self. (St. John Climacus)[130]

A spiritual mind is inevitably wrapped in spiritual understanding. Whether it is in us or not, we must never stop seeking this understanding. And when it makes its appearance, the outward senses of their own accord cease their natural action. Knowing this, one of the wise said: And thou shalt obtain a sense of the Divine. (St. John Climacus)[131]

In drawing water from a well we sometimes without noticing it bring up a frog with the water, and so in acquiring the virtues we often get involved in the vices that are imperceptibly entwined with them. The kind of thing I mean is that gluttony is entangled with hospitality; lust with love; cunning with discernment; malice with thoughtfulness; duplicity, procrastination, laziness, contradiction, wilfulness and disobedience with meekness; contempt of instruction with silence; conceit with joy; indolence with hope; harsh judgment with love again; despondency and sloth with quietness; acerbity with chastity; familiarity with humility; and behind them all as a general salve, or rather poison, follows vainglory. (St. John Climacus)[132]

Vice or passion is not originally planted in nature, for God is not the Creator of passions. But there are in us many natural virtues from Him, among which are certainly the following: mercy, for even the pagans are compassionate; love, for even dumb animals often weep at the loss of one another; faith, for we all give birth to it of ourselves; hope, for we lend, and sail, and sow, hoping for the best. So, if, as has been shown, love is a natural virtue in us, and is the bond and fulfillment of the law (Rom. 13:10), then it follows that the virtues are not far from nature. And those who plead their inability to practice them ought to be ashamed. (St. John Climacus)[133]

In all your undertakings and in every way of life, whether you are living in obedience, or are not submitting your work to anyone, whether in outward or in spiritual matters, let this be your rule and practice, to ask yourself: Am I really doing this in accordance with God's will? For example, when we, I mean beginners, carry out some task and the humility acquired from this action is not added to our soul, then in my opinion, be the matter great or small, we are not doing it according to God. For in us who are still young in the spiritual life, growth in humility is the fulfillment of the Lord's will; and for those who have reached a middle state perhaps the test is the cessation of inner conflicts; and for the perfect, an increase and abundance of the divine light. (St. John Climacus)[134]

Those who wish to learn the will of the Lord must first mortify their own will. Then, having prayed to God with faith and honest simplicity, and having asked the fathers or even the brothers with humility of heart and no thought of doubt, they should accept their advice as from the mouth of God, even if their advice be contrary to their own wish, and even if those consulted are not very spiritual. For God is not unjust, and will not lead astray souls who with faith and innocence humbly submit to the advice and judgment of their neighbor. Even if those who were asked were brute beasts, yet He who speaks is the Immaterial and Invisible One. Those who allow themselves to be guided by this rule without having any doubts are filled with great humility. For if someone expounded his problems on a harp (Ps. 48:4), how much better, do you think, can a rational mind and reasonable soul teach than an inanimate object. (St. John Climacus)[135]

Discernment is a light in darkness, the return of wanderers to the way, the illumination of those whose sight is dim. A discerning man finds health and destroys sickness. (St.John Climacus)[136]

God is not the cause or the creator of evil, and those who say that certain passions are natural to the soul have been deceived, not knowing that we have turned the constituent qualities of nature into passions. For instance, nature gives us the seed for childbearing, but we have perverted this into fornication. Nature provides us with the means of showing anger against the serpent, but we have used this against our neighbor. Nature inspires us with zeal to make us compete for the virtues, but we compete in evil. It is natural for the soul to desire glory, but the glory on high. It is natural to be overbearing, but against the demons. Joy is also natural to us, but a joy on account of the Lord and the welfare of our neighbor. Nature has also given us resentment, but to be used against the enemies of the soul. We have received a desire for pleasure, but not for profligacy. (St. John Climacus)[137]

An energetic soul rouses the demons against itself. But as our conflicts increase, so do our crowns. He who has never been struck by the enemy will certainly not be crowned. But the warrior who does not flinch despite his incidental falls will be glorified by the angels as a champion. (St. John Climacus)[138]

Our adversary, the devil, has the old-established habit of cunningly diversifying his attacks against those who have entered upon spiritual endeavor. He changes the method of attack by using different weapons against them and by adjusting himself to the person's intention.

The first method of enemy attack: Those whose will is indolent and whose thoughts are weak are attacked strongly from the very beginning by powerful temptations. The devil does this to overpower them with fear from the very first endeavor, to make the way look difficult and hard to them and to make them say: "If the beginning of the way is so grievous and hard, can anyone endure to the end the many struggles which face him?"

The second method of attack: In the case of men whom the devil sees to be full of courage, men who disregard death and undertake their work with great zeal, the devil does not at once go out to meet them, and does not engage them in battle at their first impetus, knowing that zealous warriors are not easy to overcome. . . . As soon as they begin to turn away from their first thoughts, and start inventing on their own what serves to overcome those thoughts through the seductions of speculations which spring from themselves, and when of themselves they begin to dig for their souls a moat of perdition through the wandering thoughts which are born of laziness, and bring coldness to mind and heart then the devil assaults them without mercy.

. . . The third method of enemy attack: When the enemy sees the power, such as a man acquires from God in reward for his zeal and his calling to Him with faith, he tries to find some other means to make the angel who is helping him withdraw; namely, he strives to evoke in him proud thoughts, to make him think that by his own strength he keeps himself safe from his adversary and murderer. . . .

The fourth method of enemy attack consists in the enemy beginning to oppress a man through the needs of nature (especially the need of a wife and the need to have wherewith to exist).

As soon as a man realizes his weakness and genuinely feels it, he at once rouses his soul from indolence and becomes cautious. But no one can feel his weakness unless even a small temptation, either of body or soul, is allowed to assail him and he is granted deliverance from it. For then he sees clearly the futility of his own efforts and measures, he sees that the circumspection, abstinence and guarding of his soul, through which he hoped to find security, brought him no profit and that deliverance came independently of it all. Hence he is shown that by himself he is nothing and is saved by God's help alone. (St. Isaac the Syrian)[139]

When it happens that your soul is inwardly filled with darkness and that, just as the rays of the sun are at times shut off from the earth by clouds, so the soul is deprived for a time of spiritual comfort, and when the light of grace becomes dimmed within because a cloud of passions covers the soul, and because the joy creating force is weakened in you, so that your mind is shrouded in unaccustomed darkness; then let not your thought be troubled, but be patient; read the books of the teachers, force yourself to pray—and wait for help. It will be quick in coming, it will be there before you know. For as the face of the earth is delivered by the rays of the sun from the darkness of the clouds enshrouding it, so prayer can destroy and disperse the clouds of passions in the soul and illumine the mind by the light of comfort and joy. (St. Isaac the Syrian)[140]

You should not doubt the intellect, when it begins to be strongly energized by the divine light, becomes so completely translucent that it sees its own light vividly. This takes place when the power of the soul gains control over the passions. But when St. Paul says that "Satan himself is transformed into an angel of light" (2 Cor. 11:14), he definitely teaches us that everything which appears to the intellect, whether as light or as fire, if it has a shape, is the product of the evil artifice of the enemy. So we should not embark on the ascetic life in the hope of seeing visions clothed with form or shape; for if we do, Satan will find it easy to lead our soul astray. Our one purpose must be to reach the point when we perceive the love of God fully and consciously in our heart, that is, "with all your heart, and with all your soul . . . and with all your mind" (Luke 10:27). For a man who is energized by the grace of God to this point has already left this world, though still present in it. (St. Diadochus of Photike)[141]

2. Dreams

The dreams which appear to the soul through God's love are unerring criteria of its health. Such dreams do not change from one shape to another; they do not shock our inward sense, resound with laughter or suddenly become threatening. But with great gentleness they approach the soul and fill it with spiritual gladness. As a result, even after the body has woken up, the soul longs to recapture the joy given to it by the dream. Demonic fantasies, however, are just the opposite: they do not keep the same shape or maintain a constant form for long. For what the demons do not possess as their chosen mode of life, but merely assume because of their inherent deceitfulness, is not able to satisfy them for very long. They shout and menace, often transforming themselves into soldiers and sometimes deafening the soul with their cries.

But the intellect, when pure, recognizes them for what they are and awakes the body from its dreams. Sometimes it even feels joy at having been able to see through their pranks; indeed it often challenges them during the dream itself and thus provokes them to great anger. There are, however, times when even good dreams do not bring joy to the soul, but produce in it a sweet sadness and tears unaccompanied by grief. But this happens only to those who are far advanced in humility.

We have now explained the distinction between good and bad dreams, as we ourselves heard it from those with experience. In our quest for purity, however, the safest rule is never to trust to anything that appears to us in our dreams. For dreams are generally nothing more than images reflecting our wandering thoughts, or else they are the mockery of demons. And if ever God in His goodness were to send us some vision and we were to refuse it, our beloved Lord Jesus would not be angry with us, for He would know we were acting in this way because of the tricks of the demons. Although the distinction between types of dreams established above is precise, it sometimes happens that when the soul has been sullied by an unperceived beguilement something from which no one, it seems to me, is exempt, it loses its sense of accurate discrimination and mistakes bad dreams for good. (St. Diadochus of Photike)[142]

3. In the Heart

The heart is the innermost man or spirit. Here are located self-awareness, the conscience, the idea of God and of one's complete dependence on Him, and all the eternal treasures of the spiritual life. . . . Where is the heart? Where sadness, joy, anger, and other emotions are felt, here is the heart. Stand there with attention. . . . Stand in the heart, with the faith that God is also there, but how He is there do not speculate. Pray and entreat that in due time love for God may stir within you by His grace. (St. Theophan the Recluse)[143]

His (God's) very grace writes in their hearts the laws of the Spirit. They, therefore, should not put all their trusting hope solely in the scriptures written in ink. For, indeed, divine grace writes on the "tables of the heart" (2 Cor. 3:3) the laws of the Spirit and the heavenly mysteries. For the heart directs and governs all the other organs of the body. And when grace pastures the heart, it rules over all the members and the thoughts. For there in the heart the mind abides as well as all the thoughts of the soul and all its hopes. This is how grace penetrates throughout all parts of the body. (Pseudo-Macarius)[144]

We are affected from the very bottom of the heart, so that we get at its meaning (of Holy Scripture) not by reading the text but by experience anticipating it. And so our mind will reach that incorruptible prayer . . . distinguished by the use of no words or utterances; but with the purpose of the mind all on fire . . . produced through ecstasy of heart by some unaccountable keenness of spirit, and the mind being thus affected without the aid of the sense or any visible material pours it forth to God with groanings and sighs that cannot be uttered. (St. John Cassian)[145]

When we read in the writings of the Fathers about the place of the heart which the mind finds by prayer, we must understand by this the spiritual faculty that exists in the heart. Placed by the Creator in the upper part of the heart, this spiritual faculty distinguishes the human heart from the heart of animals; for animals have the faculty of will or desire, and the faculty of fury, in the same measure as man. The spiritual faculty in the heart manifests itself—independently of the intellect—in the conscience or consciousness of our spirit, in the fear of God, in spiritual love toward God and neighbor, in feelings of repentance, humility, or meekness, in contrition of the spirit or deep sadness for our sins, and in other spiritual feelings; all of which are foreign to animals. The intellectual faculty in man's soul, though spiritual, dwells in the brain, that is to say in the head: in the same way the spiritual faculty which we term the spirit of man, though spiritual, dwells in the upper part of the heart, close to the left nipple of the chest and a little above it. Thus the union of the mind with the heart is the union of the spiritual thoughts of the mind with the spiritual feelings of the heart. (Bishop Ignatii Brianchaninov)[146]

4. Divine Providence

Be assured that your Protector is always with you—and that, in company with all other creatures, you too are under the one Master, who by a single lifting of His hand gives order and movement to all things. So stand firm and be of good cheer. Neither demons, nor dangerous beasts, nor vicious men can wreak their will on you and destroy you, unless the Ruler permits it and sets it a definite measure. So say to your soul: "I have a Protector who guards me, and no creature can rise against me without command from on high. If it be the will of my Master that the evil ones should gain mastery over the creature, I accept it without grief, since I do not wish the will of my Lord to remain unfulfilled." In this way, amid trials and temptations, you will be filled with joy, as one who knows and realizes in practice that the hand of the Master rules over him and directs him. Thus fortify your heart by trust in the Lord. (St. Isaac the Syrian)[147]

Always raise your eyes to God, for God's Providence and Protection envelop all men, but it is invisible, and reveals itself only to those who have cleansed themselves of sin, and who constantly think of God and of Him alone. Especially does God's Providence become revealed to them when, for His sake, they enter into temptation. For then they sense God's Providence, as though seeing it with physical eyes, in proportion to the measure and cause of the temptation, which overtakes each one of them, to incite them to courage, as it was with Jacob, Joshua, the three youths, Peter, and other saints, to whom God's Providence appeared in some human form, to hearten them and affirm them in righteousness. (St. Isaac the Syrian)[148]

As soon as a man rejects all visible help and human hope, and follows after God with faith and a pure heart, grace straightway follows after him and reveals its power in help of various kinds. First it reveals its power in visible things relating to the body, and helps man by ministering to it, in order that he should experience most forcefully the power of Divine Providence, which takes care of him. Having experienced help in what is visible, he becomes convinced of help in what is hidden, for here grace makes plain before him the intricacies of difficult thoughts and ideas, and so man easily discovers their meaning, their mutual relationship, their delusiveness, and how they arise from one another—and harm the soul. At the same time grace puts to shame before his eyes all the wiles of the demons and points, as with a finger, to what he would have suffered had he remained ignorant. Then is born in him the thought that he must entreat his Creator by prayer for everything both great and small. (St. Isaac the Syrian)[149]

D. Building the Body of Christ

Men, women and children, profoundly divided as to race, nation, language, manner of life, work, knowledge, honor, fortune . . . the Church recreates all of them in the Spirit. To all equally she communicates a divine aspect. All receive from her a unique nature which cannot be broken asunder, a nature which no longer permits one to take into consideration the many and profound differences which are their lot. In that way all are raised up and united in a manner which is truly catholic. In her none is in the least degree separated from the community, all are grounded, so to speak, in one another by the simple and indivisible power of faith. . . . Christ, too, is all in all, He who contains all in Himself according to the unique, infinite and all wise power of His goodness as a center upon which all lines converge that the creatures of the one God may not live as strangers or enemies one with another, having no place in common, where they may display their love and their peace. (St. Maximus the Confessor)[150]

CHAPTER FIVE

MAN'S COOPERATION: PRAXIS

All I want is to know Christ and the power of his resurrection and to share his sufferings by reproducing the pattern of his death. That is the way I can hope to take my place in the resurrection of the dead. Not that I have become perfect yet: I have not yet won, but I am still running, trying to capture the prize for which Christ Jesus captured me. I can assure you my brothers, I am far from thinking that I have already won. All I can say is that I forget the past and I strain ahead for what is still to come; I am racing for the finish, for the prize to which God calls us upward to receive in Christ Jesus. (Phil. 3:10-15)

A. The Spiritual Warfare

1. A Spiritual Battle

He who has not obtained the weapons of which we have spoken will not be able to stand in the day of battle (Eph. 6:11 ff.) but will be wounded again and again. Since he lacks those weapons he cannot live in peace and freedom, for the warfare within ourselves is not like the wars and weapons that are outside, but is far more terrible. When men fight against other men they at times fight with weapons, but at other times they withdraw and stop fighting and lay down their arms and in all security enjoy sleep and food. Often they surround themselves with fortifications and take turns to be on guard duty. Thus he who takes to flight survives; if he is taken prisoner he may perhaps escape being slain, but having exchanged his freedom for honorable servitude he may even rise to greater fame and fortune. Here it is different; warfare goes on constantly, and the soldiers of Christ must at all times be armed with their weapons. Neither by night nor by day nor for a single instant is this warfare interrupted, but even when we eat or drink or do anything (1 Cor. 10:31) we find ourselves in the thick of battle. It is incorporeal enemies that we face; they are constantly facing us even though we do not see them. They are watching us closely to see whether they can find some member of ours unprotected so that they may be able to stab it with their weapons and slay us. No one can seek protection for himself and briefly catch his breath, nor can anyone flee and be saved thereby, nor yet may we engage in the battle by relays. On all men there lies the inescapable necessity of joining in this conflict. No one may escape the alternatives of either winning and staying alive or of being overcome and dying. (St. Symeon the New Theologian)[151]

Those who are trying to lead a spiritual life have to carry on a most skillful and difficult warfare, through their thoughts every moment of their life—that is, a spiritual warfare; it is necessary that our whole soul should have every moment a clear eye, able to watch and notice the thoughts entering our heart from the evil one and repel them; the hearts of such men should be always burning with faith, humility, and love; otherwise the subtlety of the Devil finds an easy access to them, followed by a diminution of faith, or entire unbelief, and then by every possible evil, which it will be difficult to wash away even by tears. Do not, therefore, allow your heart to be cold, especially during prayer, and avoid in every way cold indifference. Very often it happens that prayer is on the lips, but in the heart cunning, incredulity, or unbelief, so that by the lips the man seems near to God, while in his heart he is far from Him. And, during our prayers, the evil one makes use of every means to chill our hearts and fill them with deceit in a most imperceptible manner to us. Pray and fortify yourself, fortify your heart.

Do not fear the conflict, and do not flee from it: where there is no struggle, there is no virtue, where there are no temptations for faithfulness and love, it is uncertain whether there is really any faithfulness and love for the Lord. Our faith, trust, and love are proved and revealed in adversities, that is, in difficult and grievous outward and inward circumstances, during sickness, sorrow, and privations. (John Cronstadt)[152]

2. Solitude

Solitude of the body is the knowledge and reduction to order of the habits and feelings. And solitude of soul is the knowledge of one's thoughts and an inviolable mind. (St. John Climacus)[153]

A friend of solitude is a courageous and unrelenting power of thought which keeps constant vigil at the doors of the heart and kills or repels the thoughts that come. He who is solitary in the depth of his heart will understand this last remark; but he who is still a child is unaware and ignorant of it. (St. John Climacus)[154]

The beginning of solitude is to throw all noise off as disturbing for the depth (of the soul). And the end of it is not to fear disturbances and to remain insusceptible to them. Though going out, yet without a word, he is kind and wholly a house of love. He is not easily moved to speech, nor is he moved to anger. The opposite of this is obvious. (St. John Climacus)[155]

The cell of the solitary is the confines of his body; he has within a shrine of knowledge. (St. John Climacus)[156]

For all who are struggling with their clay, solitude is suitable at the right time if only they have a director. For angelic strength is needed for the solitary life. I speak of those who lead a life of real solitude of body and soul. (St. John Climacus)[157]

He who has attained to solitude has penetrated to the very depth of the mysteries, but he would never have descended into the deep unless he had first seen and heard the noise of the waves and the evil spirits, and perhaps even been splashed by these waves. The great Apostle Paul confirms what we have said. If he has not been caught up into Paradise, as into solitude, he could never have heard the unspeakable words (2 Cor. 12:4). The ear of the solitary will receive from God amazing words. That is why in the book of Job that all-wise man said: "Will not my ear receive amazing things from Him?" (Job 4:12–18). (St. John Climacus)[158]

3. Virtue

Imagine virtue as the body, contemplation as the soul, and the two together as forming one perfect man, whose two parts—the senses and the mind—are made one by the spirit. Just as it is impossible for a soul to manifest its being before the forming of the body, with its members, has been completed; so too is it impossible for a soul to reach contemplation without active work in virtue. (St. Isaac the Syrian)[159]

He who has made progress in virtues and has become enriched by knowledge, already sees things as they are in their nature, and always says and does everything in accordance with sound understanding, never deviating from it. For we are virtuous or sinful according to whether we use things sensibly or stupidly. (St. Maximus the Confessor)[160]

Some virtues are of the body, others of the soul. Those of the body are: fasting, vigil, sleeping on bare earth, service, handicraft so as not to be a burden to others or to be able to give alms, and so on. Virtues of the soul are: love, magnanimity, meekness, self-mastery, prayer and so on. Thus if because of some need or because of our physical state, such as illness, or for some such reason we are unable to practice the above mentioned physical virtues, the Lord, who knows the reason for this, indulgently forgives us. But if we do not practice virtues of the soul, we shall have no excuse, for they are not subject to such obstacles. (St. Maximus the Confessor)[161]

For the substance of all the virtues is Our Lord Jesus Christ Himself. . . . All men therefore who, by constant fidelity acquire such virtue, participate without doubt in God—the substance of all the virtues. (St. Maximus the Confessor)[162]

Concerning external asceticism and what practice is better and primary, know this, beloved ones, that all the virtues are mutually bound to each other. Like a certain spiritual chain, one is dependent upon the other; prayer to love, love to joy, joy to meekness, meekness to humility, humility to service, service to hope, hope to faith, faith to obedience, obedience to simplicity.

And likewise on the opposite side the vices are bound one to the other: hatred to anger, anger to pride, pride to vainglory, vainglory to disbelief, disbelief to hardness of heart. . . . And the other parts of vice similarly are interdependent. So also on the good side the virtues are dependent upon each other and are inter-connected. (Pseudo-Macarius)[163]

Virtue needs only our will, since it is within us and springs from us. Virtue exists when the soul keeps in its natural state. It is kept in its natural state when it remains as it came into being. Now it came into being fair and perfectly straight. . . . For the soul is said to be straight when its mind is in its natural state as it was created. But when it swerves and is perverted from its natural condition, that is called vice of the soul. (St. Athanasius)[164]

4. Fasting

The Savior began the work of our salvation with fasting. In the same way all those, who follow in the footsteps of the Savior, build on this foundation the beginning of their endeavor, since fasting is a weapon established by God. Who will escape blame if he neglects this? If the Lawgiver Himself fasts, how can any of those who have to obey the Law, be exempt from fasting? This is why the human race knew no victory before fasting, and the devil was never defeated by our nature as it is; but this weapon has indeed deprived the devil of strength from the outset. . . . As soon as the devil sees someone possessed of this weapon, fear straightway falls on this adversary and tormentor of ours, who remembers and thinks of his defeat by the Savior in the wilderness; his strength is at once destroyed and the sight of the weapon, given us by the Supreme Leader, burns him up. A man armed with the weapon of fasting is always afire with zeal. He who remains therein, keeps his mind steadfast and ready to meet and repel all violent passions. (St. Isaac the Syrian)[165]

One kind of temperance is suitable for those who behave irreproachably, and another for those subject to weaknesses. For the former, a movement in the body is a signal for restraint; but the latter are affected by such movements without relief or relaxation till their very death and end. The former always wish to preserve peace of mind, and the latter propitiate God by spiritual lamentation and contrition. (St. Isaac the Syrian)[166]

The mind of a faster prays soberly, but the mind of an intemperate person is filled with impure idols. (St. Isaac the Syrian)[167]

He who cherishes his stomach and hopes to overcome the spirit of fornication, is like one who tries to put out a fire with oil. (St. Isaac the Syrian)[168]

Know that often a devil settles in the belly and does not let the man be satisfied even though he has devoured a whole Egypt and drunk a river Nile. But after taking food this unclean spirit goes away, and sends against us the spirit of fornication, telling him of our condition and saying: "Catch, catch, hound him; for when the stomach is full, he will not resist much." With a smile the spirit of fornication comes, and having bound us hand and foot by sleep, does with us all he pleases, defiling soul and body with its impurities, dreams, and emissions. (St. Isaac the Syrian)[169]

Fasting is the coercion of nature and the cutting out of everything that delights the palate, the prevention of lust, the uprooting of bad thoughts, deliverance from dreams, purity of prayer, the light of the soul, the guarding of the mind, deliverance from blindness, the door of compunction, humble sighing, glad contrition, a lull in chatter, a means to silence, a guard of obedience, lightening of sleep, health of body, agent of dispassion, remission of sins, the gate of Paradise and its delight. (St. Isaac the Syrian)[170]

Fasting gradually disperses and drives away spiritual darkness and the veil of sin that lies on the soul, just as the sun dispels the mist. Fasting enables us spiritually to see that spiritual air in which Christ, the Sun who knows no setting, does not rise, but shines without ceasing. Fasting, aided by vigil, penetrates and softens hardness of heart. Where once were the vapors of drunkenness it causes fountains of compunction to spring forth. I beseech you, brethren, let each of us strive that this may happen in us! Once this happens we shall readily, with God's help, cleave through the whole sea of passions and pass through the waves of the temptations inflicted by the cruel tyrant, and so come to anchor in the port of impassibility. (St. Symeon the New Theologian)[171]

B. Eight Capital Sins

The Fathers say that there are eight principal vices of the soul of which numerous temptations are the offspring: gluttony, fornication, covetousness, anger, sadness, acedia, vainglory and pride. (St. Nil Sorsky)[172]

There are eight principal thoughts, from which all other thoughts stem. The first thought is of gluttony; the second, of fornication; the third, of love of money; the fourth, of discontent; the fifth, of anger; the sixth, of despondency; the seventh, of vainglory; the eighth, of pride. Whether these thoughts disturb the soul or not does not depend on us; but whether they linger in us or not and set passions in motion or not—does depend on us. (Evagrius of Pontus)[173]

The war with the passions that is required of us is essentially a war of the mind. We succeed in it by denying all sustenance to the passions and so starving them out. But there is also the war of action, which consists in deliberately undertaking and performing what is diametrically opposed to our passions. For instance, to conquer avarice we should give money away freely; to fight pride we should choose some degrading occupation; to overcome a craving for amusements we should stay at home, and so on. It is true that this method used by itself does not lead directly to the aim; for when suppressed the passion may force its way inward, or retire only to give place to some other passion. But when this active struggle is united with the inner one, the two together are quickly enabled to overcome any kind of passionate attack. (St. Theophan the Recluse)[174]

1. Acedia

Acedia is akin to dejection and especially felt by wandering monks and solitaries, a persistent and obnoxious enemy to such as dwell in the desert, disturbing the monk especially about midday, like a fever mounting at a regular time, and bringing its highest tide of inflammation at definite accustomed hours to the sick soul. And so some of the Fathers declare it to be the demon of noontide which is spoken of in Psalm 90.

Then this besieges the unhappy mind, it begets aversion from the place, boredom with one's cell, and scorn and contempt for one's brethren, whether they be dwelling with one or some way off, as careless and unspiritually minded persons. Also, toward any work that may be done within the enclosure of our own lair, we become listless and inert. It will not suffer us to stay in our cell, or to attend to our reading: we lament that in all this while, living in the same spot, we have made no progress, we sign and complain that bereft of sympathetic fellowship we have no spiritual fruit; and bewail ourselves as empty of all spiritual profit, abiding vacant and useless in this place; and we that could guide others and be of value to multitudes have edified no man, enriched no man with our precept and example. We praise other and far distant monasteries, describing them as more helpful to one's progress, more congenial to one's soul's health. We paint the fellowship of the brethren there, its suavity, its richness in spiritual conversation, contrasting it with the harshness of all that is at hand, where not only is there no edification to be had from any of the brethren who dwell here, but where one cannot even procure one's victuals without enormous toil. Finally we conclude that there is no health for us so long as we stay in this place, short of abandoning the cell wherein to tarry further will be only to perish with it, and betaking ourselves elsewhere as quickly as possible.

The blessed Apostle, like a true physician of the spirit . . . busied himself to prevent the malady born of the spirit of acedia. . . . "Study to be quiet . . . and to do your own business and to work with your own hands, as is commended you." (St. John Cassian)[175]

2. Vainglory

With regard to its form, vainglory is a change of nature, a perversion of character, a note of blame. And with regard to its quality, it is a dissipation of labors, a waste of sweat, a betrayal of treasure, a child of unbelief, the precursor of pride, shipwreck in harbor, an ant on the threshing floor which, though small, has designs upon all one's labor and fruit. The ant waits for the gathering of the wheat, and vainglory for the gathering of the riches of virtue; for the one loves to steal and the other to squander. (St. John Climacus)[176]

The sun shines on all alike, and vainglory beams on all activities. For instance, I am vainglorious when I fast, and when I relax the fast in order to be unnoticed I am again vainglorious over my prudence. When well-dressed I am quite overcome by vainglory, and when I put on poor clothes I am vainglorious again. When I talk I am defeated, and when I am silent I am again defeated by it. However I throw this prickly-pear, a spike stands upright. (St. John Climacus)[177]

People of high spirit bear offense nobly and gladly, but only holy people and saints can pass through praise without harm. (St. John Climacus)[178]

It is a great work to shake from the soul the praise of men, but to reject the praise of demons is greater. (St. John Climacus)[179]

Vainglory makes those who are preferred, proud, and those who are slighted, resentful. (St. John Climacus)[180]

One who had the gift of sight told me what he had seen. "Once," he said, "when I was sitting in assembly, the demon of vainglory and the demon of pride came and sat beside me one on either side. The one poked me in the side with the finger of vainglory and urged me to relate some vision or labor which I had done in the desert. But as soon as I had shaken him off, saying: Let them be turned back and put to shame who plot evil against me (Ps. 39:15), then the demon on my left at once said in my ear: Well done, well done, you have become great by conquering my shameless mother. Turning to him, I made apt use of the rest of the verse and said: Let them be turned back and put to shame who said to me: Well done, well done (Ps. 69:3). And to my question: How is vainglory the mother of pride? he replied: Praises exalt and puff one up; and when the soul is exalted, then pride seizes it, lifts it up to heaven and casts it down to the abyss." (St. John Climacus)[181]

It is worth investigating why those who live in the world and spend their life in vigils, fasts, labors and hardships, when they withdraw from the world and begin the monastic life, as if at some trial or on the practicing ground, no longer continue the discipline of their former spurious and sham asceticism. I have seen how in the world they planted many different plants of the virtues, which were watered by vainglory as by an underground sewage pipe, and were hoed by ostentation, and for manure were heaped with praise. But when transplanted to a desert soil, inaccessible to people of the world and so not manured with foul-smelling water of vanity, they withered at once. For water-loving plants are not such as to produce fruit in hard and arid training fields. (St. John Climacus)[182]

C. A Psychology of Thoughts

1. Temptations

As a young girl, frightened by some terrifying sight, runs to her parents, clutches their garments and cries for help, so too with the soul; the more it is oppressed and driven by fear of temptations, the more it hastens to cling to God, invoking Him in ceaseless prayer. So long as, one after another, temptations continue to afflict it, it increases its supplications; but as soon as it is granted a respite, it gives itself up to dissipation of thoughts. (St. Isaac the Syrian)[183]

While the offense is still small and unripe, destroy it, before it has time to produce wide branches and has begun to ripen. Do not give yourself up to negligence, while this fault seems small to you; for later you will find in it an inhuman master and will run before it like a slave, a prisoner. A man who fights a passion at its inception quickly masters it. (St. John Climacus)[184]

In time of temptations do not leave your monastery, but endure agitation of thoughts with courage, especially those which bring sorrow and despondency; for being thus tried by afflictions providentially, you will acquire a firm hope in God. But if you leave your monastery, you will prove yourself to be inept, cowardly and inconstant. (St. Maximus the Confessor)[185]

Temptation fulfills approximately the following purpose. The gifts which our soul has received are unknown to everyone except God. They are unknown even to ourselves. Through temptations they become known. Thereafter we can no longer be ignorant of what we are: we know ourselves and can be aware, if we but co-operate, of our wrongdoings. We can also give thanks for the benefits conferred upon us and made manifest by temptations. Temptations that come upon us serve the purpose of showing us who we really are and to make manifest the things that are in our heart. This is made clear by what the Lord says in the book of Job and what is written in Deuteronomy, as follows: "Do you think I should have treated you otherwise but to make you appear just?" (Origen)[186]

2. Thoughts

If Moses, when he attempted to draw near the burning bush, was prohibited until he should remove the shoes from his feet, how should you not free yourself of every thought that is colored by passion seeing that you wish to see One who is beyond every thought and perception? (Evagrius)[187]

There are eight principal thoughts, from which all other thoughts stem. The first thought is of gluttony; the second, of fornication; the third, of love of money; the fourth, of discontent; the fifth, of anger; the sixth, of despondency; the seventh, of vainglory; the eighth, of pride. Whether these thoughts disturb the soul or not does not depend on us; but whether they linger in us or not and set passions in motion or not does depend on us. (Evagrius)[188]

This is the art of the evil one, and with these arrows he poisons every victim. And for this reason it is not safe, until the mind has had long experience of the warfare, to allow thoughts to enter into the heart; especially in the beginning, when our soul is still in sympathy with the suggestions of the demons, takes pleasure in them and follows them eagerly; but it is necessary, as soon as we are aware of the thoughts, immediately to cut them off, at the very moment of their impact and our finding them. But when after a long time the mind is practiced in this wonderful work, and knows all there is to know about it, and comes to be skilled in waging this war, so as to discriminate between thoughts correctly—and as the prophet says, is able easily to take "the little foxes" (Song of Sol. 2:15)—then it may cunningly let them enter, and fight against them with the help of Christ, expose them and throw them out. (Hesychius of Jerusalem)[189]

As it is impossible for fire and water to pass together through one channel, so it is impossible for sin to enter into the heart, unless it first knocks at the door of the heart through the fantasy of an evil suggestion.

First comes suggestion; secondly, coupling, when our thoughts and the thoughts of the wicked demons are mingled together; thirdly, merging, when thoughts of both kinds take counsel together, resolve on evil and plan what must be done; and fourthly comes the visible action, that is, the sin. If then the mind is steadfast in sobriety, pays attention to itself, and by resistance and calling on the Lord Jesus drives away the suggestion on its impact, that which would usually follow does not happen. For the evil one, being mind without body, cannot lead souls astray except by means of imagination and thoughts. From among these actions David says of suggestion: "I will early destroy all the wicked of the land" (Ps. 101:8). And the great Moses says about merging: "Thou shalt make no covenant with them" (Exod. 23:32). (Hesychius of Jerusalem)[190]

Sweet memory of God, that is, of Jesus, coupled with heart-felt wrath and beneficent contrition, can always annihilate all the fascination of thoughts, the variety of suggestions, words, dreams, gloomy imaginings and, in brief, everything with which the all-destructive enemy arms himself to sally forth, daringly seeking to devour our souls. Jesus when invoked easily burns up all this. For in no place other can we find salvation except in Jesus Christ. The Savior Himself confirmed this saying: "Without me you can do nothing" (John 15:5).

And so every hour and every moment let us zealously guard our heart from thoughts obscuring the mirror of the soul, which should contain, drawn and imprinted on it, only the radiant image of Jesus Christ, Who is the wisdom and the power of God the Father. Let us constantly seek the kingdom of heaven in the heart, and we are sure mysteriously to find within ourselves the seed, the pearl, the drink and all else, if we cleanse the eye of our mind. This is why our Lord Jesus Christ said: "The kingdom of God is within you" (Luke 17:21), meaning by this the Deity dwelling in the heart.

Sobriety cleanses conscience till it shines brightly. Being thus cleansed, conscience drives away all darkness from within, as a light which suddenly shines forth, when a veil which covered it is removed. If true and constant sobriety is continued after darkness is driven away, conscience again shows what has been forgotten or what has remained hidden without being realized.

At the same time, again by means of sobriety, it teaches invisible struggle with the enemies, waged by the mind, and the warfare of thoughts. It teaches how to throw spears in this single combat, how skillfully to shoot the darts of good thoughts (against the enemy) and how to prevent the enemy arrows from wounding the mind, by making it speed like an arrow to seek protection in Christ, and thus gain the refuge of the light of our desire, in place of the darkness of destruction. He who has tasted this light understands of what I am speaking. (Philotheus of Sinai)[191]

Guard your mind with extreme intensity of attention. As soon as you notice a (hostile) thought, immediately resist it and at the same time hasten to call on Christ our Lord to wreak vengeance. While you are still calling to Him, sweet Jesus will say: I am with you to protect you. But when by your prayer the enemies are subdued you must again diligently pay attention to your mind. Here come waves (of thoughts), more numerous than ever, again rushing against you, one after another, so that the soul is almost engulfed in them and is about to perish. But Jesus, being God, when the disciple appeals, again forbids the evil winds (of thoughts, and they become subdued). But you, having found an hour or a moment of respite from attacks of the enemy, glorify Him Who has saved you, and plunged deep into meditation upon death. (Philotheus of Sinai)[192]

D. Purity of Heart

The rule and limit of absolute and perfect purity is to be equally disposed toward animate and inanimate bodies, rational and irrational. (St. John Climacus)[193]

Not he who has kept his clay undefiled is pure, but he whose members are completely subject to his soul. (St. John Climacus)[194]

The goal of our profession is the kingdom of God. Its immediate purpose, however, is purity of heart, for without this we cannot reach our goal. We should always have this purpose in mind; and should it ever happen that for a short time our heart turns aside from the direct path, we must bring it back again at once, guiding our lives with reference to our purpose as if it were a carpenter's rule. . . .

We do everything for the sake of this immediate purpose. We give up country, family possessions and everything worldly in order to acquire purity of heart. . . . It is for love of our neighbor that we scorn wealth, lest by fighting over it and stimulating our disposition to anger, we fall away from love. When we show this disposition to anger toward our brother even in small things, we have lapsed from our purpose and our renunciation of the world is useless. The blessed Apostle was aware of this and said: "Though I give my body to be burned, and have no love, it profits me nothing" (1 Cor. 13:3). From this we learn that perfection does not follow immediately upon renunciation and withdrawal from the world. It comes after the attainment of love which, as the Apostle said, "is not jealous or puffed up, does not grow angry, bears no grudge, is not arrogant, thinks no evil" (1 Cor. 13:4, 5). All these things establish purity of heart; and it is for this that we should do everything, scorning possessions, enduring fasts and vigils gladly, engaging in spiritual reading and psalmody. . . .

Fasts and vigils, the study of Scripture, renouncing possessions and everything worldly are not in themselves perfection, as we have said; they are its tools. For perfection is not to be found in them; it is acquired through them. It is useless, therefore, to boast of our fasting, vigils, poverty and reading of Scripture when we have not achieved the love of God and our fellow men. Whoever has achieved love has God within himself and his intellect is always with God. (St. John Cassian)[195]

How can one say that a man has attained purity? When he sees all men as being good, and when none appears to him to be unclean and defiled, then he is indeed pure in heart. (St. Isaac the Syrian)[196]

CHAPTER SIX

CONTEMPLATION

If anyone loves me he will keep my word,
and my Father will love him,
and we shall come to him
and make our home with him. (John 14:23)

A. Logos Mysticism

1. Prayer

Therefore we must learn first of all that we ought always to pray and not to faint. For the effect of prayer is union with God, and if someone is with God, he is separated from the enemy. Through prayer we guard our chastity, control our temper, and rid ourselves of vanity; it makes us forget injuries, overcomes envy, defeats injustice, and makes amends for sin. Through prayer we obtain physical well-being, a happy home, and a strong, well-ordered society. Prayer will make our nation powerful, will give us victory in war and security in peace; it reconciles enemies and preserves allies. Prayer is the seal of virginity and a pledge of faithfulness in marriage; it shields the wayfarer, protects the sleeper, and gives courage to those who keep vigil. It obtains a good harvest for the farmer and a safe port for the sailor.

Prayer is your advocate in lawsuits. If you are in prison, it will obtain your release; it will refresh you when you are weary and comfort you when you are sorrowful. Prayer is the delight of the joyful as well as solace to the afflicted. It is the wedding crown of the spouses and the festive joy of a birthday no less than the shroud that enwraps us in death.

Prayer is intimacy with God and contemplation of the invisible. It satisfies our yearnings and makes us equal to the angels. Through it good prospers, evil is destroyed, and sinners will be converted. Prayer is the enjoyment of things present and the substance of the things to come. Prayer turned the whale into a home for Jonas; it

brought Ezechias back to life from the very gates of death; it transformed the flames into a moist wind for the three children. Through
prayer the Israelites triumphed over the Amalecites and 185,000
Assyrians were slain in one night by the invisible sword. Past history
furnishes thousands of other examples besides these which make it
clear that of all the things valued in this life nothing is more precious
than prayer. (St. Gregory of Nyssa)[197]

Someone approaches God in prayer, but failing to appreciate the
exalted greatness whom he is addressing, unwittingly insults His
majesty with nothing but base petitions. It is just as if a very poor
and uneducated man who thought earthenware precious, approached a king who had decided to distribute riches and honors.
But the poor man would not make requests worthy of the king, but
ask from so great a personage to take clay and make it into something according to his own mind. In the same way the man who
makes prayer without being properly taught, will not lift himself up
to the height of the Giver, but wants the Divine power to descend to
the mean, earthly level of his own desires. Therefore he offers un-
ruly cravings to Him who sees into the hearts, not desiring Him to
heal the perverse movements of his mind, but to make them worse,
for through the help of God the evil desire would become a fact.
Because someone gives me pain and my heart hates him it says to
God: Strike him; almost crying out: Let my own passion be in Thee,
and may my wickedness pass over into Thee. Obviously, just as in
human fights one cannot support one of the parties without sharing
in the anger of the person who is infuriated against his opponent,
thus it is also clear that he who tries to set God against his enemy
asks Him to share his own angry excitement. But this means that
the Divine should succumb to passion, behave in a human manner
and change from His own natural goodness into the ferocity of a
beast. (St. Gregory of Nyssa)[198]

Prayer by reason of its nature is the converse and union of man
with God, and by reason of its action upholds the world and brings
about reconciliation with God; it is the mother and also the daughter
of tears, the propitiation for sins, a bridge over temptations, a wall
against afflictions, a crushing of conflicts, work of angels, food of all
the spiritual beings, future gladness, boundless activity, the spring
of virtues, the source of graces, invisible progress, food of the soul,
the enlightening of the mind, an axe for despair, a demonstration of
hope, the annulling of sorrow, the wealth of monks, the treasure of

solitaries, the reduction of anger, the mirror of progress, the realization of success, a proof of one's condition, a revelation of the future, a sign of glory. For him who truly prays, prayer is the court, the judgment hall and the tribunal of the Lord before the judgment to come. (St. John Climacus)[199]

Let your prayer be completely simple. For both the publican and the prodigal son were reconciled to God by a single phrase. (St. John Climacus)[200]

The attitude of prayer is one and the same for all, but there are many kinds of prayer and many different prayers. Some converse with God as with a friend and master, interceding with praise and petition not for themselves but for others. Some strive for more (spiritual) riches and glory and for confidence in prayer. Others ask for complete deliverance from their adversary. Some beg to receive some kind of rank; others for complete forgiveness of debts. Some ask to be released from prison; others for remission of accusations. (St. John Climacus)[201]

Do not attempt to talk much when you pray lest your mind be distracted in searching for words. One word of the publican propitiated God, and one cry of faith saved the thief. Loquacity in prayer often distracts the mind and leads to fantasy, whereas brevity makes for concentration. (St. John Climacus)[202]

Try to lift up, or rather, to shut off your thought within the words of your prayer, and if in its infant state it wearies and falls, lift it up again. Instability is natural to the mind, but God is powerful to establish everything. If you persevere indefatigably in this labor, He who sets the bounds to the sea of the mind will visit you too, and during your prayer will say to the waves: Thus far shalt thou come and no further (Job 38:11). Spirit cannot be bound; but where the Creator of the spirit is, everything obeys. (St. John Climacus)[203]

The beginning of prayer consists in banishing the thoughts that come to us by single ejaculations the very moment that they appear; the middle stage consists in confining our minds to what is being said and thought; and its perfection is rapture in the Lord. (St. John Climacus)[204]

Prepare your self for your set times of prayer by unceasing prayer in your soul, and you will soon make progress. I have seen these who shone in obedience and who tried, as far as they could, to keep in mind the remembrance of God, and the moment they stood in prayer they were at once masters of their minds, and shed streams of tears; because they were prepared for this beforehand by holy obedience. (St. John Climacus)[205]

The highest state of prayer, it is said, is when the mind while praying leaves the flesh and the world and is completely devoid of matter and form. He who keeps this state inviolate truly prays without ceasing. (St. Maximus the Confessor)[206]

Prayer is a continual intercourse of the spirit with God. What state of soul then is required that the spirit might thus strain after its Master without wavering, living constantly with him without intermediary? (3)

Stand resolute, fully intent on your prayer. Pay no heed to the concerns and thoughts that might arise the while. They do nothing better than disturb and upset you so as to dissolve the fixity of your purpose. (9)

Strive to render your mind deaf and dumb at the time of prayer and then you will be able to pray. (11)

Prayer is the fair flower of meekness and mildness. (14)

Prayer is the fruit of joy and of thanksgiving. (15)

Prayer is the exclusion of sadness and despondency. (16)

When an angel makes his presence felt by us, all disturbing thoughts immediately disappear. The spirit finds itself clothed in great tranquillity. It prays purely. At other times, though, we are beset with the customary struggle and then the spirit joins the fight. It cannot so much as raise its eyes for it is overtaken by diverse passions. Yet if only the spirit goes on striving it will achieve its purpose. When it knocks on the door hard enough it will be opened. (30)

Pray not to this end, that your own desires be fulfilled. You can be sure they do not fully accord with the will of God. Once you have learned to accept this point, pray instead that "thy will be done" in me. In every matter ask him in this way for what is good and for what confers profit on your soul, for you yourself do not seek this so completely as he does. (31)

Do not be overanxious and strain yourself so as to gain an immediate hearing for your request. The Lord wishes to confer greater favors than those you ask for, in reward for your perseverance in praying to him. For what greater thing is there than to converse intimately with God and to be preoccupied with his company? Undistracted prayer is the highest act of the intellect. (34)

Prayer is an ascent of the spirit to God. (35)

Whether you pray along with the brethren or alone, strive to make your prayer more than a mere habit. Make it a true inner experience. (41)

When you pray keep your memory under close custody. Do not let it suggest your own fancies to you, but rather have it convey the awareness of your reaching out to God. Remember this—the memory has a powerful proclivity for causing detriment to the spirit at the time of prayer. (44)

The state of prayer can be aptly described as a habitual state of imperturbable calm *(apatheia)*. It snatches to the heights of intelligible reality the spirit which loves wisdom and which is truly spiritualized by the most intense love. (52)

The man who strives after true prayer must learn to master not only anger and his lust, but must free himself from every thought that is colored by passion. (53)

The man who loves God constantly lives and speaks with him as a Father. He turns aside from every thought that is tinged with passion. (54)

If you are a theologian you truly pray. If you truly pray you are a theologian. (60)

When your spirit withdraws, as it were, little by little from the flesh because of your ardent longing for God, and turns away from every thought that derives from sensibility or memory or temperament and is filled with reverence and joy at the same time, then you can be sure that you are drawing near that country whose name is prayer. (61)

The Holy Spirit takes compassion on our weakness, and though we are impure he often comes to visit us. If he should find our spirit praying to him out of love for the truth he then descends upon it and dispels the whole army of thoughts and reasonings that beset it. And too he urges it on to the works of spiritual prayer. (62)

If you long to pray then avoid all that is opposed to prayer. Then when God draws near he has only to go along with you. (65)

When you are praying do not fancy the Divinity like some image formed within yourself. Avoid also allowing your spirit to be impressed with the seal of some particular shape, but rather, free from all matter, draw near the immaterial Being and you will attain to understanding. (66)

Stand guard over your spirit, keeping it free of concepts at the time of prayer so that it may remain in its own deep calm. Thus he who has compassion on the ignorant will come to visit even such an insignificant person as yourself. That is when you will receive the most glorious gift of prayer. (69)

You will not be able to pray purely if you are all involved with material affairs and agitated with unremitting concerns. For prayer is the rejection of concepts. (70)

Do not set your heart on what seems good to you but rather what is pleasing to God when you pray. This will free you from disturbance and leave you occupied with thanksgiving in your prayer. (89)

By true prayer a monk becomes another angel, for he ardently longs to see the face of the Father in heaven. (113)

Do not by any means strive to fashion some image or visualize some form at the time of prayer. (114)

Do not cherish the desire to see sensibly angels or powers or even Christ lest you be led completely out of your wits, and taking a wolf for your shepherd, come to adore the demons who are your enemies. (115)

Let me repeat this saying of mine that I once expressed on some other occasions: Happy is the spirit that attains to perfect formlessness at the time of prayer. (117)

Happy is the spirit which, praying without distraction, goes on increasing its desire for God. (118)

Happy is the spirit that becomes free of all matter and is stripped of all at the time of prayer. (119)

Happy is the spirit that attains to complete unconsciousness of all sensible experience at the time of prayer. (120)

Do you wish to pray? Then banish the things of this world. Have heaven for your homeland and live there constantly—not in mere word but in actions that imitate the angels and in a more god-like knowledge. (142)

The value of prayer is found not merely in its quantity but also in its quality. This is made clear by those two men who entered the temple, and also by this saying: "When you pray do not do a lot of empty chattering" (Luke 18:10; Matt. 6:7). (151)

When you give yourself to prayer, rise above every other joy— then you will find true prayer. (153) (Evagrius)[207]

We are affected from the very bottom of the heart, so that we get at its meaning (of Holy Scripture) not by reading the text but by experience anticipating it. And so our mind will reach that incorruptible prayer . . . distinguished by the use of no words or utterances; but with the purpose of the mind all on fire . . . produced through ecstasy of heart by some unaccountable keenness of spirit, and the mind being thus affected without the aid of the sense or any visible material pours it forth to God with groanings and sighs that cannot be uttered. (St. John Cassian)[208]

There are three methods of attention and prayer, by which the soul is uplifted and moves forward, or is cast down and destroyed. Whoever employs these methods at the right time and in the right way, moves forward; but whoever employs them unwisely and at the wrong time is cast down. . . .

The distinctive features of the first method are as follows: if a man stands at prayer and, raising his hands, his eyes and his mind to heaven, keeps in mind Divine thoughts, imagines celestial blessings, hierarchies of angels and dwellings of the saints, assembles briefly in his mind all that he has learned from the Holy Scriptures and ponders over all this while at prayer, gazing up to heaven, and thus inciting his soul to longing and love of God, at times even shedding tears and weeping, this will be the first method of attention and prayer. . . .

The second method is this: a man tears his mind away from all sensed objects and leads it within himself, guarding his senses and collecting his thoughts, so that they cease to wander amid the vanities of this world; now he examines his thoughts, now ponders over the words of the prayer his lips utter, now pulls back his thoughts, if, ravished by the devil, they fly toward something bad and vain, now with great labor and self-exertion strives to come back into himself, after being caught and vanquished by some passion. The distinctive feature of this method is that it takes place in the head, thought fighting against thought. . . .

The beginning of this third method is not gazing upward to heaven, raising one's hands or keeping one's mind on heavenly things . . . the third method of attention and prayer is the following: the mind should be in the heart a distinctive feature of the third method of prayer. It should guard the heart while it prays, revolve, remaining always within, and thence, from the depths of the heart, offer up prayers to God. When the mind, there, within the heart, at last tastes and sees that the Lord is good, and delights therein, then it will no longer wish to leave this place in the heart. . . . You should observe three things before all else: freedom from all cares, not only cares about bad and vain but even about good things, or in other words, you should become dead to everything; your conscience should be clear in all things, so that it denounces you in nothing; and you should have complete absence of passionate attachment, so that your thought inclines toward nothing worldly. Keep your attention within yourself (not in your head, but in your heart). Keep your mind there (in the heart), trying by every possible means to find the place where the heart is, in order that, having found it, your mind should constantly abide there. . . . From that moment onward, from whatever side a thought may appear, the mind immediately chases it away, before it has had time to enter, and become a thought or an image, destroying it by Jesus' name, that is, Lord Jesus Christ, have mercy upon me! . . . One of the holy fathers says: "Sit in your cell and this prayer will teach you everything." (Nicephorus)[209]

2. Contemplation

Prayer is one thing, and contemplation in prayer is another, although prayer and contemplation mutually engender one another. Prayer is sowing, contemplation the reaping of the harvest, when the reaper is filled with wonder at the ineffable sight of the beautiful ears of corn, which have sprung up before him from the little naked seeds that he sowed. (St. Isaac the Syrian)[210]

The next stage (in prayer) which follows this, is when a man, progressing in the good life and approaching the experience and practice of contemplation, is granted from above the grace to taste the sweetness of spiritual knowledge.

The beginning of this stage is the following: first a man is convinced of God's Providence for men, he is illumined with love for the Creator and is filled with wonder alike at the wise ordering of sentient beings and at God's great care for them.

This is the beginning of Divine sweetness in him and the kindling of his love for God, which flames in the heart and burns up the passions of soul and body. This love, accompanied by great zeal and good conscience, begins to flare up suddenly—and a man is intoxicated, as with wine, and his heart made captive to God.

Thereupon this force begins to gain strength and firmness in him, in proportion to his effort to lead a good life, to guard himself, to spend his time in reading and prayer. (St. Isaac the Syrian)[211]

The highest state of pure prayer has two forms. One belongs to men of active life, the other to men of contemplative life. One is engendered in the soul by fear of God and good hope; the other by love of God and extreme purity. The sign of the first order is when a man collects his mind, freeing it of all worldly thoughts, and prays without distraction and disturbance, as if God Himself were present before him, as indeed He is. The sign of the second is when, in the very act of rising in prayer, the mind is ravished by the Divine boundless light and loses all sensation of itself or of any other creature, and is aware of Him alone, who, through love, has produced in him this illumination. In this state, moved to understand words about God, he receives pure and luminous knowledge of Him. (St. Maximus the Confessor)[212]

By fulfilling the commandments, the mind becomes stripped of passions; by spiritual contemplation of the visible it is stripped of passionate representations of things; by knowledge of the invisible it withdraws from contemplation of visible things; finally, by knowledge of the Holy Trinity it abandons even the knowledge of things invisible. (St. Maximus the Confessor)[213]

When the soul undergoes such spiritual activity and subjects itself to God and through direct union approaches the Divinity, it is enlightened in its movements by an intense light and the mind experiences a feeling of joy of the happiness that awaits us in the life to come. Then an indescribable sweetness warms the heart, the whole body feels its repercussions and man forgets not only any given passion, but even life itself and thinks that the kingdom of heaven consists of nothing other than this ecstatic state. Here he experiences that the love of God is sweeter than life and the knowledge of God sweeter than honey. (St. Nil Sorsky)[214]

B. Experiencing the Trinity

1. Trinity

There is one God, the Father, of whom the One Son is begotten and from whom the One Holy Spirit flows; Unity unconfounded and Trinity undivided; Mind without beginning, Sole Begetter of the One Word, who is essentially without beginning, and the Source of the One, everlasting Life, that is, the Holy Spirit. (St. Maximus the Confessor)[215]

The Old Testament proclaimed the Father openly, and the Son more obscurely. The New Testament manifested the Son, and suggested the Deity of the Spirit. Now the Spirit Himself dwells among us, and supplies us with a clearer demonstration of Himself. For it was not safe, when the Godhead of the Father was not yet acknowledged, plainly to proclaim the Son; nor when that of the Son was not yet received to burden us further (if I may use so bold an expression) with the Holy Ghost; lest perhaps people might, like men loaded with food beyond their strength, and presenting eyes as yet too weak to bare it to the sun's light, risk the loss even of that which was within the reach of their powers; but that by gradual additions, and, as David says, Goings up, and advances and progress from glory to glory (Ps. 84:7), the Light of the Trinity might shine upon the more illuminated. (St. Gregory Nazianzus)[216]

We acknowledge the Trinity, holy and perfect, to consist of the Father, the Son and the Holy Spirit. In this Trinity there is no intrusion of any alien element or of anything from outside, nor is the Trinity a blend of creative and created being. It is a wholly creative and energizing reality, self-consistent and undivided in its active power, for the Father makes all things through the Word and in the Holy Spirit, and in this way the unity of the holy Trinity is preserved. Accordingly, in the Church, one God is preached, one God who is above all things and through all things and in all things. God is above all things as Father, for he is principal and source; he is through all things through the Word; and he is in all things in the Holy Spirit.

. . . Even the gifts that the Spirit dispenses to individuals are given by the Father through the Word. For all that belongs to the Father belongs also to the Son, and so the graces given by the Son in the Spirit are true gifts of the Father. Similarly, when the Spirit dwells in us, the Word who bestows the Spirit is in us too, and the Father is present in the Word. This is the meaning of the text: My Father and I will come to him and make our home with him. For where the light is, there also is the radiance; and where the radiance is, there too are its power and its resplendent grace.

This is also Paul's teaching in his second letter to the Corinthians: The grace of our Lord Jesus Christ and the love of God and the fellowship of the Holy Spirit be with you all. For grace and the gift of the Trinity are given by the Father through the Son in the Holy Spirit. Just as grace is given from the Father through the Son, so there could be no communication of the gift to us except in the Holy Spirit. But when we share in the Spirit, we possess the love of the

Father, the grace of the Son and the fellowship of the Spirit himself. (St. Athanasius)[217]

When the Lord says, "I and my Father are one," He means their oneness of essence; and when He says, "the Father is in me, and I in him" He shows the inseparability of the Hypostases. . . . According to the teaching of the great Gregory we should preserve the unity of God and profess three Hypostases, each with His distinctive property. For, according to his teaching, the Trinity is divided but indivisibly; and is combined but dividedly. A wonderful union and division! But where is the wonder if the Father and the Son were combined and divided as man and man are combined and divided, and nothing more? (St. Maximus the Confessor)[218]

> And, as for those who have managed to participate in Your secrets,
> —in an immaterial sensation to share materially
> in Your mysteries, formidable and for all unspeakable,
> and to recognize, in visible things, the invisible glory
> and the strange mystery which has taken place in the world,
> they are still less numerous well do I know it!
> They are the ones who have received pure contemplation,
> from the One who was in the beginning, before all creation,
> begotten of the Father, and with the Spirit, Son, God and Word,
> triple light in unity but unique light in the three.
> Two aspects of a unique light: Father, Son and Spirit,
> for it is indivisible in the three Persons, without confusion,
> these three persons in whom, according to the divine nature, there is but
>   one power,
> one glory, one authority and one will.
> For all three appear to me, in one unique face,
> like two beautiful eyes filled with light.
> How will the eyes see without the face, tell me?
> But, without eyes, it is useless to speak of the face,
> deprived as it is of the essential, or, better still, of everything!
> Likewise the sun, were one to extract from it the light which is its beauty,
> would disappear first, and, after it, would disappear the entire creation
> which receives light and vision from it.
> Thus in the order of the intelligible: if God were deprived of one of the
>   two,
> either of the Son or of the Spirit, He would no longer be Father.
> He would no longer even be living, separated from the Spirit who gives
>   life and being to everyone.
> Let every truly rational creature adore then . . .

the Divine Nature in three hypostases transcending all explanation. (St. Symeon the New Theologian)[219]

Trinity is simply unity; it is not merged together—it is three in one. The One three-hypostatical God has the three hypostases perfectly distinct in Himself.

God is known and understood in everything in three hypostases. He holds all things and provides for all things through His Son in the Holy Spirit; and no one of Them, wherever He is invoked, is named or thought of as existing apart or separately from the two others.

Just in the same way, man has mind, word and spirit; and the mind cannot be without the word, nor the word without the spirit, but the three are always in one another, yet exist in themselves. The mind speaks by means of words, and the word is manifested through the spirit. This example shows that man bears in himself a feeble image of the ineffable prototype, the Trinity, thus demonstrating that he has been made in God's image.

Mind is the Father, word is the Son, spirit is the Holy Spirit, as the divine fathers teach in this example, expounding the dogmatic teaching of the consubstantial and pre-existing Trinity, of one God in three persons, thus transmitting to us the true faith as an anchor of hope. According to the Scriptures, to know the One God is the root of immortality, and to know the dominion of the three-in-one is the whole and entire truth. The word of the Gospel on this subject can be understood thus: "This is life eternal, that they might know thee, the only true God" in three hypostases, "and Jesus Christ, whom thou hast sent" in two natures and two wills (John 17:3). (St. Gregory of Sinai)[220]

2. The Indwelling Trinity

Now it is the proper substance of the Holy Spirit who dwells in the just and who sanctifies them and it belongs only to the Three Persons of the Holy Trinity, to be able, by their substance, to penetrate into souls. (St. Didymus of Alexandria)[221]

It is untrue to say that we cannot be one with God except by union of will. For above that union there is another union more sublime and far superior, which is wrought by the communication of the Divinity to man, who, while keeping his own nature, is, so to speak, transformed into God, just as iron plunged into fire becomes fiery, and while remaining iron seems changed into fire. . . . Union with God cannot exist otherwise than by participation with the Holy Spirit, diffusing in us the sanctification proper to Himself, imprinting and engraving on our souls the divine likeness. (St. Cyril of Alexandria)[222]

Accordingly we are all one in the Father and in the Son and in the Holy Spirit; one, I say, in unity of relationship of love and concord with God and one another . . . one by conformity in godliness, by communion in the sacred body of Christ, and by fellowship in the one and Holy Spirit and this is a real, physical union. (St. Cyril of Alexandria)[223]

C. True Theology

1. Knowledge

There are three modes by which knowledge ascends and descends. These modes are: body, soul, spirit. Knowledge is the gift of God to the nature of rational beings and was bestowed on them at their very creation. In its nature it is as simple and indivisible as sunlight, but corresponding to its application it undergoes changes and divisions. Listen to the order of this application.

1. The first degree of knowledge. When knowledge follows desires of the flesh, it embraces the following modes: wealth, vainglory, adornment, bodily comfort, care for book-learning . . . and all the other things which crown the body in this visible world. Because of these distinctive features knowledge becomes opposed to faith. . .

2. The second degree of knowledge. When a man renounces the first degree, he becomes occupied with thoughts and desires of the soul; then, in the light of the nature of his soul, he practices the following excellent deeds: fasting, prayer, alms, reading of the Divine Scriptures, virtuous life, struggle with passions and so on. For all the good deeds, all the excellent features seen in the soul and the wonderful means used for serving in the house of Christ in this second degree of knowledge are the work of the Holy Spirit, who lends power to its action. . . . But even here knowledge is still material and multiple. It contains only the way which leads and speeds us toward faith. There is yet a higher degree of knowledge.

3. The third degree of knowledge is the degree of perfection. Hear now how a man becomes finer, acquires that which is of the spirit, and in his life comes to resemble the invisible powers, which perform their service not through sensory actions but through vigi-

lance of mind. When knowledge soars above earthly things and the cares of earthly activities, when it begins to experience thoughts belonging to what is within and hidden from the eyes, when it surges upward and follows faith in its solicitude, for the life to come, in its desire for what was promised us, and in searching deeply into the mysteries that are hidden; then faith itself absorbs this knowledge, is transformed and begets it anew, so that this knowledge becomes all spirit. (St. Isaac the Syrian) [224]

2. Apophatic Theology: Knowing by Not Knowing

By thy persistent commerce with the mystic visions, leave behind both sensible perceptions and intellectual efforts, and all objects of sense and intelligence, and all things not being and being, and be raised aloft unknowingly to the union as far as attainable, with Him who is above every essence and knowledge . . . for by the resistless and absolute ecstasy in all purity, from thyself and all, thou wilt be carried on high, to the superessential ray of the Divine darkness, when thou hast cast away all, and become free from all. (Dionysius Pseudo-Areopagite)[225]

Then he (Moses) is freed from them who are both seen and seeing, and enters into the gloom of the *Agnosia;* a gloom veritably mystic, within which he closes all perceptions of knowledge and enters into the altogether impalpable and unseen, being wholly of Him who is beyond all, and of none, neither himself nor other; and by inactivity of all knowledge, united in his better part to the altogether Unknown, and by knowing nothing, knowing above mind. (Dionysius Pseudo-Areopagite)[226]

Now the doctrine we are taught here is as follows. Our initial withdrawal from wrong and erroneous ideas of God is a transition from darkness to light. Next comes a closer awareness of hidden things, and by this the soul is guided through sense phenomena to the world of the invisible. And this awareness is a kind of cloud, which overshadows all appearances, and slowly guides and accustoms the soul to look toward what is hidden. Next the soul makes progress through all these stages and goes on higher, and as she leaves below all that human nature can attain, she enters within the secret chamber of the divine knowledge, and here she is cut off on all sides by the divine darkness. Now she leaves outside all that can be grasped by sense or by reason, and the only thing left for her contemplation is the invisible and the incomprehensible. And here

God is, as the Scriptures tell us in connection with Moses: But Moses went to the dark cloud wherein God was (Exod. 20:21). (St. Gregory of Nyssa)[227]

The Bride is surrounded with the divine night in which the Bridegroom comes near without showing Himself . . . but by giving the soul a certain sense of His presence while fleeing from clear knowledge. (St. Gregory of Nyssa)[228]

And thus the soul, slipping at every point from what cannot be grasped, becomes dizzy and perplexed and returns once again to what is connatural to it, content now to know merely this about the Transcendent, that it is completely different from the nature of things that the soul knows. (St. Gregory of Nyssa)[229]

For the sacred text is here teaching us that spiritual knowledge first occurs as an illumination in those who experience it. Indeed, all that is opposed to piety is conceived of as darkness; to shun the darkness is to share in the light. But as the soul makes progress, and by a greater and more perfect concentration comes to appreciate what the knowledge of truth is, the more it approaches this vision, and so much the more does it see that the divine nature is invisible. It thus leaves all surface appearances, not only those that can be grasped by the senses but also those which the mind itself seems to see, and it keeps on going deeper until by the operation of the spirit it penetrates the invisible and incomprehensible, and it is there that it sees God. The true vision and the true knowledge of what we seek consists precisely in not seeing, in an awareness that our goal transcends all knowledge and is everywhere cut off from us by the darkness of incomprehensibility. Thus that profound evangelist, John, who penetrated into this luminous darkness, tells us that no man hath seen God at any time (John 1:18), teaching us by this negation that no man—indeed, no created intellect—can attain a knowledge of God. (St. Gregory of Nyssa)[230]

And then it (God's presence in darkness) breaks forth, even from the things that are beheld and from those that behold them, and plunges the true initiate into the darkness of unknowing wherein he renounces all the apprehensions of his understanding and is enwrapped in that which is wholly intangible and invisible, belonging wholly to him that is beyond all things and to none else (whether himself or another), and being through the passive stillness of all his reasoning powers united by his highest faculty to Him that is wholly unknowable, of whom thus by a rejection of all knowledge he possesses a knowledge that exceeds his understanding. (Dionysius Pseudo-Areopagite)[231]

For those who have been purified by *hesychia* know that the Divine surpasses these contemplations and these initiations and so possesses that grace supra-intelligible and super-additional in a way that surpasses us; they possess it not because they do not see after the fashion of those who practice negative theology, but because there is in the very vision which they know, something which surpasses vision, by undergoing negation and not by conceiving it. Just as the act of undergoing and seeing divine things differs from cataphatic theology and is superior to it, so does the act of undergoing negation in spiritual visions, negation linked to the transcendence of the Object, differ from negative theology and is superior to it. (St. Gregory Palamas)[232]

3. Theology

Our intellect often finds it hard to endure praying because of the straitness and concentration which this involves; but it joyfully turns to theology because of the broad and unhampered scope of divine speculation. Therefore, so as to keep the intellect from expressing itself too much in words or exalting itself unduly in its joy, we should spend most of our time in prayer, in singing psalms and reading the Holy Scriptures, yet without neglecting the speculations of wise men whose faith has been revealed in their writings. In this way we shall prevent the intellect from confusing its own utterances with the utterances of grace, and stop it from being led astray by self-esteem and dispersed through over-elation and loquacity. In the time of contemplation, we must keep the intellect free of all fantasy and image, and so ensure that with almost all our thoughts we shed tears. . . . There is, moreover, a prayer which is above even the broadest scope of speculation; but this prayer is granted only to those who fully and consciously perceive the plenitude of God's grace within them.

At the start of the spiritual way, the soul usually has the conscious experience of being illumined with its own light through the action of grace. But, as it advances further in its struggle to attain theology, grace works its mysteries within the soul for the most part without its knowledge. Grace acts in these two ways so that it may first set us rejoicing on the path of contemplation, calling us from ignorance to spiritual knowledge, and so that in the midst of our struggle it may then keep this knowledge free from arrogance. . . .

Spiritual knowledge teaches us that, at the outset, the soul in pursuit of theology is troubled by many passions, above all by anger and hatred. This happens to it not so much because the demons are arousing these passions, as because it is making progress. . . . The theologian whose soul is gladdened and kindled by the oracles of God comes, when the time is ripe, to the realm of dispassion; for it is written: "The oracles of the Lord are pure, as silver when tried in fire, and purged of earth" (Ps. 12:6). The gnostic, for his part, rooted in his direct experience of spiritual knowledge, is established above the passions. The theologian, if he humbles himself, may also savor the experience of spiritual knowledge, while the gnostic, if he acquires faultless discrimination, may by degrees attain the virtue of theological contemplation. These two gifts, theology and *gnosis,* never occur in all their fullness in the same person; but theologian and gnostic each marvel at what the other enjoys to a greater degree, so that humility and desire for holiness increase in both of them. That is why the Apostle says: "For to one is given by the Spirit the principle of wisdom; to another the principle of spiritual knowledge by the same Spirit" (1 Cor. 12:8). (St. Diadochus of Photike)[233]

D. A Diaphanous God

He preserves his soul undefiled, who compels his mind to think only of God and of His perfections, who uses his speech for rightly interpreting and expounding these perfections, and who has taught his senses to look rightly on the visible world and all therein and to proclaim to the soul the greatness of the intelligence there concealed. (St. Maximus the Confessor)[234]

My thoughts dwelt constantly on the Jesus Prayer and I felt a great joy. From that time on I began to experience occasionally a great many different sensations in my heart and my mind. Now and then my heart would brim over with happiness overwhelmed by such lightness, freedom and solace that I was all changed and enraptured. At times I felt a glowing love for Jesus Christ and all God's creatures; and my eyes filled with tears of gratitude to God, who poured His grace on me, a great sinner. *(The Pilgrim)*[235]

After these words I looked in his face and there came over me an even greater reverential awe. Imagine in the center of the sun, in the dazzling brilliance of his midday rays, the face of the man who talks with you. You see the movement of his lips and the changing expression of his eyes, you hear his voice, you feel someone grasp your shoulders; yet you do not see the hands, you do not even see yourself or his figure, but only a blinding light spreading several years around and throwing a sparkling radiance across the snow blanket on the glade and into the snowflakes which besprinkled the great elder and me. Can one imagine the state in which I then found myself? *(A Conversation of St. Seraphim of Sarov with Motovilov)*[236]

CHAPTER SEVEN

THE NEW MAN

God, create a clean heart in me,
put into me a new and constant spirit,
do not banish me from your presence,
do not deprive me of your holy spirit.

Be my savior again, renew my joy,
keep my spirit steady and willing;
and I shall teach transgressors the way to you,
and to you the sinners will return.

... Sacrifice gives you no pleasure,
were I to offer holocaust, you would not have it.
My sacrifice is this broken spirit,
you will not scorn this crushed and broken heart.

Show your favor graciously to Zion,
rebuild the walls of Jerusalem. (Ps. 51:10-13, 16-18)

A. Hesychasm: Holistic Integration

Our glorious teachers and preceptors, in whom lives the Holy Spirit, wisely teach us all, especially those who have wished to embrace the field of divine silence and consecrate themselves to God, having renounced the world to practice hesychasm with wisdom, and to prefer prayer to the Lord above any other work, or care, begging His mercy with undaunted hope. Such men should have, as their constant practice and occupation, the involving of His holy and most sweet name, bearing it always in the mind, in the heart and on the lips. They should force themselves in every possible way to live, breathe, sleep and wake, walk, eat and drink with Him and in Him, and in general so to do all that they have to do. For as in His absence all harmful things come to us, leaving no room for anything to profit the soul, so in His presence all evil is swept away, no good is ever lacking and everything becomes possible, as the Lord Himself says: "He that abides in me, and I in him, the same brings forth much fruit: for without me you can do nothing" (John 15:5). Thus unworthy as we are, we too call with faith on this most terrible and most worshipful name; and with His aid daringly set sail and launch forth on these writings. (The Monks Callistus and Ignatius)[237]

Sobriety is a spiritual art, which, with long and diligent practice and with the help of God, releases man completely from passionate thoughts and words and from evil deeds. And as it proceeds, it gives a sure knowledge of God the Incomprehensible, as far as this can be reached; and it gives in secret a solution of Divine and secret mysteries. It is the doer of every commandment in the Old and New Testament; and the giver of every blessing in the life to come. In itself it is, in essence, purity of heart; which on account of its greatness and its high qualities or to speak more exactly, on account of our inattention and our carelessness, is very rare among monks today, it is this which Christ calls blessed, saying: "Blessed are the pure in heart: for they shall see God" (Matt. 5:8). Being then such as it is, it is bought for a great price. Sobriety, if it be constant in a man, becomes his guide to a righteous and God pleasing life. It is also a ladder towards contemplation; and it teaches us to govern rightly the movements of the three parts of the soul and to guard the senses securely, and increases daily the four great virtues, wisdom, courage, abstinence and justice. (Hesychius of Jerusalem)[238]

1. Passionlessness

St. Basil the Great says of passionlessness: "He who has become a lover of God and is wishing to participate, however imperfectly, in the passionlessness of God, in spiritual sanctity, serenity, quietness and meekness, and to taste the joy and gladness born of them, must strive to lead his thoughts far away from every material passion which may trouble the soul, and to contemplate Divine things with a clear and unshaded eye, insatiably enjoying the Divine light. A man who has implanted this habit and disposition in his soul becomes akin to God, in as far as it is possible for him to be like God, and is loved and welcomed by Him as one who has courageously undertaken this great and difficult work, and has become capable of conversing with God in spite of his nature being compounded with matter, by sending to Him his thought pure and stripped of any admixture of carnal passions." This is on passionlessness.

As regards human passionlessness St. Isaac writes thus: "Passionlessness does not mean not feeling passions, but not accepting them. Thanks to the many and varied virtues, both evident and hidden, acquired by the saints, passions lost power in them and so could not be easily roused to attack the soul. So thought need no longer keep its attention on passions; for all its time is filled with thinking, studying and investigating the most perfect contemplations, which are consciously set in motion in the mind."

Whenever passions begin to move and be excited, the mind is suddenly lifted away from them by some realization of Divine things which has entered it, and passions remain without effect, as St. Mark said: "When by the grace of God the mind practices works of virtue and comes near to knowledge, it is little capable of feeling what comes from the worst and unwise part of the soul. For this knowledge makes it soar on high and estranges it from everything that is in the world. By their chastity, by the subtlety, lightness and sharpness of their mind, as well as by their deeds, the mind of saints becomes purified and filled with light, for their flesh has withered through works of silence and their long abiding in it. Therefore contemplation comes easily and swiftly to each one of them and, abiding in them, leads them in wonder to the depths of the object of their contemplation. . . . For when the soul does not make friends with passions of thinking about them, then, since it is constantly occupied with another concern, the power of passions is unable to hold spiritual feelings in its grip." (The Monks Callistus and Ignatius)[239]

B. The Jesus Prayer

Some of the fathers taught that the prayer should be said in full: "Lord, Jesus Christ, Son of God, have mercy upon me." Others advised saying half, thus: "Jesus, Son of God, have mercy upon me," or "Lord Jesus Christ, have mercy upon me," or to alternate, sometimes saying it in full and sometimes in a shorter form. Yet it is not advisable to pander to laziness by changing the words of the prayer too often, but to persist a certain time as a test of patience. Again, some teach the saying of the prayer with the lips, others with and in the mind. In my opinion both are advisable. For at times the mind, left to itself, becomes wearied and too exhausted to say the prayer mentally; at other times the lips get tired of this work. Therefore both methods of prayer should be used with the lips and with the mind. But one should appeal to the Lord quietly and without agitation, so that the voice does not disturb the attention of the mind and does not thus break off the prayer, until the mind is accustomed to this doing, and, receiving force from the Spirit, firmly prays within on its own. There there will be no need to say the prayer with the lips; indeed, it will be impossible, for he who reaches this stage is fully content with mental doing of the prayer and has no wish to leave it. (St. Gregory of Sinai)[240]

After quoting the evidence of many holy fathers concerning inner life, the blessed Nicephorus says the following from his own experience: "You know, brother, how we breathe: we breathe the air in and out. On this is based the life of the body and on this depends its warmth. So, sitting down in your cell, collect your mind, lead it into the path of the breath along which the air enters in, constrain it to enter the heart together with the inhaled air, and keep it there. Keep it there, but do not leave it silent and idle; instead give it the following prayer: 'Lord, Jesus Christ, Son of God, have mercy upon me.' Let this be its constant occupation, never to be abandoned. For this work, by keeping the mind free from dreaming, renders it unassailable to suggestions of the enemy and leads it to Divine desire and love. Moreover, brother, strive to accustom your mind not to come out too soon; for at first it feels very lonely in that inner seclusion and imprisonment. But when it gets accustomed to it, it begins on the contrary to dislike darting among external things. For the kingdom of God is within us, and for a man who has seen it within, and having found it through pure prayer, has experienced it, everything outside loses its attraction and value. . . ." These are the words of this blessed father, uttered for the purpose of teaching the mind, under the influence of this natural method, to abandon its usual circling, captivity and dispersion and to return to attention to itself; and through such attention to reunite with itself and in this way to become one with the prayer and, together with the prayer, to descend into the heart and to remain there for ever. (The Monks Callistus and Ignatius)[241]

The great Chrysostom also says: "I implore you, brethren, never to break or despise the rule of this prayer." And a little further: "A monk when he eats, drinks, sits, officiates, travels or does any other thing must continually cry: 'Lord, Jesus Christ, Son of God, have mercy upon me!' so that the name of Lord Jesus, descending into the depths of the heart, should subdue the serpent ruling over the inner pastures and bring life and salvation to the soul. He should always live with the name of Lord, Jesus, so that the heart absorbs the Lord and the Lord the heart, and the two become one." And again: "Do not estrange your heart from God, but abide in Him and always guard your heart by remembering our Lord Jesus Christ, until the name of the Lord becomes rooted in the heart and it ceases to think of anything else. May Christ be glorified in you." (The Monks Callistus and Ignatius)[242]

The prayer of Jesus is said like this: Lord Jesus Christ, Son of God, have mercy on me, a sinner. Originally it was said without the addition of the word sinner: this word was added to the other words of the prayer later. This word, remarks St. Nil Sorsky, which implies a consciousness and confession of the fall, is fitting for us and pleasing to God who has commanded us to offer prayers in acknowledgment and confession of our sinfulness. The Fathers allow beginners, in deference to their weakness, to divide the prayer into two halves, and sometimes to say, Lord Jesus Christ, have mercy on me, a sinner, and sometimes, Son of God, have mercy on me, a sinner. But this is only a concession or indulgence, and not at all an order or rule requiring unfailing compliance. It is much better to say constantly the same, whole prayer without distracting and bothering the mind with changes or with concern about changes. . . . St. Gregory the Sinaite forbids frequent change, saying: "Trees that are often transplanted do not take root." (Ignatius Brianchaninov)[243]

Insanity can come from the Jesus Prayer only if people, while practicing it, fail to renounce the sins and wicked habits which their conscience condemns. This causes a sharp inner conflict which robs the heart of all peace. As a result the brain grows confused and a man's ideas become entangled and disorderly. (St. Theophan the Recluse)[244]

The monk Basil and the elder Paissy Velitchkovsky say that many of their contemporaries harmed themselves by misusing material aids. And in later times cases of derangement caused in this way were frequently met. In fact they are met even now. . . . One is bound to meet them. They are the inevitable consequence of ignorant, self-directed, conceited, premature and proud zeal, and finally of a complete lack of experienced directors. (Ignatius Brianchaninov)[245]

I began to seek the place of my heart in the manner Symeon the New Theologian taught. With my eyes closed I looked upon it in thought, i.e., in imagination. I tried to see it as it is in the left side of my breast and to listen attentively to its beating. At first I did it several times a day for half an hour, and failed to see anything but darkness. Then I succeeded in picturing my heart and the movement in it, and I learned how to bring in and out of it the Jesus Prayer, timing it with my breathing. In this I followed the teaching of Sts. Gregory of Sinai, Callistus and Ignatius. While inhaling, I saw my heart in my mind and said: "Lord Jesus Christ." In breathing out, I said: "Have mercy on me." This I did for an hour at a time, later for two hours, then as long as I was able to. Finally, I succeeded in doing it almost all day long. If things were hard to manage and I fell prey to laziness and doubt, I hastened to open the *Philocalia* and to read passages dealing with the action of the heart, and then once more I felt a fervent and eager desire for the Prayer.

About three weeks later I noticed that my heart ached. Afterward this pain was transformed to the delightful sensation of warmth, comfort and peace. This incited me still further and urged me to the saying of the Prayer with greater care. My thoughts dwelt constantly on it and I felt a great joy. From that time on I began to experience occasionally a great many different sensations in my heart and my mind. Now and then my heart would brim over with happiness overwhelmed by such lightness, freedom and solace that I was changed and enraptured. At times I felt a glowing love for Jesus Christ and all God's creatures; and my eyes filled with tears of gratitude to God, who poured His grace on me a great sinner. As for my mind, so dull before, it sometimes received such an enlightenment that I was able to understand easily and to meditate upon things which hitherto had been beyond my comprehension. Now and then a sensation of delightful warmth would spread from my heart throughout my whole being, and I would be profoundly moved in recognizing God's presence in all things. Again, when I called upon the Name of Jesus I would be overwhelmed with bliss, and the meaning of "The Kingdom of Heaven is within you" would become clear to me.

From these and other, similar, comforting experiences I drew the conclusion that the results of inner prayer are threefold: it manifests itself in the spirit, in feelings and in revelations; the spirit is filled by a mellowness that comes from the love of God, inward calmness, exultation of mind, purity of thoughts and sweet remembrance of God. The feelings convey to us a delightful warmth of the heart, a joyful exultation, lightness and vigor, enjoyment of life and insensibility to pain and sorrow. The revelation brings us enlightenment of the mind, understanding of the Holy Scriptures and of the speech of all creatures, freedom from vanities, awareness of the sweetness of the inner life and cognizance of the nearness of God and of His love for mankind.

After having spent some five months in solitude and prayer which filled me with sweet sensations, I grew so used to it that I practiced it constantly. In the end I felt that it was going on by itself in my mind and heart, not only while I was awake but also in my sleep. It never ceased for a single moment in whatever business I might have been doing. My soul gave thanks to God, and my heart melted away in continuous joy. *(The Pilgrim)*[246]

You have read about the Jesus Prayer, have you not? And you know what it is from practical experience. Only with the help of this prayer can the necessary order of the soul be firmly maintained; only through this prayer can we preserve our inner order undisturbed even when distracted by household cares. This prayer alone makes it possible to fulfill the injunction of the Fathers: the hands at work, the mind and heart with God. When this prayer becomes grafted in our heart, then there are no inner interruptions and it continues always in the same, evenly flowing way.

The path to achievement of a systematic interior order is very hard, but it is possible to preserve this or a similar state of mind during the various and inevitable duties you have to perform; and what makes it possible is the Jesus Prayer when it is grafted in the heart. How can it be so grafted? Who knows? But it does happen. He who strives is increasingly conscious of this engrafting, without knowing how it has been achieved. To strive for this inner order, we must walk always in the presence of God, repeating the Jesus Prayer as frequently as possible. As soon as there is a free moment, begin again at once, and the engrafting will be achieved.

One of the means of renewing the Jesus Prayer and bringing it to life is by reading, but mainly about prayer. (St. Theophan the Recluse)[247]

C. *Penthos:* Weeping in Exile

1. Tears

First pray for the gift of tears, so that through sorrowing you may tame what is savage in your soul. And having confessed your transgressions to the Lord, you will obtain forgiveness from Him.

Pray with tears and all you ask will be heard. For the Lord rejoices greatly when you pray with tears.

If you shed tears during your prayer, do not exalt yourself, thinking you are better than others. For your prayer has received help so that you can confess your sins readily and make your peace with the Lord through your tears. Therefore do not turn the remedy for passions into a passion, and so again provoke to anger Him who has given you this grace. (Evagrius)[248]

One of the brethren asked Abba Poemen, saying, "Father, what shall I do in the matter of my sins?" The old man said unto him, "Whosoever wisheth to blot out his offenses can do so by weeping, and he who wisheth to acquire good works can do so by means of weeping; for weeping is the path which the Scriptures have taught us, and the fathers have also wept continually, and there is no other path except that of tears." (Abba Poemen)[249]

Greater than Baptism itself is the fountain of tears after Baptism, even though it is somewhat audacious to say so. For Baptism is the washing away of evils that were in us before, but sins committed after Baptism are washed away by tears. As Baptism is received in infancy we have all defiled it, but we cleanse it anew with tears. And if God in His love for mankind had not given us tears, few indeed and hard to find would be those in the state of grace. (St. John Climacus)[250]

In the case of tears as in everything else our good and just Judge will certainly take into consideration the strength of our nature. For I have seen small tear-drops shed with difficulty like drops of blood, and I have also seen fountains of tears poured out without difficulty. And I judged those toilers more by their toil than by their tears, and I think that God does too. (St. John Climacus)[251]

When you reach the realm of tears, then know that your mind has left the prison of this world, has put its foot on the path of a new age and has begun to smell the scent of new and wondrous air. Tears begin to flow because the birth of the spiritual child is near. Grace, the common mother of all, wishes mysteriously to bring forth a divine image into the light of the life to come. But these tears are of a different order from those which come from time to time to those practicing silence (sometimes during contemplation, sometimes during reading or at the time of prayer). I am not speaking of this type of tears, but of such as flow unceasing day and night.

The eyes of a man who has reached this degree become like a

spring of water for up to two years and more after which he comes to the stilling of thoughts. After the stilling of thoughts, as far as nature permits it in part, there comes that rest of which St. Paul speaks (Heb. 4:3). In this peaceful tranquillity the mind begins to contemplate mysteries. Then the Holy Spirit begins to reveal to him heavenly things and God comes to dwell in him and resurrects in him the fruit of the Spirit. When you enter the realm of stillness of thoughts, the profusion of tears is taken from you—tears come to you in moderation and at the proper time. (St. Isaac the Syrian)[252]

> Clean the stains of my soul and give me tears of penance,
> loving tears out of love, tears of salvation,
> tears that clean the darkness of my mind,
> making me light so that I may see You,
> Light of the world,
> Enlightenment to my repentant eyes. (St. Symeon the New Theologian)[253]

If a man who possesses within him the light of the Holy Spirit is unable to bear its radiance, he falls prostrate on the ground and cries out in great fear and terror, as one who sees and experiences something beyond nature, above words or reason. He is then like a man whose entrails have been set on fire, and, unable to bear the scorching flame, he is utterly devastated by it and deprived of all power to be in himself. But, through constant watering and cooling by tears, the flame of divine desire in him burns all the brighter, producing yet more copious tears and, being washed by their flow, he shines with ever greater radiance. And when the whole of him is aflame and he becomes as light, the words of John the Divine are fulfilled: "God unites with gods and is known by them." (St. Symeon the New Theologian)[254]

Without tears our dried heart could never be softened, nor our soul acquire spiritual humility and we would not have the force to become humble. For he who has not such dispositions cannot be united to the Holy Spirit and without such union with the Holy Spirit after purification, one can no longer expect knowledge and contemplation of God nor merit to be instructed in the hidden virtues of humility. (St. Symeon the New Theologian)[255]

2. Mercy

And what is a merciful heart? The burning of the heart on account of all creation, on account of people and birds and animals and demons, and for *every* created being. Because of their remembrance, the eyes fill with tears. Great and intense mercy grasps the heart and wrings it out, for he who is merciful is not able to bear or hear or see any harm or the slightest sorrow which takes place in the created world. This holds true on behalf of those who harm him. For these he offers prayers continually with tears for their protection and for their redemption. He does the same thing even for the snakes which crawl upon the ground. All of this he does out of his great mercy, which moves in his heart without measure in the likeness of God. (St. Isaac the Syrian)[256]

When the saints become perfect, they are both absorbed into God in the outpouring of love for Him, as well as into love for their fellow human beings. The saints themselves seek this sign of their union with God, that is, that they have the passionate desire to be merciful to their neighbor. Thus did our fathers, the monks, do when growing in the perfection and likeness of God, always receiving in themselves the fullness of life in Jesus Christ. . . . Let it further be said that those who love this world cannot realize love for their fellow human beings. For when one obtains love, he is, together with it, clothed in God. (St. Isaac the Syrian)[257]

Why is it that, whereas the priest (in the Divine Liturgy) asks the faithful to pray for so many different things, the faithful in fact ask for one thing, only mercy? Why is this the sole cry they send forth to God?

In the first place, as we have already said, it is because this prayer implies both gratitude and confession. Secondly, to beg God's mercy is to ask for his kingdom, that kingdom which Christ promised to give to those who seek for it, assuring them that all things else of which they have need will be added unto them. Because of this, this prayer is sufficient for the faithful, since its application is general.

How do we know that the kingdom of God is signified by his mercy? In this way: Christ, speaking of the reward of the merciful, and of the recompense of kindness which they will receive from him, in one place says that they shall obtain mercy, and in another that they shall inherit the kingdom; thus proving that God's mercy and the inheritance of the kingdom are one and the same thing. "Blessed are the merciful, for they shall obtain mercy," he says. And elsewhere, as if to explain himself and to show that it means to obtain mercy, he declares: "Then shall the King say unto them on his right hand (by whom he means the merciful): Come, ye blessed

of my Father, inherit the kingdom prepared for you from the foundation of the world." (Nicholas Cabasilas)[258]

God gave us His own Son; but you will not even share your bread
with Him who was given us and put to death for your sake.

On account of you the Father did not spare Him though He was
indeed His Son; you disregard Him when He is wasting away with
starvation, even though you would be spending on Him what is
really His, spending it moreover for your own good. What can be
worse than such injustice? He was given up for you, put to death for
you, went about hungry for you; you would be giving only what is
His, giving moreoever for your own benefit; even so, you refuse to
give.

What stone could be more insensitive than such men, for despite
so many inducements they persist in this satanic cold-heartedness.
He was not satisfied only to endure death on a cross; He chose to
become poor and homeless, a beggar and naked, to be thrown into
prison and suffer sickness, so that in this way too He might invite
you to join Him.

"If you will make Me no return for having suffered for you, at
least have pity on My poverty. If not that, be moved at least by My
sickness and imprisonment. If none of these elicit your compassion,
at least grant Me this, because it is so small a request. I want
nothing expensive, just a little bread, shelter, a few kind words. If all
this leaves you unmoved, at least improve your conduct for the
kingdom of heaven's sake, for all the rewards I have promised. Or is
this too of no account in your eyes? Well, at least out of natural pity
you might feel upset when you see Me naked; and remember how I
was naked on the cross, which I suffered for your sake; or, if not
this, then recall the poverty and nakedness I endure today in the
poor. Once I was in fetters for you; I am still in fetters for you, so
that whether by those earlier bonds or by these present ones, you
might be moved to show some feeling for Me. I fasted for you and I
go hungry again, still for your sake; I thirsted as I hung upon the
cross, and I am thirsty again in the poor of today. In one way or
another, I would draw you to Myself; for your soul's sake, I would
have you compassionate.

"You are bound to Me by innumerable favors, and now I ask you
to make some return. Not that I demand it as My due. I reward you
as though you were acting out of generosity; for your trifling ges-
tures, I am giving you a kingdom.

"I do not say: 'Put an end to My poverty,' or 'Make over to Me your wealth, although it was for you that I became poor.' All I ask for is a little bread, clothing and a little comfort in My hunger.

"If I am in prison, I do not ask you to set Me free of My chains and release Me; all I ask is that, for My sake, you should visit someone in prison. This will be favor enough; in return I bestow upon you heaven. I released you from the heaviest chains; it will be enough for Me if you visit Me in prison.

"I could, of course, reward you without any of this; but I want to be in your debt, so that, along with your reward, you may have confidence in yourself." (St. John Chrysostom)[259]

3. Repentance

Repentance is the renewal of baptism. Repentance is a contract with God for a second life. A penitent is a buyer of humility. Repentance is constant distrust of bodily comfort. Repentance is self-condemning reflection, and carefree self-care. Repentance is the daughter of hope and the renunciation of despair. A penitent is an undisgraced convict. Repentance is reconciliation with the Lord by the practice of good deeds contrary to the sins. Repentance is purification of conscience. Repentance is the voluntary endurance of all afflictions. A penitent is the inflicter of his own punishments. Repentance is a mighty persecution of the stomach, and a striking of the soul into vigorous awareness. (St. John Climacus)[260]

Do not be surprised that you fall every day; do not give up, but stand your ground courageously. And assuredly the angel who guards you will honor your patience. While a wound is still fresh and warm it is easy to heal, but old, neglected and festering ones are hard to cure, and require for their care much treatment, cutting, plastering and cauterization. Many from long neglect become incurable. But with God all things are possible. (St. John Climacus)[261]

Nothing equals or excels God's mercies. Therefore he who despairs is committing suicide. A sign of true repentance is the acknowledgment that we deserve all the troubles visible and invisible, that come to us, and even greater ones. Moses, after seeing God in the bush, returned again to Egypt, that is to darkness and to the brick-making of Pharoah, symbolical of the spiritual Pharoah. But he went back again to the bush, and not only to the bush but also up the mountain. Whoever has known contemplation will never despair of himself. Job became a beggar, but he became twice as rich again. (St. John Climacus)[262]

It is a good thing to repent, and so is the benefit that comes from it. The Lord Jesus Christ, our God, knowing this and forseeing all things, said: "Repent, for the Kingdom of heaven is at hand" (Matt. 4:17). Do you want to learn why it is impossible for us to be saved without repentance, a heartfelt repentance such as the word of Scripture requires from us? Listen to the apostle himself as he proclaims: . . . "We must appear before the judgment seat of Christ, so that each one may receive good or evil, according to what he has done in the body" (2 Cor. 5:10). . . . Let us repent with all our heart and cast away not only our evil deeds, but also the wicked and unclean thoughts of our hearts and obliterate them in accordance with that which is written: "Rend your hearts and not your garments" (Joel 2:13). Tell me: What use is it if we distribute all our goods to the poor, but fail to make a break with evil and to hate sin? What use is it if, while we do not actively commit bodily sin, we mentally engage in shameful and unclean thoughts and invisibly commit sin and are governed and controlled by restrained passions of soul? I beseech you, let us cast away, together with our wealth, the habit of servitude to the evils we have mentioned. Nor let us stop at this, but let us eagerly wash away their defilement with tears of penitence. (St. Symeon the New Theologian)[263]

D. Attention: Inner Attentiveness

You should know that attention must never leave the heart. . . . What is important is not the position of the body but the inner state. Our whole aim is to stand with attention in the heart, and look toward God, and cry out to Him. (St. Theophan the Recluse)[264]

St. Paul also writes of attention and circumspect firmness: "See then that ye walk circumspectly, not as fools, but as wise, redeeming the time, because the days are evil" (Eph. 5:15-16). And St. Isaac says: "O wisdom! how wonderful thou art. How far seeing and provident! Blessed is he who has acquired thee, for he is freed from the carelessness of youth. . . . Love of wisdom means always to be watchfully attentive in small, even the smallest actions. Such a man gains the treasure of great peace; he is unsleeping so that nothing adverse may befall him, and cuts off its causes beforehand; he suffers a little in small things, thus averting great suffering. And further: the Wise One therefore says, "Be sober and watch over your life; for sleep of the mind is akin to real death and is its image." And the blessed Basil says: "He who is careless in small things cannot be trusted to be zealous in great things." (The Monks Callistus and Ignatius)[265]

Collected thoughts and concentrated attention make the mind pray unceasingly, purely and undistractedly, as St. Nilus says: "Attention seeking prayer will find prayer; for what most naturally follows upon attention is prayer, and it is upon prayer that our greatest efforts should be directed." (The Monks Callistus and Ignatius)[266]

Attention is a sign of sincere repentance. Attention is the appeal of the soul to itself, hatred of the world and ascent toward God. Attention is renunciation of sin and acquisition of virtue. Attention is an undoubting certainty of the remission of sins. Attention is the beginning of contemplation, or rather its necessary condition; for, through attention, God comes close and reveals Himself to the mind. Attention is serenity of the mind, or rather its standing firmly planted and not wandering, through the gift of God's mercy. Attention means cutting off thoughts, it is the abode of remembrance of God and the treasure house of the power to endure all that may come. Therefore attention is the origin of faith, hope and love; since he who has no faith cannot bear all the afflictions coming from without, and he who does not suffer them willingly cannot say: "He is my refuge and my fortress" (Ps. 91:2); and he who has not the Almighty as his refuge cannot be truly sincere in his love for Him. (Nicephorus the Solitary)[267]

CHAPTER EIGHT

INSERTED INTO CHRIST

Since you have been brought back to true life with Christ, you must look for the things that are in heaven, where Christ is, sitting at God's right hand. Let your thoughts be on heavenly things, not on the things that are on the earth, because you have died, and now the life you have is hidden with Christ in God. But when Christ is revealed—and he is your life—you too will be revealed in all your glory with him. (Col. 3:1-4)

A. The Indwelling Christ

O immensity of ineffable glory, O excess of love! He who contains all things dwells in the interior of a corrupt and mortal man, whose every possession is in the power of Him who inhabits him. Man indeed becomes truly like a woman carrying a child. O stupendous prodigy, of an incomprehensible God, works and mysterious incomprehensible! A man bears consciously in himself God as light, Him who has produced and created all things, holding even the man who carries Him. Man carries Him interiorly as a treasure which transcends words, written or spoken, any quality, quantity, image, matter and figure, shaped in an inexplicable beauty, all entirely simple as light, He who transcends all light. (St. Symeon the New Theologian)[268]

Listen, now, to still more formidable marvels!
We become members of Christ—and Christ becomes our members,
Christ becomes my hand, Christ, my miserable foot;
and I, unhappy one, am Christ's hand, Christ's foot!
I move my hand, and my hand is the whole Christ
—since, do not forget it, God is indivisible in His divinity—
I move my foot and behold it shines like That One!
Do not accuse me of blasphemy, but welcome these things

and adore Christ who makes you such
since, if you so wish, you will become a member of Christ,
and similarly all our members individually
will become members of Christ and Christ our members,
and all which is dishonorable in us He will make honorable
by adorning it with His divine beauty and His divine glory,
since living with God at the same time, we shall become gods,
no longer seeing the shamefulness of our body at all,
but made completely like Christ in our whole body,
each member of our body will be the whole Christ
. . . It is truly a marriage which takes place, ineffable and divine:
God unites Himself with each one yes, I repeat it,
it is my delight and each one becomes one with the Master. (St. Symeon
   the New Theologian)[269]

The problem of our life is union with God, and sin completely prevents this; therefore flee from sin as from a terrible enemy, as from the destroyer of the soul, because to be without God is death and not life. Let us therefore understand our destination; let us always remember that our common Master calls us to union with Himself.

Be so sure of the Lord's nearness to you that you may feel when praying to God that you touch Him, not only with your thought and heart, but also with your mouth and tongue. "The Word is nigh thee, even in thy mouth, and in thy heart"; that is, God.

That our union with God in the future world will come to pass, and that it will be for us the source of light, peace, joy, and beatitude, this we partly recognize by experience when in the present life. During prayer, when our soul is wholly turned toward God, and is united to Him, we feel happy, calm, easy, and joyful, like children resting on their mother's breast, or, I would rather say, we experience a sensation of inexpressible well-being. "It is good for us to be here." Therefore struggle unremittingly to obtain future everlasting bliss, the beginning of which you know by experience even in the present life but bear in mind that these beginnings are only earthly, imperfect, which we see now only in part, as "through a glass darkly." How will it be with us then when we shall indeed be most truly united to God, when the images and shadows shall pass away, and the kingdom of truth and vision will come? Oh, we must labor unceasingly all our life, until death, for future blessedness, for our future union with God.

Remember that you are always walking in the presence of the sweetest Lord Jesus. Say to yourself oftener: "I wish so to live that my life may gladden my Beloved, crucified for my sake on the Cross. Above all, I will take for the companion and friend of my life my Holy Beloved, Who instills everything into my heart, making me thirst for the salvation of all, rejoicing with those who rejoice, and weeping with those who weep." This will especially comfort my Comforter, Christ. (John Cronstadt)[270]

The mind of Christ, which the saints receive according to the words "We have the mind of Christ" (1 Cor. 2:16), comes, not by our losing our own mental power, nor as essentially and personally passing into our mind (taking its place), but as illumining, by its quality, the power of our mind and transporting its action into singleness with itself. In my opinion, a man has the mind of Christ, if he thinks of all things in the spirit of Christ and is brought by all things to thought of Him. (St. Maximus the Confessor)[271]

B. The Eucharist

I believe, Lord, and profess that You are in truth the Christ, the Son of the living God, come to the world to save sinners, of whom I am the greatest. I believe also that this is really Your Sacred Body and that this is really Your Precious Blood. And so I pray to You, have mercy on me and pardon my offenses, deliberate and indeliberate, in word and deed, remembered and long-forgotten; and grant that I may without condemnation share Your sacred mysteries, for the remission of sins and for eternal life. Amen.

This day receive me, Son of God, to eat Your sacramental supper; for I shall not betray the sacrament to Your enemies, nor give You a kiss like Judas, but like the thief acknowledge You: Remember me, Lord, in Your kingdom.

May this sharing in Your holy mysteries, Lord, be for me not to judgment or to damnation, but to the healing of soul and body. (Byzantine Liturgy of St. John Chrysostom)[272]

O my Creator, who have freely given me Your Flesh as good, O Fire which consumes the unworthy, consume me not. Enter, rather, into my members, into every part of me, into my very heart and soul. Burn up the thorns of all my sinning; cleanse my soul, sanctify my imagination; bind firmly together my joints and bones; illumine the five senses of my body; fix my entire being in the fear of You. Guard, protect and shelter me always from every deed and word which stains the soul. Cleanse, wash, adorn me; set me on the right path, give me understanding and enlightenment. Let me prove to be the dwelling place of Your Spirit alone, and in no way the dwelling place of sin. Let every passion and every evil deed take flight, as from a fire, from this house of Yours, when what I have received enters in. I set before You the prayers of all the saints: of the leaders of the angelic hosts, of Your forerunner, of the wise Apostles and, above all, of Your pure and spotless Mother. In Your compassion, accept their prayers, O my Christ, and make Your servant a child of light. It is You alone, O Blessed One, who bring holiness and light to our souls, and each day we give You the glory which befits You as God and Master. (St. Simeon Metaphrastes)[273]

Now the true Bread who "strengthens the heart of man" (Ps. 104:15) and came down from heaven bringing us life (John 6:32–33) will suffice for all things. He will intensify our eagerness and take away the inborn sluggishness of the soul. Him we must seek in every way in order that we may feed on Him and ward off hunger by constantly attending this banquet. Nor should we unnecessarily abstain from the holy table and thus greatly weaken our souls on the pretext that we are not really worthy of the Mysteries. Rather, we must resort to the priests (for Confession) on account of our sins so that we may drink of the cleansing Blood. . . .

Christ's Blood, then, closes the doors of our senses and allows nothing to pass through them which is able to harm us. Nay more, by sealing the doors it wards off the destroyer (cf. Exod. 12:13) and makes the heart into which it has been poured a temple of God. It is better than the walls of Solomon, which are a type of that Blood, in that it prevents the evil idol, "the abomination of desolation in the holy place" (Matt. 24:15), from being set up. (Nicholas Cabasilas)[274]

I am writing to all the Churches and I enjoin all, that I am dying willingly for God's sake, if only you do not prevent it. I beg of you, do not do me an untimely kindness. Allow me to be eaten by the beasts, which are my way of reaching to God. I am God's wheat, and I am to be ground by the teeth of wild beasts, so that I may become the pure bread of Christ. (St. Ignatius of Antioch)[275]

I have no taste for corruptible food nor for the pleasures of this life. I desire the Bread of God, which is the Flesh of Jesus Christ, who was of the seed of David; and for drink I desire His Blood, which is love incorruptible. (St. Ignatius of Antioch)[276]

Therefore, in order that we may become of His Body, not in

desire only, but also in very fact, let us become commingled with that Body. This, in truth, takes place by means of the food which He has given us as a gift, because He desired to prove the love which He has for us. It is for this reason that He has shared Himself with us and has brought His Body down to our level, namely, that we might be one with Him as the body is joined with the head. This, in truth, is characteristic of those who greatly love. . . . Moreover, Christ has done even this to spur us on to greater love. And to show the love He has for us He has made it possible for those who desire, not merely to look upon Him, but even to touch Him and consume Him and to fix their teeth in His Flesh and to be commingled with Him; in short, to fulfill all their love. Let us, then, come back from that table like lions breathing out fire, thus becoming terrifying to the Devil, and remaining mindful of our Head and of the love which He has shown for us. (St. John Chrysostom)[277]

I speak of that union which comes in the Mysteries
(the Sacrament of Holy Communion).
for, purified by repentance
and by the torrents of tears,
I receive in Communion
the Body divinized as being that of God.
I too become god
in this inexpressible union.
See what a mystery!
The soul then and the body . . .
are one being in two essences.
Therefore these are one and two
in communion with Christ
and drinking His blood,
they are united to two essences,
united in this way to the essences of my God,
they become god by participation.
They are called by the same name as that of Him
in whom they have participated on a level of essence.
They say that coal is fire
and the iron is black.
Yet then the iron is immersed in the fire
it appears as fire.
If it then appears as such,
we also can call it by that name.
We see it as fire,
we can call it fire.

If you have never known this in your own experience
do not distrust the experiences
of those who describe them to you. (St. Symeon the New Theologian)[278]

Through one body, His own, He blesses, by a mysterious communion, those who believe in Him, and He makes them con-corporal
with Himself and with one another. Who can now separate them or
deprive them of their "physical" union? They have been bound
together into unity with Christ by means of His one holy body. For if
we all eat of the one bread we all become one body, since there can
be no division in Christ. . . . Since we are all united with the one
Christ through His sacred body, and since we all receive Him who is
one and indivisible into our own bodies, we ought to look upon our
members as belonging to Him rather than to ourselves. (St. Cyril of
Alexandria)[279]

Most clearly moreover, He said: "This is my body . . . this is my
blood." Lest you think that these things are a figure, rather than
that they are truly offered to be transformed by the mysterious
power of Almighty God into the body and blood of Christ, having
been made partakers of which, we take on the vivifying and sanctifying power of Christ. (St. Cyril of Alexandria)[280]

If mere contact with the sacred flesh of Jesus gives life to a dead
body, should we not experience effects still more wonderful when
we receive the sacred Eucharist? Surely it must completely transform those who receive it into its own perfection, i.e., into immortality. . . . Corruptible as we are in the flesh, we lose our weakness by
this "mingling" and we are transformed into what is proper to the
Eucharist, that is, into life. (St. Cyril of Alexandria)[281]

O, you of virtue, I beg you, consider attentively who is He whom
you dare to receive into yourself? It is God Himself three times holy.
With whom do you wish to form the most intimate union? With Him
who has created us. Be seized with fright and tremble. For the
divine fire touches your mouth, soiled by your useless and dissonant
words through your impurities. . . . Your tongue has spread evils
and injustices. And by what do you wish to be refreshed? By the
blood of the terrible Judge. . . . Holding your hands joined in the
form of the cross and placed over your breast, incline a bit your
head and recite the prayer: "I believe, O Lord, and confess . . ." to
the end. Recite it with all your heart, with sighings, fear, trembling
and compunction of heart. Tremble as you stand erect and reflect

on what you are doing in order not to eat the flesh of the Lord and not to drink His blood onto your condemnation. Ask of God most merciful that even as this moment when He visits you by His grace you can show compunction, tenderness and burning tears. (Nazarus of Valaam)[282]

C. Light from Light

1. Light

He, however, who is united to God by faith and recognizes Him by action is indeed enabled to see Him by contemplation. He sees things of which I am not able to write. His mind sees strange visions and is wholly illuminated and becomes like light, yet he is unable to conceive of them or describe them. His mind is itself light and sees all things as light, and the light has life and imparts light to him who sees it. He sees himself wholly united to the light, and as he sees he concentrates on the vision and is as he was. He perceives the light in his soul and is in ecstasy. In his ecstasy he sees it from afar, but as he returns to himself he finds himself again in the midst of the light. He is thus altogether at a loss for words and concepts to describe what he has perceived in his vision. (St. Symeon the New Theologian)[283]

Let no one deceive you! God is light (1 John 1:5), and to those who have entered into union with Him He imparts of His own brightness to the extent that they have been purified. When the lamp of the soul, that is, the mind, has been kindled, then it knows that a divine fire has taken hold of it and inflamed it. How great a marvel! Man is united to God spiritually and physically, since the soul is not separated from the mind, neither the body from the soul. By being united in essence man also has three hypostases by grace. He is a single god by adoption with body and soul and the divine Spirit of whom he has become a partaker. Then is fulfilled what was spoken by the prophet David, "I have said, ye are gods, and ye are all the sons of the Most High" (Ps. 82:6), that is, sons of the Most High according to the image of the Most High and according to His likeness (Gen. 1:26). We become the divine offspring of the Divine Spirit (John 3:8), to whom the Lord rightly said and continues to say, "Abide in Me, that you may bring forth much fruit" (John 15:4, 8). . . . It is evident that just as the Father abides in His own Son (John 14:10) and the Son in His Father's bosom (John 1:18) by nature, so those who have been born anew through the divine Spirit (John 3:3, 5) and by His gift have become the brothers of Christ our God and sons of God and gods by adoption, by grace abide in God and God in them (1 John 4:12 ff.). (St. Symeon the New Theologian)[284]

I fell prostrate on the ground, and at once I saw, and behold, a great Light was immaterially shining on me and seized hold of my whole mind and soul, so that I was struck with amazement at the unexpected marvel and I was, as it were, in ecstasy. . . . I conversed with this Light. The Light itself knows it; it scattered whatever mist there was in my soul and cast out every earthly care. It expelled from me all material denseness and bodily heaviness that made my members to be sluggish and numb. What an awesome marvel! . . . Besides, there was poured into my soul in unutterable fashion a great spiritual joy and perception and a sweetness surpassing every taste of visible objects, together with a freedom and forgetfulness of all thoughts pertaining to this life. In a marvelous way there was granted to me and revealed to me the manner of the departure from this present life. Thus all the perceptions of my mind and my soul were wholly concentrated on the ineffable joy of that Light. (St. Symeon the New Theologian)[285]

> Hail, gladdening Light, of his pure glory pour'd
> who is the immortal Father, heavenly blest,
> holiest of holies, Jesus Christ, the Lord.
> Now we are come to the sun's hour of rest,
> the lights of evening round us shine,
> we hymn the Father, Son and Holy Spirit divine.
> Worthiest art thou at all times to be sung
> with undefiled tongue,
> Son of our God, giver of life, alone!
> Therefore in all the world thy glories, Lord, they own. (Phos Hilaron)[286]

When both the intellect and the heart are united in prayer, and when the thoughts of the soul are not scattered, the heart is warmed by a spiritual heat, the Light of Christ enlightens it and fills the interior man with peace and joy. (St. Seraphim of Sarov)[287]

2. Transformation

Whoever approaches God and truly desires to be a partner of Christ must approach with a view to this goal, namely, to be changed and transformed from his former state and attitude and become a good and new person, harboring nothing of "the old man" (2 Cor. 5:17). . . . For indeed our Lord Jesus Christ came for this reason, to change and transform and renew human nature and to recreate this soul that had been overturned by passions through the transgression. He came to mingle human nature with His own Spirit of the Godhead.

A new mind and a new soul and new eyes, new ears, a new spiritual tongue and, in a word, new men; this was what He came to effect of those who believe in Him. Or new wineskins, anointing them with His own light of knowledge so that He might pour into them new wine which is His Spirit. For He says: "new wine must be put into new wineskins" (Matt. 9:17). (Pseudo-Macarius)[288]

The soul that is penetrated with the examples of Christ and cooperates with the grace of the sacraments sees itself transformed. And this transformation, which is the true virtue, the true sanctity, resides in the will and in no way in the miracles or extraordinary charisms. (Nicholas Cabasilas)[289]

Therefore man comes at the end of all creatures as a certain natural link joining through his own members himself with the other creatures and joining in himself those things which naturally are very distinct from one another. By union with God Who is the universal cause Who made creatures distinct from one another in the beginning, man can then gradually and orderly progress through means to the end in a sublime ascension. . . .

Then man makes one earth by uniting paradise with his inhabited world through chaste conversation. His united world then becomes no longer distinct by reason of the diversity of so many parts, but rather it is brought together into a synthesis so that man no longer suffers proliferation into separated parts. Then heaven and earth are united through a virtuous life similar to that of angels. Man no longer is bound down by his bodily condition but rises through an elevation of his soul to the invisible presence of God. He thus is able to make his own way by discerning what is prior and then go back to the material creation, to the things that are secondary.

Then man unites the things known to his intellect and those known to his senses through a knowledge similar to that of the angels who see all of creation, not as separated into known and unknown, but man, become like to angels, is able to know by a knowledge that is the greatest infusion of true wisdom and given only to the worthy to know the difficult and the ineffable. Thus uniting created nature with the Uncreated through charity . . . man shows all as one and the same through the power of grace. He sees all things in God, first as flowing from God into existence and secondly through them, rising to God as to the end of all moved creatures and the fixed and stable ground of their being, Who is the end of every rule and law, the end of every word and mind and of every nature, and infinite and unbound goal of all beings. (St. Maximus the Confessor)[290]

Whereas the angels are appointed to serve the Creator and have as their only mission to be under authority (it not being given to them to rule over inferior beings unless they are sent to do this by the Preserver of all things) man is preordained not only to be ruled, but to rule over all that which is on the earth. (St. Gregory Palamas)[291]

God placed him (man), great in littleness (a microcosm), on the earth a new Angel, a mingled worshipper, fully initiated into the visible creation, but only partially into the intellectual; King of all upon earth, but subject to the King above; earthly and heavenly; temporal and yet immortal; visible and yet intellectual; halfway between greatness and lowliness; in one person combining spirit and flesh; spirit, because of the favor bestowed on him; flesh, because of the height to which he had been raised; the one that he might continue to live and praise his Benefactor, the other that he might suffer, and by suffering, be put in remembrance and corrected if he became proud of his greatness. (St. Gregory Nazianzus)[292]

D. Resurrection

1. Glory

God rejoices from all eternity in the sublimity of His glory . . . glory is the revelation, the manifestation, the reflection, the garment of interior perfection. God revealed Himself to Himself from all eternity in the eternal generation of His consubstantial Son and by the eternal procession of His consubstantial Spirit, and thus the unity in the holy Trinity shone with an essential, imperishable glory that is unchanging. God the Father is the "Father of Glory" (Eph. 1:17); the Son of God is the "brightness of his glory" (Heb. 1:3) and "possessed the glory of the Father before the world was" (John 17:5); so too the Spirit of God is the "Spirit of glory" (1 Pet. 4:14).

God lives in this glory that is His own, intrinsic to Him, in perfect happiness above all glory, needing no witness, unable to allow any division. But as in His mercy and His infinite love He desires to share His beatitude and make happy those who participate in His glory, He calls forth His infinite perfections and reveals them in His creatures; His glory is resplendent in the heavenly powers, reflected in man, clothing the visible world with a garment of magnificence; He gives His glory to those whom He allows to participate in it and receive it; it then returns again to Him. This eternal circulation of the divine glory, as it were, constitutes the blessed life, the happiness of creatures. (Metropolitan Philaret of Moscow)[293]

Abba Lot went to Abba Joseph, and said unto him, "Father, according to my strength I sing a few Psalms, and I pray a little, and my fasting is little, and my prayers and silent meditation are few, and as far as lieth in my power I cleanse my thoughts, what more can I do?" Then the old man stood up, and spread out his hands toward heaven and his fingers were like unto ten lamps of fire, and he said unto him, "if thou wishest, let the whole of thee be like unto fire." (*The Wit and Wisdom of the Christian Fathers of Egypt*)[294]

With this radiance the blessed ones live, and at death the light does not depart from them. The righteous constantly have light, and they come to that new life shining with it. At the time of universal judgment they will run to Him with whom they will have been all the time. It will then happen that for each of those who rise to life the wholeness of the body will be preserved as its bones and parts and members come together with its head.

When freedom appears they will rush to Christ with an irresistible motion in order that they may receive their proper place. Accordingly Paul, as he shows that this rush cannot be restrained, calls it a "carrying up" (rapture), for he says, "we shall be carried off in the clouds to meet the Lord in the air" (1 Thess. 4:14). . . . This signifies that there is nothing human which will be able to delay, but that it is Christ Himself who will draw them, Christ Himself who will carry them off, He who cannot be subservient to time. (Nicholas Cabasilas)[295]

2. Resurrection

But as for you, my beloved, have no doubt as to the Resurrection of the dead. For the living mouth of God testifies: "I cause to die and I make alive" (Deut. 32:39). And both of them proceeded out of one mouth. And as we are sure that He causes to die, and we see it; so also it is sure and worthy of belief, that He makes alive. And from all that I have explained to you, receive and believe that in the day of the Resurrection your body shall arise in its entirety, and you shall receive from our Lord the reward of your faith, and in all that you have believed, you shall rejoice and be made glad. (Aphrahat)[296]

There is a twofold death; and so twofold must be our resurrection. In Christ there was but one death. For Christ did not sin; but for us He suffered this single death. For He was not subject to death, since He was never a debtor to sin, and so neither was He liable to death. And so from a single death He rose in a single Resurrection from the dead. But we who have died a twofold death rise by a twofold resurrection. Until now we have risen in baptism, and we have risen with Him through baptism. This resurrection is deliverance from our sins; the second is the resurrection of the body. He has given us the greater; we await the lesser. The first is greater than the second. For it is a greater thing to be delivered from our sins than for the body to see resurrection. Through this the body fell: because it sinned. If then this was the cause of its fall, to be freed from sin is the cause of its rising again. (St. John Chrysostom)[297]

Glorious is our Paschal Festival; and truly splendid this great assembly of the Christian people. And within this holy mystery are contained things both old and new. The celebration of this week, or rather its joyfulness, is shared by such a multitude, that not alone does man rejoice on earth, but even the powers of heaven are united with us in joyful celebration of Christ's Resurrection. For now the Angels, and the hosts of the Archangels, also keep holiday this day, and stand waiting for the triumphant return from this earth of Christ our Lord, who is King of heaven. And the multitude of the Blessed likewise rejoice, proclaiming the Christ who was begotten before the day star rose (Ps. 109:3). The earth rejoices, now washed by divine blood. The sea rejoices, honored as it was by His feet upon its waters. And ever more let each soul rejoice, who is born again of water and the Holy Spirit; and at last set free from the ancient curse! (St. Proclus, Patriarch of Constantinople)[298]

Shine, shine, O New Jerusalem, for the glory of the Lord has shone upon you. Rejoice and be glad, O Sion! And you, O Immaculate, O Mother of God, exult with joy in the resurrection of your Son.

Christ is risen, and He has crushed death and raised the dead; rejoice, therefore, O Nations of the earth! Shine, shine, O New Jerusalem, for the glory of the Lord has risen over you. Cry out now and rejoice, O Sion; and you, the pure one, the Mother of God, exult in the resurrection of the One to whom you gave birth.

On this day the whole creation rejoices and exults, for Christ is risen and Hades despoiled.

O Christ, how noble, dear and sweet is Your divine voice; for You have made us a truthful promise to abide with us for ever and ever. And we the faithful hold on to this promise as to an anchor of hope. We exult in joy.

On this day, the Master has despoiled Hades, for He has raised those who for ages had been firmly chained in it.

O Christ, how noble, dear and sweet is Your divine voice; for You have made us a truthful promise to abide with us for ever and ever. And we the faithful hold on to this promise as to an anchor of hope; we exult in joy. (Hirmos of the Easter Service of the Byzantine Rite attributed to St. John Damascene)[299]

Most men believe in the resurrection of Christ, but very few have a clear vision of it. Those who have no vision thereof cannot even adore Christ Jesus. . . . That most sacred formula which is daily on our lips does not say, "Having *believed* in Christ's resurrection," but, "Having *beheld* Christ's resurrection let us worship the Holy One, the Lord Jesus, who alone is without sin." How then does the Holy Spirit urge us to say, "Having beheld Christ's resurrection," which we have not seen, as though we had seen it, when Christ has risen once for all a thousand years ago, and even then without anybody's seeing it? Surely Holy Scripture does not wish us to lie? Rather, it urges us to speak the truth, that the resurrection of Christ takes place in each of us who believes, and that not once, but every hour, so to speak, when Christ the Master arises in us, resplendent in array (Ps. 93:1) and flashing with the lightnings of incorruption and Deity. For the light-bringing coming of the Spirit shows forth to us, as in early morning, the Master's resurrection, or, rather, it grants us to see the Risen One Himself. Therefore we say, "The Lord is God and He has given us light" (Ps. 118:27), and we allude to His second Coming and add these words, "Blessed is He that comes in the Name of the Lord" (Ps. 118:26). Those to whom Christ has given light as He has risen, to them He has appeared spiritually, He has been shown to their spiritual eyes. When this happens to us through the Spirit He raises us up from the dead and gives us life. He grants us to see Him, who is immortal and indestructible. More than that, He grants clearly to know Him who raises us up and glorifies us with Himself, as all the divine Scripture testifies. (St. Symeon the New Theologian)[300]

CHAPTER NINE

A FERTILE DESERT

I have been crucified with Christ, and I live now not with my
own life but with the life of Christ who lives in me. The life I
now live in this body I live in faith; faith in the Son of God
who loved me and who sacrificed himself for my sake. I
cannot bring myself to give up God's gift. (Gal. 2:19-21)

A. Monasticism

1. Monks

Of all the orders of the initiated, the highest is the holy order of
the monks, which has been cleansed by a complete purification. By
means of its integral power and the absolute purity of its activities, it
has acquired the ability to contemplate with spiritual vision and
communion every sacred work as far as permissible. Conducted by
the perfecting powers of the bishops, instructed by their divine illu-
minations and pontifical traditions in the sacred rites of the holy
mysteries which they view in due measure, it is proportionately
raised up by the sacred understanding of these things to the most
consummate perfection. Our divine leaders deem these men worthy
of holy titles. Some call them "devotees," others, "monks," because of their pure service and cult of God as well as on account of
their undivided and unified life, which unifies them by holy combina-
tions of their differences into godlike unity and perfection of divine
love. Therefore, sacred law has imposed on them a perfecting
grace, and deemed them worthy of a certain sanctifying invocation
that is not pontifical . . . but consecratory, being used by the holy
priests in hierarchical initiation of second rank. (Dionysius Pseudo-
Areopagite)[301]

Let us prepare as offerings for the King desirable fruits, fasting
and prayer. Let us guard His pledge in purity, that He may trust us
over all His treasury. For whosoever deals falsely with His pledge,
they suffer him not to enter into the treasure-house. Let us be care-

ful of the body of Christ, that our bodies may rise at the sound of the trumpet. Let us hearken to the voice of the bridegroom, that we may go in with Him into the bride-chamber. Let us prepare the marriage gift for His bridal day, and let us go forth to meet Him with joy. Let us put on holy raiment, that we may recline in the chief place of the elect. Whosoever puts not on wedding raiment, they cast him out into outer darkness. Whosoever excuses himself from the wedding shall not taste the feast. Whosoever loves fields and merchandise, shall be shut out of the city of Saints. Whosoever does not bear fruit in the vineyard, shall be uprooted and cast out to torment. Whosoever has received money from his Lord, let him return it to its Giver with its increase. Whosoever desires to become a merchant, let him buy for himself the field and the treasure that is in it. Whosoever receives the good seed, let him purge his land from thorns. Whosoever desires to be a fisherman, let him cast forth his net at every time. Whosoever is training for the conflict, let him keep himself from the world. Whosoever wishes to go down to the battle, let him take unto him armor wherewith to fight, and let him purify himself at every time. Whosoever adopts the likeness of angels, let him be a stranger to men. Whosoever takes upon him the yoke of the saints, let him remove from him getting and spending. . . . Whosoever loves virginity, let him become like Elijah. Whosoever takes up the yoke of the Saints, let him sit and be silent. Whosoever loves peace, let him look for His Master as the hope of life. (Aphrahat)[302]

Have you not come to fight against invisible foes? Did you not come here to take up the warfare against your passions? For what reason did you wish to be enlisted and take your place in the ranks of Christ's soldiers? Was it to receive rations and pay on the same terms as they, and to sit at their table like those who on the stage eat their fill and get drunk? If that is what you think, woe are you on the day of judgment, when Christ comes "to repay every man for what he has done" (Matt. 16:27). Then He will require of His monks, who have pledged themselves to Him "in the presence of many witnesses," the vows they have promised to perform and observe before the holy altar and His holy angels. What are the questions to which we must reply? Is this not why we have approached the holy altar and this holy assembly? Is it with a desire for embracing the monastic life and the angelic way of living? And what do we answer to this question? "Yes, reverend father." The priest then says to us, "You know, brethren, that inasmuch as you have come to be numbered with the servants of Christ the King you have prepared yourselves for trials. Know well, then, that from now on especially the enemy will set in motion every device against you. You must therefore be hungry and thirsty and cold, be dishonored and spat upon, be slapped in the face and be mocked, and endure all painful things that are in accordance with God. . . . Do we not promise to suffer and endure all things and pronounce the answer "Yes, reverend father" to every question about the endurance of afflictions? Do we not before God and the angels agree to observe self-control, vigils and prayers and obedience till death to our superior and the whole community? (St. Symeon the New Theologian)[303]

We should pursue the middle way, at a fitting time. The holy writings testify that the middle way has no pitfalls. And the fitting time is after we have acquired wisdom in the company of other men. For the middle way it is required that one, or at the most two brothers share our abode, according to the teaching of St. John Climacus. He tells us that there are three excellent forms of monastic life; the life of solitude, cohabitation with one or two brothers observing silence, and community life. The middle way—that is, silence in the company of one or two brothers—is the most practicable, for it is perilous for a man to be alone. If he is plunged into *accidie,* or overcome by sleep or indolence or despair, there is no one to lift him up. And St. John Climacus quotes the words of our Lord Himself: "Where there are two or three gathered together in my name, there am I in the midst of them." (St. Nil Sorsky)[304]

2. Flight from the World

The difference between Christians and the rest of men is neither in country, nor in language nor in customs. . . . They dwell in their own fatherlands, but as temporary inhabitants. They take part in all things as citizens, while enduring the hardships of foreigners. Every foreign place is their fatherland, and every fatherland is to them a foreign place. Like all others, they marry and beget children; but they do not expose their offspring. Their board they set for all, but not their bed. Their lot is cast in the flesh; but they do not live for the flesh. They pass their time on earth; but their citizenship is in heaven. They obey the established laws, and in their private lives they surpass the laws.

They love all men; by all they are persecuted. They are unknown, they are condemned. They are put to death, and they gain life. They are poor but make many rich; they are destitute, but have an abundance of everything. They are dishonored, and in their dishonor they are made glorious. They are defamed, but they are vindicated. They are reviled, and they bless. They are insulted, and they pay homage. When they do good, they are punished as evil-doers; and when they are punished they rejoice as if brought to life. They are made war upon as foreigners by the Jews, and they are persecuted by the Greeks; and yet, those who hate them are at a loss to state the cause of their hostility. (*Letter to Diognetus*)[305]

When you hear that it is necessary to withdraw from the world, to leave the world, to purify yourself from all that belongs to the world, you must first learn and understand the term world, not in its every-day meaning, but in its purely inward significance. When you understand what it means and the different things that this term includes, you will be able to learn about your soul—how far removed it is from the world and what is mixed with it that is of the world. "World" is a collective name, embracing what are called passions. When we want to speak of passions collectively, we call them "the world"; when we want to distinguish between them according to their different names, we call them passions.

When you have learned what the world means, then, by discerning all that is implied in this term, you will also learn what ties you to the world and in what you are freed from it. I will say, more briefly, that the world is carnal life and minding of the flesh. Therefore a man is seen to be free of the world inasmuch as he has wrenched himself free of this. (St. Isaac the Syrian)[306]

The world of Christians is of a special kind, their style of living, their thinking, their speech and all their actions. That of men of this world is completely different. There is a great difference between them. The inhabitants of this world, the children of this age, are like wheat in a sieve. They are being sifted by restless thoughts of this world. They are constantly tossed to and fro by earthly cares, desire and absorption in a variety of material concerns. . . . For Christians live in another world, eat from another table, are clothed different-ly, enjoy different enjoyment, different dialogue and different mentality. Because of this they exceed all other men. This power already they are considered worthy to enjoy in their souls through the Holy Spirit. Therefore, also in the resurrection their bodies will be worthy to receive those eternal blessings of the Holy Spirit. They will be permeated with that glory which their souls in this life have already experienced. (Pseudo-Macarius)[307]

Let us then, dear brethren, flee from the world and "the things that are in the world" (1 John 2:15). For what have we in common with the world and the men who are in the world? Let us run, let us pursue, until we have laid hold of something that is permanent and does not flow away, for all things perish and pass away like a dream, and nothing is lasting or certain among things that are seen. The sun, the stars, heaven and earth, all things pass away; of all things man alone abides. What, then, among visible things can profit us at the time when we must needs die, when we depart from the hence to the rest that is in the world beyond, when we leave all these things behind? If visible things pass away, what do they avail us when we depart and abandon this body as dead? When the soul abandons its own body it can neither see by means of it nor be seen by any other. From that time on it deals only with the things that are invisible and has no concern for the things that are here. Before it lies a twofold life and destiny, either that of the kingdom, heaven and eternal glory, or else the opposite, that of hell and the fiery punishment. It is one of these that it receives from God as its eternal inheritance, as it deserves for its deeds in this life. (St. Symeon the New Theologian)[308]

But what is "the world"? What are "the things that are in the world"? Listen! It is not gold, silver, or horses, or mules. All these things that serve our physical needs we ourselves possess. It is not meat, nor bread, nor wine, for we ourselves partake of these things and eat them in moderation. It is not houses, nor baths, nor fields, nor vineyards, nor suburban properties, for great and small monasteries consist of these. So what is the world? It is sin, brethren, and attachment to things and passions. Let John the Theologian, the disciple beloved by Christ (John 13:23), speak of "the things that are in the world." He says: "Do not love the world or the things in the world . . . for all that is in the world, the lust of the flesh and the lust of the eyes and the pride of life, is not of the Father but is of the world" (1 John 2:15 f.). If we, then, who have left all the world behind and fled from it and have become naked do not beware of these things, what would it profit us merely to have withdrawn from the world? From whatever place we have come out and and wherever we arrive, we shall find the same things. Whatever the place, men cannot live alone. Everywhere we make use of things that we need for sustaining our bodies. Everywhere there are women and children, and wine and every kind of fruit; physical sustenance consists in these and similar things. But if we have "the lust of the flesh and the lust of the eyes" and the pride of our thoughts, how shall we be able in their midst to escape from any kind of sin, without in any way being harmed by its sting? . . . Thus he who is given to anger must not give way to it. He who pleads in his defense should not add any mental reservation in his heart to what he speaks; he who seeks justice for himself must be dead to the world in the disposition of his heart. He who has once attained to that state must eagerly seek and desire not even to spare his own body. Those who contend in the spiritual contest have attained this state, and in every generation still do so. (St. Symeon the New Theologian)[309]

B. Martyrdom

Great and excellent is the martyrdom of Jesus. He surpassed in affliction and in confession all who were before or after. And after Him was the faithful martyr Stephen whom the Jews stoned. Simon Peter also and Paul were perfect martyrs. And James and John walked in the footsteps of their Master Christ. Also others of the apostles thereafter in diver places confessed and proved true martyrs. And also concerning our brethren who are in the West, in the days of Diocletian there came great affliction and persecution to the whole Church of God, which was in all their region. The Churches were overthrown and uprooted, and many confessors and martyrs made confession. And the Lord turned in mercy to them after they were persecuted. And also in our days these things happened to us also on account of our sins; but also that what is written might be fulfilled, even as our Redeemer said:—These things are to be. The Apostle also said:—Also over us is set this cloud of confession (Heb. 11:1); which is our honor, wherein many confess and are slain. (Aphrahat)[310]

Again, we know that, since we have been persuaded by Jesus to abandon idols and polytheism which is really atheism, the Enemy cannot persuade us to accept idolatry; but he tries to force it upon us. And so with this in view he sets upon those who come within his power and makes either martyrs or idolaters of them who are brought to trial. Even now he keeps on repeating: "All this will I give thee, if falling down thou wilt adore me." Let us take care, therefore, never to adore idols or obey demons: for the idols of the

Gentiles are demons. How monstrous is it to give up the sweet yoke
of Christ and His light burden to submit oneself once more to the
yoke of demons and to carry the burden of the gravest sins! . . .

They that kill us, therefore, kill only the life of the body, as is
clearly signified by the words, fear ye not them that kill the body—
expressed in the same terms by Matthew and Luke. When they
have slain the body, they cannot, even if they wished it, slay the
soul: they have no more that they can do. For how can the soul be
slain when it has been given life by the very fact of martyrdom? . . .
He who will have had witness borne to Him, will in return bear
witness to us before God and His Father; and He Himself will bear
witness in heaven to him who has borne witness to Him on earth.
(Origen)[311]

Let us speak about the different kinds of Baptism, that we may
come out thence purified. Moses baptized but it was in water, and
before that in the cloud and in the sea. This was typical as Paul
says: the Sea of the water, and the cloud of the Spirit; the Manna,
of the Bread of Life; the Drink, of the Divine Drink. John also
baptized; but this was not like the baptism of the Jews, for it was
not only in water, but also "unto repentance." . . . Jesus also baptized, but in the Spirit. This is the perfect Baptism . . . I know also a
fourth Baptism that by martyrdom and blood, which also Christ
Himself underwent, and this one is far more august than all the
others, inasmuch as it cannot be defiled by after-stains. (St. Gregory
Nazianzus)[312]

C. Spiritual Guidance

1. Direction

Those of us who wish to go out of Egypt and to fly from Pharaoh,
certainly need some Moses as a mediator with God and from God,
who, standing between action and contemplation, will raise hands of
prayer for us to God, so that guided by Him we may cross the sea of
sin and rout the Amalek of the passions. That is why those who
have surrendered themselves to God deceive themselves if they
suppose that they have no need of a director. Those who came out
of Egypt had Moses as their guide, and those who fled from Sodom
had an angel. The former are like those who are healed of the
passions of the soul by the care of physicians: these are they who
come out of Egypt. The latter are like those who long to put off the

uncleanness of the wretched body. That is why they need a helper, an angel, so to speak, or at least one equal to an angel. For in proportion to the corruption of our wounds we need a director who is indeed an expert and a physician. (St. John Climacus)[313]

When motives of humility and real longing for salvation decide us to bend our neck and entrust ourselves to another in the Lord, before entering upon this life, if there is any vice and pride in us, we ought first to question and examine, and even, so to speak, test our helmsman, so as not to mistake the sailor for the pilot, a sick man for a doctor, a passionate for a dispassionate man, the sea for a harbor, and so bring about the speedy shipwreck of our soul. But when once we have entered the arena of religion and obedience we must no longer judge our good manager in any way at all, even though we may perhaps see in him some slight failings, since he is only human. Otherwise, by sitting in judgment we shall get no profit from our subjection. (St. John Climacus)[314]

It is dangerous for an inexperienced soldier to leave his regiment and engage in single combat. And it is not without peril for a monk to attempt the solitary life before he has had much experience and practice in the struggle with the animal passions. The one subjects his body to danger, the other risks his soul. Two are better than one, says Scripture. That is to say, It is better for a son to be with his father, and to struggle with his attachments with the help of the divine power of the Holy Spirit. He who deprives a blind man of his leader, a flock of its shepherd, a lost man of his guide, a child of its father, a patient of his doctor, a ship of its pilot, imperils all. And he who attempts unaided to struggle with the spirits gets killed by them. (St. John Climacus)[315]

2. Spiritual Direction

Brother, constantly call on God that He may show you a man who is able to direct you well, one whom you ought to obey as though he were God Himself, whose instruction you must carry out without hesitation, even if what he enjoins on you appears to you to be repugnant and harmful. If your heart is moved by grace to even greater confidence in the spiritual father whom you already have, do what he tells you and be saved. It is better for you to be called a disciple of a disciple rather than to live by your own devices and gather the worthless fruits of your own will. If the Holy Ghost sends you to another, do not hesitate at all, for we hear that it was Paul who planted, and Apollos who watered, and that Christ gives the growth (1 Cor. 3:6). So, brother, do as we have said, and go to the man whom God shows you, either mystically in person, or externally through His servant. You should look on him and speak to him as to Christ Himself, and so revere Him and be taught by Him what is profitable. . . . If he brings you to the mountain, climb it with eagerness, for I know well that you will enjoy the vision of Christ transfigured and shining more brightly than the sun with the light of the Godhead. (St. Symeon the New Theologian)[316]

Indeed, you should also confess the thoughts of your heart to your spiritual father every hour, if possible. But if not, do not put it off till evening, but after the morning office examine yourself (1 Cor. 4:3) and confess all that has befallen you. Have unhesitating faith in him, even if the whole world reproach and abuse him. Even were you yourself to see him committing fornication, do not take offense or diminish your faith in him, for you obey Him who said, "Judge not, and you will not be judged" (Luke 6:37). (St. Symeon the New Theologian)[317]

D. Crucified with Christ

1. Trials

God often permits virtuous men to be tried by something; He permits temptations to rise up against them on all sides, strikes them in their body like Job, casts them into poverty, lets them be shunned by mankind, strikes them in their acquisitions; only their souls are not visited by harm. And, indeed, it is impossible that when we walk in the way of righteousness tribulation should not be met with, and that the body should not be exhausted by pain and labor, and yet remain steadfast, if only we desire to live in virtue. If a man proceeds on his way according to God and meets with something of this kind, it is not right for him to deviate from his way; but he must accept what comes with joy and without questioning, and render thanks to God for sending him this blessing and for being beset by trials for His sake; for God thus lets him share in the sufferings of the prophets, apostles and other saints, who endured tribulations for the sake of this way. Whether these trials come from men, demons or the flesh, let it be a cause for thanksgiving. For God cannot show His favor to a man, who desires to dwell with Him, except by sending him trials for the sake of truth; just as no man can become worthy of this greatness—that is, to be beset by trials and to rejoice without the grace of Christ. (St. Isaac the Syrian)[318]

Through love for God, such as the saints show by suffering for the sake of His name, their heart acquires the *daring* to look at God, their face uncovered, and to ask of Him with hope. Great is the power of daring prayer. Therefore, God lets His saints be tried by every kind of affliction, and lets them too have experience of His help in practice and of how greatly He takes care of them. Through trials and temptations they gain wisdom, and through experience acquire knowledge of all things to protect them from mockery by demons. If God exercised them only in that which is good, they would lack training in the other part and would be blind in battles. (St. Isaac the Syrian)[319]

If a man is not first tried by experience of evil, he has no taste in the good; so, when he meets with good in evil, he lacks knowledge to make use of it, as his own property. How pleasing is knowledge derived in actual deed from experience and practice, and what power it gives to a man who has acquired it in himself through long practice; these things are learned by those who have experienced the help of such knowledge, have seen alike the impotence of their nature and the assistance of Divine power, and are convinced. For they learn this only when, by first withholding the power of His help, God brings them to realize the impotence of their own nature, the difficulties of temptations, the cunning of the enemy, to realize what it is they are fighting, what their own nature is, how well they were protected by Divine power, how much they have advanced on the way, how high the power of God has lifted them, and how helpless they are in struggling against any passion, when this power of God is withdrawn from them. Through all this they acquire humility, draw nearer to God, begin to expect His help and to abide in prayer. Where could they have found all this, if they had not experience of much evil through falling into this evil with God's sanction? As the Apostle says: "And lest I should be exalted above measure through the abundance of the revelations, there was given to me a thorn in the flesh, the messenger of Satan" (2 Cor. 12:7). But by frequent experience of Divine help in temptations, a man acquires firm faith, which makes him unafraid and gives him a good heart in trials. (St. Isaac the Syrian)[320]

Trials which come when a man enters upon righteous life and

when his life grows in righteousness, differ from trials which are allowed to come to teach a proud heart.

Trials to the soul, which come from the rod of the spirit and serve progress and growth, trials through which the soul is taught, tested and brought to spiritual endeavor are the following: laziness, heaviness in the body, infirmity of the member, despondency, confusion of thoughts, apprehensiveness caused by bodily exhaustion, temporary desertion of hope, darkening of thoughts, lack of human help, scarcity of the bodily necessities of life, and other similar things.

These trials bring to the soul a feeling of loneliness and defenselessness, darkening of heart and humility. Yet the Divine Providence proportions these trials to the strength and needs of those who suffer them. In them are blended both comfort and defeat, light and darkness, struggle and help, in short, straitness and spaciousness. And this is a sign that, with God's help, a man is making progress. (St. Isaac the Syrian)[321]

There are two means of mounting the cross: one is crucifixion of the body, the other, ascent into contemplation. The first is the outcome of freedom from passions, and the second the effect of active works of the spirit.

The mind does not submit if the body is not submissive to it. The kingship of the mind is the crucifixion of the body; and the mind does not submit to God, unless freedom has submitted to reason. He who submits to God is near to having all things submissive to him. (St. Isaac the Syrian)[322]

As wax cannot take the imprint of a seal unless it is warmed or softened thoroughly, so a man cannot receive the seal of God's holiness unless he is tested by labors and weaknesses. That is why the Lord says to St. Paul: "My grace is sufficient for you: for My power comes to its fullness in your weakness"; . . . By weaknesses the Apostle means the attacks made by the enemies of the cross, attacks which continually fell upon him and all the saints of that time, to prevent them from being "unduly elated by the abundance of revelations," as he says himself (2 Cor. 12:7). Because of their humiliations they persevered still more in the life of perfection, and when they were treated with contempt they preserved the divine gift in holiness. But by weaknesses we now mean evil thoughts and bodily illnesses. In those times, since their bodies were submitted to deadly tortures and other afflictions, men pursuing the spiritual way were raised far above the passions which normally attack human nature as a result of sin. . . . So we should fulfill our inward martyrdom before God with confidence and patience, for it is written: "I waited patiently for the Lord; and He heard me" (Ps. 40:1). (St. Diadochus of Photike)[323]

2. Vigils

Do not consider that among all the practices of a monk there is anything more important than night vigil. If a monk is free from the distraction of physical occupations and of cares for transitory things, the mind, by its help, is quick to soar on high as on wings and to rise to delighting in God. If a monk keeps vigil of the mind with good judgment, he will appear, as it were, incorporeal. It is impossible that those who spend their whole life in this occupation should be left by God with no reward for their sobriety, watchfulness of heart and careful directing of their thoughts toward Him. A soul which labors at keeping vigil will have the eyes of Cherubim, to keep them constantly raised on high and to contemplate heavenly visions. (St. Isaac the Syrian)[324]

CHAPTER TEN

PUTTING ON THE MIND OF CHRIST

In your minds you must be the same as Christ Jesus:
His state was divine,
yet he did not cling
to his equality with God
but emptied himself
to assume the condition of a slave,
and become as men are;
and being as all men are,
he was humbler yet,
even to accepting death,
death on a cross.
But God raised him high
and gave him the name
which is above all other names
so that all beings
in the heavens, on earth and in the underworld,
should bend the knee at the name of Jesus
and that every tongue should acclaim
Jesus Christ as Lord,
to the glory of God the Father. (Phil. 2:5-11)

A. Obedience to God's Will

Obedience is absolute renunciation of our own life, clearly expressed in our bodily actions, or, conversely, obedience is the mortification of the limbs while the mind remains alive. Obedience is unquestioning movement, voluntary death, simple life, carefree danger, spontaneous defense by God, fearlessness of death, a safe voyage, a sleeper's progress. Obedience is the tomb of the will and the resurrection of humility. A corpse does not argue or reason as to what is good or what seems to be bad. For he who has devoutly put the soul of the novice to death will answer for everything. Obedience is an abandonment of discernment in a wealth of discernment. (St. John Climacus)[325]

It is absolutely indispensable for those of us who wish to retain undoubting faith in our superiors to write their good deeds indelibly in our hearts and constantly remember them, so that when the demons sow among us distrust toward them, we may be able to silence them by what is preserved in our memory. For the more faith flourishes in the heart, the more alacrity the body has in service. But he who has stumbled on distrust has already fallen; for all that does not spring from faith, is sin (Rom. 14:23). The moment any thought of judging or condemning your superior occurs to you, leap away from it as from fornication. Whatever you do, give that snake no license, no place, no entry, no power; but say to that serpent: "Listen, deceiver, I have no authority to judge of my superior, but he has been appointed to sit in judgment of me. It is not I who am to be his judge, but he is deputed to be mine." (St. John Climacus)[326]

He who is sometimes obedient to his father and sometimes disobedient is like a person who sometimes puts lotion in his eyes and sometimes quicklime. For it is said, When one builds and another pulls down, what profit have they had but the labor? (Eccles. 34:23). (St. John Climacus)[327]

From obedience comes humility, as we have already said earlier. From humility comes discernment as the great Cassian has said with beautiful and sublime philosophy in his chapter on discernment. From discernment comes insight, and from insight comes foresight. And who would not follow this fair way of obedience, seeing such blessings in store for him? It was of this great virtue of obedience that the good Psalmist said: "Thou hast in Thy goodness prepared for the poor" (Ps. 67:10) obedient soul, O God, Thy presence in his heart. (St. John Climacus)[328]

Now the health of the soul is the accomplishment of the Divine Will, just as, on the other hand, the disease of the soul that ends in death is the falling away from this good Will. We fell ill when we forsook the wholesome way of life in Paradise and filled ourselves with the poison of disobedience, through which our nature was conquered by this evil and deadly disease. Then there came the true Physician who cured the evil perfectly by its opposite, as is the law of medicine. For those who had succumbed to the disease because they had separated themselves from the Divine Will, He frees once more from their sickness by uniting them to the Will of God. For the words of the prayer brings the cure of the disease which is in the soul. For He prays as if His soul was immersed in pain, saying, Thy Will be done. Now the Will of God is the salvation of men. (St. Gregory of Nyssa)[329]

Harm has come to us from transgressing the commandments. It follows, therefore, that health is restored by keeping them. Without keeping commandments, without first of all following this road which leads to purity of soul, we must not even hope or aspire for the soul to be purified. Do not say that God can grant us purification of soul through grace, even without our keeping the command-ments. This is for the Lord to judge, and the Church does not direct that we should ask for such a thing. The Jews, at the time of their return from Babylon to Jerusalem, traveled by the natural way; but Ezekiel arrived there by supernatural means and it was by Divine revelation that he was made a witness of the renewal that was to come. So too with purity of soul. Some going by the road that many have trodden, through keeping commandments, in a life of many labors, arrive by sweat and blood at purity of soul; others are grant-ed it by the gift of grace. The wonderful thing is that it is not permissible to ask in prayer for purity to be granted us by grace, nor to refuse to lead a life of practicing the commandments. For when the rich man asked the Lord: "Master, what shall I do to inherit eternal life?" (Luke 10:25), the Lord said clearly: keep the commandments. When the rich man persisted, wishing to know more, He said: "If thou wilt be perfect, go and sell that thou hast, and give to the poor, and thou shalt have treasure in heaven; and come and follow me" (Matt. 19:21). This means: become dead to all that you have, and then live in Me; depart from the old world of passions, then enter the new world of the spirit. For by saying: take up your cross (Matt. 16:24), the Lord taught man to die to all things in the world. And when a man has killed the old man in himself, or his passions, He says to him: "Follow me." The old man cannot go the way of Christ. (St. Isaac the Syrian)[330]

Resisting God in his desire to prevent God's will, that is, His commandments from being done, Satan fights against God through us by attempting to put obstacles to their fulfillment. But again, God wishes His holy will, that is, as I have said, His Divine and life-giving commandments, to be done by us; so by a movement of His hand He defeats through us the pernicious intention of the evil one. The insane desire of the enemy to resist God by instigating transgressions of His commandments is defeated by God through human weakness. And look, is it not so? All Divine commandments lay down laws for the tripartite soul and give it health through their ordinances. He who follows them strictly has the three parts truly sane and sound. At the same time the devil, day and night, wages an unending war against the same three parts of the soul. If Satan wages war against these three parts, it is clear that thereby he fights against Christ's commandments, for, through these commandments Christ imposes laws on the tripartite soul, that is, the excitable, the desiring and the thinking powers of the soul. Look now: the threat that "whosoever is angry with his brother without a cause shall be in danger of the judgment" (Matt. 5:22), and the commandments that follow are remedies for the excitable part. This and other commandments, given together with it, the enemy tries to overthrow within by means of thoughts of arguing, spite and envy. This adversary knows that the ruler of the excitable part is the thinking power. Consequently he directs his first arrows against it by means of thoughts, as I have said, of suspicion, envy, argumentativeness, quarrelsomeness, deceit, vanity and presses the mental power to abandon its natural authority and relinquish the reins of government to excitation itself, thus leaving it with no government. . . . Thus this destroyer of souls attains his evil ends only when he finds a man ready to transgress the Divine commandments under the influence of thoughts introduced into his heart. (Philotheus of Sinai)[331]

B. Humility

Humility even without efforts gains forgiveness for many trespasses; but without humility even efforts are vain and may lead to much harm. What salt is for any food, humility is for every virtue. To acquire it, a man must always think of himself with contrition, self-belittlement and painful self-judgment. But if we acquire it, it will make us sons of God. (St. Isaac the Syrian)[332]

Someone was asked: "How can a man acquire humility?" He said: "By constant remembrance of one's trespasses and of the nearness of death, by poor clothes, by always preferring the last place and by gladly undertaking the lowest and most degrading tasks on every occasion: by not being disobedient, by keeping silence, by not liking to go to meetings, by wishing to remain unknown, and not elected for any post, by never keeping a single thing entirely at his own disposal, by hating conversations with a number of people, and by not liking gains, and above all by being in his mind above blaming and accusing any man, and above envy—by not being a man who lays his hand on others but who suffers the hands of others being laid on him, and does his own work in solitude and carries no cares in the world except himself. To be more brief: the life of a stranger in this world, poverty and solitude—these are the things which give birth to humility and purify the heart. (St. Isaac the Syrian)[333]

A humble man does not dare even to pray or petition God about something, and does not know what to ask for; he simply keeps all his senses silent and waits only for mercy and for whatever the Most Worshipful Majesty may be pleased to send him. When he bows down with his face to the earth, and the inner eyes of his heart are raised to the gates of the Holy of Holies, where He dwells Whose abode is darkness, before Whom the Seraphims close their eyes, he dares only to speak and pray thus: "May Thy will be done upon me, O Lord!" (St. Isaac the Syrian)[334]

Humility is a certain mysterious force, which perfected saints receive when they have completed their life. This force is given by the power of grace only to those who are perfect in virtue, for this virtue includes all in itself. (St. Isaac the Syrian)[335]

If anyone should ask how to acquire humility, we would answer: "It is enough for the disciple that he be as his master, and the servant as his lord" (Matt. 10:25). See how much humility was shown by Him Who has given us this commandment and Who gives us this gift; imitate Him and you will acquire it. (St. Isaac the Syrian)[336]

Humility is followed by self-mastery and restraint in everything. Through constant self-restraint, humility comes to contemplation and adorns the soul with chastity; whereas vanity, through constant turmoil and confusion of thoughts, gathers impure treasures from everything it meets, and defiles the heart. It looks with unseemly eyes at the nature of things, and fills the mind with shameful images; but humility brings spiritual harmony through contemplation and urges its possessor to glorify God. (St. Isaac the Syrian)[337]

Let all who are led by the Spirit of God enter with us into this spiritual and wise gathering, holding in their spiritual hands the God-inspired tablets of knowledge. We have met, we have investigated, and we have probed the meaning of this precious inscription. And one said: "It means constant oblivion of one's achievements." Another: "It is the acknowledgement of oneself as the last of all and the greatest sinner of all." And another: "The mind's recognition of one's weakness and impotence." Another again: "In fits of rage it means to forestall one's neighbor and be first to stop the quarrel." And again another: "Recognition of divine grace and divine mercy." And again another: "The feeling of a contrite soul, and the renunciation of one's own will." But when I had listened to all this and had attentively and soberly considered it, I found that I had not been able to comprehend the blessed sense of that virtue from what had been said. Therefore, last of all, having gathered what fell from the lips of those learned and blessed fathers as a dog gathers the crumbs that fall from the table, I too gave my definition of it and said: "Humility is a nameless grace in the soul, its name known only to those who have learned it by experience. It is unspeakable wealth, a name and gift from God, for it is said: Learn not from an angel, not from man, and not from a book, but from Me, that is, from Me indwelling, from My illumination and action in you, for I am meek and humble in heart and in thought and in spirit, and your souls shall find rest from conflicts and relief from arguments." (St. John Climacus)[338]

He who has taken humility as his bride is above all gentle, kind, full of compunction, sympathetic, calm, bright, compliant, inoffensive, wide awake, not indolent and (why say more?) free from passion; for the Lord remembered us in our humility, and delivered us from our enemies (Ps. 135:23-24), and our passions and impurities. (St. John Climacus)[339]

Know, beloved, that the valleys shall stand deep in corn and spiritual fruit. This valley is a soul low and humble among the mountains, that is, it is filled with labors and virtues, and always remains lowly and steadfast. David did not say, "I have fasted," "I have kept vigil," or "I have lain on the bare earth," but "I humbled myself, and soon the Lord saved me" (Ps. 115:5). (St. John Climacus)[340]

All visible things get their light from the sun, and all that is done according to reason gets its force from humility. Where there is no light, everything is dark; where there is no humility, all that we have is rotten. (St. John Climacus)[341]

It is one thing to be humble, another to strive for humility, and another to praise the humble. The first belongs to the perfect, the second to the truly obedient, and the third to all the faithful. (St. John Climacus)[342]

Humility is the door of the Kingdom that introduces those who draw near to it. And I think that the Lord was speaking of this door when He said: He shall enter and shall pass out of life without fear, and shall find pasture and green grass in paradise. All who have entered the monastic life by any other door are thieves and robbers of their own life. (St. John Climacus)[343]

If we sincerely wish to guard our mind in the Lord, we have need of great humility, first in relation to God and, second, in relation to men. We should always strive to make our heart contrite, seeking for and putting into practice every means for humbling it. It is well known that what renders the heart humble and contrite is memory of our former life in the world, if it is recollected by us as it should be. Another thing is memory of all our sins from youth onward; if the mind examines them in detail, this recollection habitually makes us humble, brings tears and moves us to a whole-hearted gratitude to God; so too does a constant and active (deeply felt) memory of death which gives birth to sweetness, glad mourning and sobriety of mind.

The thing which pre-eminently humbles our mind and disposes us to keep our eyes downcast to the ground is memory of the passion of our Lord Jesus Christ, if a man goes over it in his memory and remembers it in detail. This also engenders tears. In addition our soul is made truly humble by the great mercies of God toward us personally, if we examine and enumerate them in detail; for our fight is with proud demons (who are ungrateful to God). (Philotheus of Sinai)[344]

C. Faith, Hope, and Love

1. Faith

Faith is compounded of many things, and by many kinds is it brought to perfection. For it is like a building that is built up of many pieces of workmanship and so its edifice rises to the top. And know, my beloved, that in the foundation of the building stones are laid, and so resting upon stones the whole edifice rises until it is perfected. Thus also the true Stone, our Lord Jesus Christ, is the foundation of all our faith. And on Him, on this Stone, faith is based. And resting on faith all the structure rises until it is completed. For it is the foundation that is the beginning of all the building. For when any one is brought nigh unto faith, it is laid for him upon the Stone, that is our Lord Jesus Christ. And his building cannot be shaken by the waves, nor can it be injured by the winds. By the stormy blasts it does not fall, because its structure is reared upon the rock of the true Stone. And in this that I have called Christ the Stone, I have not spoken, of my own thought, but the Prophets beforehand called Him the Stone. (Aphrahat)[345]

First a man believes, and when he believes, he loves. When he loves, he hopes. When he hopes, he is justified. When he is justified, he is perfected. When he is perfected, he is consummated. And when his whole structure is raised up, consummated, and perfected, then he becomes a house and a temple for a dwelling place of Christ. (Aphrahat)[346]

Let us draw near then, my beloved, to faith, since its powers are so many. For faith raised up to the heavens Enoch, and conquered the Deluge. It caused the barren to bring forth. It delivered from the sword. It raised up from the pit. It enriched the poor. It released the captives. It delivered the persecuted. It brought down the fire. It divided the sea. It cleft the rock, and gave to the thirsty water to drink. It satisfied the hungry. It raised the dead, and brought them up from Sheol. It stilled the billows. It healed the sick. It conquered hosts. It overthrew walls. It stopped the mouths of lions, and quenched the flame of fire. It humiliated the proud, and brought the humble to honor. All these mighty works were wrought by faith. (Aphrahat)[347]

Grace is not merely faith, but also active prayer. For the latter shows in practice true faith, made living by Jesus, for it comes from the Spirit through love. And so forth is dead and lifeless in a man who does not see it active in himself. More than that—a man has no right to be called faithful, if his faith is a bare word and if he has not in him a faith made active by love or the Spirit. Thus faith must be made evident by progress in works, or it must act in the light and shine in works, as the divine Apostle says: "Show me thy faith without thy works, and I will show thee my faith by my works" (James 2:18), thus showing that the faith of grace is made evident by works performed in accordance with the commandments, just as the commandments are fulfilled in deed and are made bright through the faith which is in grace. Faith is the root of the command-ments, or rather the spring, whose water feeds their growth. It has two aspects: profession and grace, remaining at the same time essentially one and indivisible. (St. Gregory of Sinai)[348]

For knowledge is a state of mind that results from demonstration; but faith is a gift which leads on from what is undemonstrable to what is universal and simple, to what is neither concomitant to matter, nor matter itself, nor subject to matter. (Clement of Alexandria)[349]

Such a change as this, by which someone comes from unbelief to belief, and, while hoping and fearing, yet believes, is of divine origin. Indeed, faith appears to us to be the first inclination toward salvation; after which hope and repentance and even fear, advancing in company with moderation and patience, lead us on to love and to knowledge. (Clement of Alexandria)[350]

2. Hope

The heart finds no respite from labors and stumblings, until hope enters it and brings it peace and joy. Lips we worship said of hope: "Come unto me, all ye that labor and are heavy laden, and I will give you rest" (Matt. 11:28). The light of the mind gives birth to faith; faith gives birth to the comfort of hope; hope makes strong the heart. (St. Isaac the Syrian)[351]

A firm and trustworthy basis for hope of the deification of human nature is God's Incarnation, which makes of man a god in the same measure as God Himself became man. For it is clear that He who became man without sin can also deify nature, without transforming it into the Deity, raising it to Himself in the measure that He humbled Himself for man's sake. Speaking of this mystery the great Apostle says, "That in the ages to come he might show the exceeding riches of his grace in his kindness toward us through Christ Jesus" (Eph. 2:7). (St. Maximus the Confessor)[352]

The root of every good work is the hope of the resurrection; for the expectation of a reward nerves the soul to good work. Every laborer is prepared to endure the toils if he looks forward to the reward of these toils. But they who labor without reward—their soul is exhausted with their body. . . . He that believes his body will remain for the resurrection is careful of his garment and does not soil it in fornication; but he that has no faith in the resurrection gives himself to fornication, and abuses his own body as if it belonged to another. A great precept and teaching of the Holy Catholic Church, therefore, is belief in the resurrection of the dead—great and most necessary, but contradicted by many, although it is rendered credible by the truth. (St. Cyril of Jerusalem)[353]

Let that which tranquillizes my thoughts and my heart be committed to writing as a memorial to me of the constant peace of my heart amidst the cares and vanities of life. What is it? It is the Christian saying, full of living trust and wonderful soothing power: "The Lord is everything to me." This is the priceless treasure! This is the precious jewel, possessing which we can be calm in every condition, rich in poverty, generous and kind to other people in the time of our wealth, and not losing hope even after having sinned. "The Lord is everything to me." He is my faith, my trust, my love, my strength, my power, my peace, my joy, my riches, my food, my drink, my raiment, my life—in a word, mine all. Thus man, the Lord is everything to you; and you must be everything to the Lord. And, as all your treasure is contained in your heart and in your will, and God requires from you your heart, having said: "My Son, give Me thy heart," therefore, in order to fulfill God's gracious and perfect will, renounce your own corrupt, passionate, seductive will; do not know your own will, know only God's will. "Not my will, but Thy will be done."

. . . The means for confirming and strengthening Christian hope in us are—prayer, especially frequent sincere prayer, the confession of our sins, the frequent reading of the Word of God, and, above all, the frequent communion of the holy, life-giving mysteries of the Body and Blood of Christ. (John Cronstadt)[354]

3. Love

Love is that good disposition of the soul in which it prefers nothing that exists to knowledge of God. But no man can come to such a state of love if he be attached to anything earthly . . . when urged by love the mind soars to God, it has not sensation either of itself or of anything existing. Illumined by the limitless Divine light, it is insensible to all the created, just as is the physical eye to stars in the light of the sun. (St. Maximus the Confessor)[355]

He who loves God cannot but love every man as himself, although the passions of those who are not yet purified find no favor with him. Therefore when he sees them converted and reformed, he rejoices with great and ineffable joy. (St. Maximus the Confessor)[356]

He who loves God must of necessity love his neighbor too. And such a man cannot hoard possessions, but so manages them as to please God, giving to each man what he needs. (St. Maximus the Confessor)[357]

The works of love are diligently to do good to one's neighbor, to be magnanimous, patient and to use things with good judgment. (St. Maximus the Confessor)[358]

Perfect love does not divide human nature, which is one, according to men's different characters; but looking always on this nature, it loves all men equally; it loves the good as friends and the wicked as enemies, doing good to them, being longsuffering, enduring things caused by them, never returning evil for evil, but even suffering for them if occasion demands, in order, if possible, to make friends even of them. But if this proves impossible, it still retains its good disposition toward them, always showing the fruits of love equally to all men. Thus our Lord God Jesus Christ, showing His love for us, suffered for the whole of mankind and gave equally to all the hope of resurrection, although each one makes himself worthy either of glory or of the torment of hell. (St. Maximus the Confessor)[359]

What a man loves, that he desires to grasp with all his strength; and all that obstructs him in this he pushes aside, lest he lose it. Thus a lover of God applies himself to pure prayer and casts out every passion which hinders this end. (St. Maximus the Confessor)[360]

Men love one another, either commendably or reprehensibly, for the following five reasons: either for the sake of God, as a virtuous man loves all men and is loved even by those who are not virtuous; or from nature, as parents love their children and are loved by them; or from vanity, as a man praised loves his praiser; or for the sake of gain, as a rich man is loved for what is received from him; or from love of lust, as a man who serves his stomach and what is below it loves the giver of feasts. The first of these is commendable, the second is intermediate, the others are passionate. (St. Maximus the Confessor)[361]

If you hate some, neither love nor hate others and love some moderately but others very intensely, then learn from this unequalness that you are still far from perfect love, which enjoins equal love for all men. (St. Maximus the Confessor)[362]

He who is perfect in love and has reached the summit of passionlessness knows no difference between his own people and strangers or between believer and infidel, between bond and free, or even male and female. Being above the tyranny of passions and seeing one human nature, he looks equally on all men and is equally disposed toward them all. There is in him "neither Jew nor Greek, there is neither bond nor free, there is neither male nor female, but all in all is Christ" (Gal. 3:28). (St. Maximus the Confessor)[363]

If a man's mind is constantly bent toward God, his desire too increases in its longing for God, and the whole of his excitable power is transformed into love of God. For the mind, becoming wholly luminous through its long participation in Divine illumination, and having subdued and mastered its desiring part, effects a transformation, as has been said, into continual longing and unfailing love for God—translating it entirely from the earthly to the Divine. (St. Maximus the Confessor)[364]

Time is divided into three parts. Faith extends over all three, hope over one, and love over two. Faith and hope have limits, but love, uniting with what is beyond the endless, and ever increasing, remains through endless ages. Therefore "the greatest of these is charity" (1 Cor. 13:13). (St. Maximus the Confessor)[365]

Love of God loves always to give wings to the mind to speak of God and Divine things; and love of neighbor disposes it always to think well of him. (St. Maximus the Confessor)[366]

Many have said much about love, yet if you seek it, you will find it only among the disciples of Christ. For they alone had true love to teach them the love of which it is said, "And though I have the gift of prophecy, and understand all mysteries, and all knowledge; . . . and have not charity . . . it profiteth me nothing" (1 Cor. 13:2-3). For he who has love has God Himself, for "God is love" (1 John 4:16). To Him be glory for ages, of ages. Amen. (St. Maximus the Confessor)[367]

There is a love like a small lamp, fed by oil, which goes out when the oil is ended; or like a rain-fed stream which goes dry, when rain no longer feeds it. But there is a love, like a spring gushing from the earth, never to be exhausted. The first is human love; the second is Divine, and has God as its source. (St. Isaac the Syrian)[368]

The rightful door leading to contemplation is love. In all ascents to revelations of knowledge and to contemplations of the mysteries, it is Divine love that leads in and out those who have acquired it. So first we must acquire love, and thereupon contemplation of the spiritual will be natural for us. Realise the wisdom of the blessed Paul when, putting aside all the gifts bestowed by grace, he asked for the most essential—the one by which all gifts are received and preserved, that is, love (1 Cor. 13). Love is the place of revelations; and in this place contemplation is revealed to us by itself. Just as with the progress of natural growth the soul receives more and more knowledge about things existing in the world, and learns new things from day to day; so in spiritual things a man receives spiritual contemplation and Divine perception, and learns this in proportion to the growth of his mind in wise living. And when it comes to the realm of love, it contemplates the spiritual in its rightful place. (St. Isaac the Syrian)[369]

Love for God is by nature hot, and when it grips a man beyond measure, it throws the soul into ecstasy. A man who feels this love exhibits a remarkable change: his face becomes fiery and joyful, and his body is warmed; fear and shame leave him; a terrible death he counts as joy; the contemplation of his mind allows no kind of interruption in his thought of the celestial; he is aware of no impulse excited by objects, for, even if he does something, he is quite insensible of it—so ravished is his mind in contemplation, and his thought is always as it were conversing with someone. (St. Isaac the Syrian)[370]

By no other virtue, by no other fulfillment of the Lord's commandment, can anyone be known as a disciple of Christ, for He says, "By this will all men know that you are My disciples, if you have love for one another" (John 13:55). It is for this reason that "the Word became flesh and dwelt among us" (John 1:14). For this reason He was incarnate; He willingly endured His life-giving sufferings, in order that He might deliver man, His own creature, from the bonds of hell, and restore him and lead him up to heaven. Moved by love the apostles ran that unceasing race and cast on the whole world the fishhook and net of the word to drag it up from the deep of idolatry and bring it safe into the port of the kingdom of heaven. Moved by love the martyrs shed their blood that they might not lose Christ. Moved by it our God bearing Fathers and teachers of the world eagerly laid down their own lives for the Catholic and apostolic Church. (St. Symeon the New Theologian)[371]

There are ten distinctive marks which are symptoms of the initiated's love of God. The first is that he longs after seeing his Lord. And because essential seeing takes place only after departure from this life, it is necessary for him who seeks his Lord to resemble Paul and like him to desire to depart in order to be with Christ.

The second is, that he does not fulfill his own will, but that of his

Lord, as the true one has said: "If you love me, keep my commandments" (John 4:15). The third is that he hates the whole world in order to possess the One only. . . . The fourth is that the lips constantly administer the name of his Lord. For every one who loves something often thinks of it and his tongue does not cease to mention it, as David who loved the law of his Lord meditated upon it the whole day.

The fifth is that he finds consolation in solitude and the abode in the small cell, rejecting the sight of the world and hating intercourse and speech. Because, as Mar Isaac the Syrian says, the consummation of excellency is lonely intercourse, and the quiet dwelling of the mind upon God. The sixth is that he is not spiteful on account of the worldly things which escape him, but that he regrets, on the contrary, every hour he passes in idleness.

The seventh is that he finds enjoyment in the labors of asceticism though they be heavy and wearying. . . . The eighth is that he is full of mercy toward the good, and scornful and severe against the bad, as also his Lord is just and loving justness and His face looks toward uprightness, but His soul hates the unjust and those who love unjustness.

The ninth is that he prays constantly, that his love may not abate and his gifts may not diminish. . . . The tenth is that he conceals his love as much as he can, though the signs thereof are not concealed in him. (Bar Hebraeus)[372]

4. Alms

He who bestows alms, imitating God, does not distinguish good from bad, righteous from wicked in their bodily needs. He gives alike in all, according to their need; though he prefers a virtuous to a sinful man for the good disposition of his will.

Love is made manifest not merely through giving away one's possessions, but even more so by teaching the word of God and by bodily service. (St. Maximus the Confessor)[373]

The Lord will demand from us an account of our help to the needy according to what we have and not according to what we have not (2 Cor. 8:12). If, then, from fear of God I distribute in a short space of time what I might have given away over many years, on what grounds can I be accused, seeing that I now have nothing? On the other hand, it might be argued: "Who now will give help to the needy that depend on regular gifts out of my modest means?"

A person who argues in this way must learn not to insult God because of his own love of money. God will not fail to provide for His own creation as He has done from the beginning; for before this or that person was prompted to give help, the needy did not lack food or clothing. Understanding this, we should reject, in a spirit of true service, the senseless presumption which arises from wealth and we should hate our own desires—which is to hate our own soul (Luke 14:26). Then, no longer possessing wealth which we enjoy distributing, we shall begin to feel our worthlessness intensely, because we find we cannot now perform any good works. Certainly, provided there is some good in us, we gladly obey the divine command and, as long as we are well off, we enjoy giving things away. But when we have exhausted everything an ill-defined gloom and a sense of abasement come over us, because we think we are doing nothing worthy of God's righteousness. In this deep abasement the soul returns to itself, so as to procure through the labor of prayer, through patience and humility what it can no longer acquire by the daily giving of help to the needy. . . . God is not prepared to grant the gift of theology to anyone who has not first prepared to give away all his possessions for the glory of the Gospel; then in godly poverty he can proclaim the riches of the divine kingdom. (St. Diadochus of Photike)[374]

"Thou shalt love thy neighbor as thyself." We ought to have all things in common. As the sun, the air, fire, water, and earth are common to us all, so ought also (in part) food and drink, money, books, and (in general) all the Lord's gifts to be shared in common; for they are given in common to all, and yet are easily divisible for distribution among many. For we have nothing of our own, but everything belongs to God. And it is not just for the rich to keep their superfluity in their treasuries when there are so many poor people in need of the means of existence, of necessary clothing and dwellings.

However, it is just that the laborious should enjoy abundance, and that the idle should endure poverty and misery. Therefore, if we know that some are poor only through their own idleness and laziness, with such we are not obliged to share the abundance earned by our labor. "If any man will not work," says the Apostle Paul, "neither let him eat." But the crying poverty arising from old age, exhaustion, from sickness, from fruitless and badly paid labor, from really difficult conditions of life, from a numerous family, from bad harvest, we must always hasten to help, especially those of us who are rich. We must be guided by the history of the times of the Apostles, by the example of the early Church.

Concerning modern works of charity. If you enjoy earthly blessings in full measure, and if you give to the needy, but indulge yourself still more, it means that you do good works without the least self-denial. Your works of charity are not great. But what else do we find? What are so-called works of charity? People arrange different entertainments with a charitable object—that is, they intentionally wish before all to serve their sinful flesh, and the Devil, and only afterward their neighbor and God. But this is no charity at all! Such works only bear the name of charity. "Let us do evil, that there may come good." "Woe to you that are filled, for you shall hunger! Woe to you that laugh, for you shall mourn and weep!"

That man is of a noble and elevated spirit who mercifully and generously scatters his gifts upon all, and rejoices when he has an opportunity of doing good and giving pleasure to everybody without thinking of being rewarded for it. That man is of noble and elevated spirit who never grows conceited and haughty toward those who frequent him and avail themselves of his bounties, does not neglect them in any respect, does not underrate them in any degree in his thoughts, but esteems them as he esteemed them at their first meeting with him or much higher than at that time. As it is, it often happens that, having become accustomed to them, we speedily grow tired of them, and reckon them as nothing: we often place a man lower than a beloved animal or a beloved object.

Bear in your heart continually the words, "Christ is Love," and endeavor to love all, sacrificing for the sake of love, not only your possessions, but even yourself.

Lord! teach me to bestow charity willingly, kindly, joyfully, and to believe that by bestowing it I do not lose, but gain, infinitely more than that which I give. Turn my eyes away from hard-hearted people who do not sympathize with the poor, who meet poverty with indifference, who judge, reproach, brand it with shameful names, and weaken my heart, so that I may not do good, so that I, too, may harden my heart against poverty. O my Lord, grant that every charity I bestow may be profitable, and may not do harm! Lord, accept Thyself charity in the person of Thy poor. Lord, deign to help me to build a house for the poor in this town, concerning which

I have already many times prayed to Thee, the all-merciful, almighty, most wise, wonderful! (John Cronstadt)[375]

D. Divine Counsels

1. Chastity

Not he is chaste in whom shameful thoughts stop in time of struggle, work and endeavor, but he who by the trueness of his heart makes chaste the vision of his mind, not letting it stretch out toward unseemly thoughts. And while the honesty of his conscience testifies, in what his eyes see, that he is true to the law of purity, modesty hangs like a veil in the secret place of thoughts and his innocence, like a chaste virgin, is kept inviolate for Christ by faith. (St. Isaac the Syrian)[376]

Weaken your flesh by hunger and vigil, and practice without laziness psalmody and prayer—and the consecration of chastity will descend upon you, bringing with it love. (St. Maximus the Confessor)[377]

Someone told me of an extraordinarily high degree of purity. He said: "A certain man, on seeing a beautiful body, thereupon glorified the Creator, and from that one look he was moved to the love of God and to a fountain of tears. And it was wonderful to see how what would have been the cause of destruction for one was for another the supernatural cause of a crown." If such a person always feels and behaves in the same way on similar occasions, then he has risen immortal before the general resurrection. (St. John Climacus)[378]

Chastity is the name which is common to all the virtues. (St. John Climacus)[379]

2. Detachment

The man who really loves the Lord, who has made a real effort to find the coming Kingdom, who has really begun to be troubled by his sins, who is really mindful of eternal torment and judgment, who really lives in fear of his own departure, will not love, care or worry about money, or possessions, or parents, or worldly glory, or friends, or brothers, or anything at all on earth. But having shaken off all ties with earthly things and having stripped himself of all his cares, and having come to hate even his own flesh, and having stripped himself of everything, he will follow Christ without anxiety or hesitation, always looking heavenward and expecting help from there, according to the word of the holy man: My soul sticks close behind Thee (Ps. 62:9), and according to the ever-memorable author who said: I have not wearied of following Thee, nor have I desired the day (or rest) of man, O Lord (Jer. 17:16). (St. John Climacus)[380]

Let us pay close attention to ourselves so that we are not deceived into thinking that we are following the strait and narrow way when in actual fact we are keeping to the wide and broad way. The following will show you what the narrow way means: mortification of the stomach, all-night standing, water in moderation, short rations of bread, the purifying draught of dishonor, sneers, derision, insults, the cutting out of one's own will, patience in annoyances, unmurmuring endurance of scorn, disregard of insults, and the habit, when wronged, of bearing it sturdily; when slandered, of not being indignant; when humiliated, not to be angry; when condemned, to be humble. Blessed are they who follow the way we have just described, for theirs is the Kingdom of Heaven. (St. John Climacus)[381]

No one will enter the heavenly bridechamber wearing a crown unless he makes the first, second and third renunciation. I mean the renunciation of all business, and people, and parents; the cutting out of one's will; and the third renunciation, of the conceit that dogs obedience. "Come ye out from among them, and be ye separate," saith the Lord, "and touch not the unclean world" (2 Cor. 6:17). For who amongst them has ever worked any miracles? Who has raised the dead? Who has driven out devils? No one. All these are the victorious rewards of monks, rewards which the world cannot receive; and if it could, then what is the need of asceticism or solitude? (St. John Climacus)[382]

CHAPTER ELEVEN

THE WORSHIPING COMMUNITY

Let us, who here mystically represent the Cherubim in singing the thrice-holy hymn to the life-giving Trinity, let us now
lay aside every earthly care . . . so that we may welcome
the King of the universe who comes escorted by invisible
armies of angels. Alleluia, alleluia, alleluia! (*The Cherubim
Hymn* of the Byzantine Liturgy of St. John Chrysostom)

A. Liturgy

On the Day of the Lord gather together, break bread and give
thanks after confessing your transgressions so that your sacrifice
may be pure. Let no one who has a quarrel with his neighbor join
you until he is reconciled, lest your sacrifice be defiled. For this is
that which was proclaimed by the Lord: "In every place and time
let there be offered to Me a clean sacrifice. For I am a Great King,"
says the Lord, "and My name is wonderful among the Gentiles."
(Didache)[383]

O King of glory, no one is worthy to come to You, to draw near
to You, to serve You, when he is bound down by the desires and
pleasures of the flesh; for to serve You is something grand and
awe-inspiring even for the heavenly powers themselves. And yet,
because of Your ineffable and boundless love for mankind, You
became man without changing or diminishing Your Divinity; You
became our High Priest, and, as Master of all, You granted to us
the priestly power of offering up this public sacrifice without any
new shedding of blood. It is You alone, O Lord our God, who are
Master over all things in heaven and on earth—You who are borne
upon the throne of the Cherubim, You who are the Lord of the
Seraphim and King of Israel, You alone who are holy and resting

among the holy. Still, I make my prayer to You, who alone are good and graciously ready to hear me; turn Your eyes toward me, Your sinful and unprofitable servant, and cleanse my soul and heart from any thought of evil. By the power of the Holy Spirit, make me worthy—since I am clothed with the grace of the priesthood to stand before Your holy altar and consecrate Your sacred and immaculate Body and precious Blood. It is to You, then, that I come with my head bowed low and I beseech You not to turn Your face away from me, nor to exclude me from the number of Your children but rather allow these gifts to be offered to You by me, Your sinful and unworthy servant. For it is really You who offer and are given back to us, Christ our God, and to You we give glory, with Your eternal Father and with Your most holy and gracious and life-giving Spirit, now and always and for ever and ever. Amen. (The Priest's Prayer before the Great Entrance of St. John Chrysostom's Liturgy of the Byzantine Rite)[384]

The chief thing in prayer for which we must care above all is lively, clear-sighted faith in the Lord: represent Him vividly before yourself and within you—then ask of Jesus Christ in the Holy Ghost whatever you desire and you will obtain it. Ask simply, without the slightest doubt—then your God will be everything to you, accomplishing in an instant great and wonderful acts, as the sign of the cross accomplishes great wonders. Ask for both spiritual and material blessings not only for yourself, but for all believers, for the whole body of the Church of Christ. . . .

When you are praying, either inwardly only, or both inwardly and outwardly, be firmly convinced that the Lord is there, by you and within you, and hears every word, even if only said to yourself, even when you only pray mentally; speak from your whole heart, without in the least justifying yourself; have faith that the Lord will have mercy upon you and you will not remain unforgiven. This is true. It is taken from experience. (John Cronstadt)[385]

During the oblation, the whole Church, in heaven and upon earth—the Church of the first-born, inscribed in the heavens, and the Church militant, fighting against the enemies of salvation upon earth—is typically represented assembled around the Lamb, who took upon Himself the sins of the world. What a great spectacle, enrapturing and moving the soul! It is possible that I too am the joint heir with the saints, if I remain faithful to the Lamb until death? Are not all my brethren too members of this heavenly holy assemblage, and joint-heirs of the future kingdom? Oh, how widely my heart should expand in order to contain all within itself, to love all, to care for all, to care for the salvation of all as for mine own! This is wisdom and the highest wisdom. Let us be simple; let us walk in simplicity of heart with all. Let us remember our high calling and election and let us continually aspire to the honor of God's heavenly calling through Christ Jesus. "We are the children of God . . . heirs of God, and joint-heirs with Christ." (John Cronstadt)[386]

B. Icons

We do not make obeisance to the nature of wood, but we revere and do obeisance to Him who was crucified on the Cross. . . . When the two beams of the Cross are joined together I adore the figure because of Christ who on the Cross was crucified, but if the beams are separated, I throw them away and burn them. (Leontius of Neapolis)[387]

Of old God the incorporeal and uncircumscribed was not depicted at all. But now that God has appeared in the flesh and lived among men, I make an image of the God who can be seen. I do not worship matter but I worship the Creator of matter, who for my sake became material and deigned to dwell in matter, who through matter effected my salvation. I will not cease from worshipping the matter through which my salvation has been effected. (St. John Damascene)[388]

Matter is endowed with a divine power through the prayer made to those who are depicted in image. (St. John Damascene)[389]

PRAYER OF BLESSING OF AN ICON OF THE HOLY TRINITY

Oh, Lord God, who are glorified in the blessed Trinity, You who cannot be reached by the mind nor expressed by word, who were not seen by any man in any place, only as we have learned from the Holy Scriptures and the God-revealing teachings of the Apostles, so do we believe and so do we confess You, God the Father without beginning, and Your consubstantial Son and Your coessential Spirit enthroned with You; and as the ancient Scriptures inform us of Your appearance in the image of the three Angels, which occurred to that most renowned patriarch Abraham, so in the new grace the Father manifested Himself in the voice, the Son in flesh in the Jordan, and the Holy Spirit in the form of a dove . . . therefore in order to always remember You, the one adorable God, we not only confess You with our lips, but also paint Your image, not in order to make this a divinity, but that by looking at it with our corporeal eyes, we may see You, our God, with our intellectual eyes, and that by venerating it we may glorify and praise You, our Creator, Redeemer and Sanctifier, and recall Your innumerable good works: because the honor paid to an image passes on to the prototype.

Presenting therefore this icon today before Your majesty with the pious motivation which we have intended, we ask and pray and make ourselves pleasing to Your bounteous generosity, look mercifully upon it and send down Your heavenly blessing, and in Your thrice-holy name, bless† and sanctify† it, so that those who do piously venerate it and do in front of it humbly bow and faithfully pray to You may find mercy, and receive grace, and be free from all misery and tribulations, and obtain pardon of sins, and become worthy of the heavenly kingdom, by Your grace and generosity and love-of-mankind, the One God glorified in the Trinity, the Father and the Son and the Holy Spirit, to whom be glory, now and always for ages and ages. (*Evkholohion ily Trebnyk* [Book of Blessings and Rituals])[390]

C. *Theotokos:* Mother of God

But to this what was the reply of the honored virgin, the heavenly chamber, the holy mountain, the sealed fountain, kept for Him only who had sealed it? "Since," says she, "thou hast clearly explained that the Holy Ghost shall come upon me, I no longer demur, I no longer object. Be it unto me according to thy word. If I am judged worthy for the Lord, I will gladly serve His will. If the Builder desires the thing built to become a temple to the Builder, let Him construct a house unto Himself as He has pleased. If the Creator rests on His creature, let Him mold in me His flesh as He knows how and wishes. Behold the handmaid of the Lord: be it unto me according to thy word. Let thy words be unto me fulfilled in the act. Let thy words be unto me in accordance with the deeds."

. . . As for us, what shall we offer to the Virgin? What words of praise shall we weave for her? What other, than those whose beginning Gabriel has first provided to us, saying, "Hail much graced one, the Lord is with thee. Blessed art thou among women, and blessed is the fruit of thy womb." Hail, because we see the sun of righteousness rising out of thee, illuminating both the heavenly and the earthly order, driving away the murk of error, and irradiating the universe with the splendor of Grace. Hail, much graced one, because having raised for us without husbandry the soul-nourishing grain, thou hast destroyed the seeds of the soul-corrupting growth. Hail, because thou hast brought to all of us the ambrosia of the life-giving bread, baked in thy flaming womb as in an oven, having removed like yeast the pest of the death-giving food. Hail, because thou hast made the tree of life bear fruit for us, which withers the offshoots of the tree of decay and yields the sweetness of knowledge. Hail, much-graced one, because thou hast stored away the pearl of great price, conveying the wealth of salvation to the ends of the universe. Blessed art thou among women, because thou hast requited the discomfiture of woman's transgression, having turned the reproach of deceit into a laudation of the sex; because in thee, a virgin, He who first molded Adam out of virgin earth, today remolds man from thy virginal blood; because, having woven the fleshy garment of the Word, thou hast covered up the nakedness of the first-formed. Why should I enumerate each count? Hail, much-graced one, because super-human things were wrought in thee, and the blessing of all good things has bloomed for us through thy pregnancy. (Photius, Patriarch of Constantinople)[391]

But who was worthy to serve as the minister of the mystery? Who was worthy to become the mother of God, and lend flesh to Him who is rich in everything? Clearly it was she who this day strangely issued from Joachim and Anna, the barren root, whose nativity we are celebrating in splendor, whose birth is the prelude to the greatest mystery—I mean the birth of the Word in the flesh—, and for whom this public and holy celebration is held. It was needful, yea needful, that she who from the very cradle had by a superior reason preserved her body pure, her soul pure, her thoughts pure, should be marked out to be the Creator's mother. It was needful that she who had been brought to the temple as an infant, who had trodden the untrodden places, should appear as a living temple for Him who gave her life. It was needful that she who had been born in a wondrous manner from a sterile womb, and had removed her parents' reproach, should also make good the failure of her forefathers: for she, the descendant, was able to repair the ancestral defeat, who brought forth the Savior of our race by a husbandless birth, and molded His body. It was needful that she who formed herself beautifully with spiritual comeliness should appear as a chosen bride, fitting for the heavenly Bridegroom. It was needful that she who with her virtuous ways, as with stars, had likened herself to the heavens, should be revealed to all the faithful as giving rise to the sun of righteousness. It was needful that she who dyed herself once with the dye of her virginal blood should serve as the purple of the universal Emperor. Oh, what a miracle! Whom the entire creation cannot contain, the Virgin's belly bears without being straitened. Whom the Cherubim do not dare to behold, the Virgin carries in her arms of clay. From the barren and fruitless womb comes forth the holy mountain, from which has been cut without hands a precious cornerstone, Christ our God, who has crushed the temples of the demons and the palaces of Hell together with their domination. The living and heavenly oven is being forged on earth, wherein the Creator of our clay, having baked the first-fruits with a divine fire and burned up the crop of tares, makes unto Himself a bread of wholly pure flour. But what is one to say, what would one not experience, sailing over the high sea of the Virgin's gifts and achievements? One fears and rejoices, one is calm and excited, one is hushed again and cries out, one cowers and expands, sometimes drawn by fear, sometimes by love. (Photius, Patriarch of Constantinople)[392]

God the Christ is born and, by assuming flesh with a rational soul, becomes man—He, who from non-being has given being to all that is, and to whom the Virgin gave birth supernaturally, losing no attributes of virginity. For as He became man without changing His nature or losing His power; so also He both makes her a mother and preserves her a Virgin who gave Him birth, simultaneously denoting one miracle by another and veiling one by the other. In Himself, in His essence, God is always hidden in mystery; and if at times He emerges from His essential mystery, He does so in such manner that, by its very manifestation, He makes it even more mysterious. Thus He makes the Virgin a bearing Mother in such a way that the very giving of birth itself makes the bonds of virginity indissoluble. (St. Maximus the Confessor)[393]

> I shall not be jealous, My Son,
> that Thou art with me,
> and also with all men.
> Be Thou God to him
> that confesses Thee,
> and be thou Lord to him
> that serves Thee,
> and Brother to him
> that loves Thee,
> that Thou mayest gain all!

When Thou didst dwell in me,
Thou didst also dwell out of me,
and when I brought Thee forth openly,
Thy hidden might was not removed from me.
Thou art within me
and Thou art without me,
O Thou that makest Thy Mother amazed.
For when I see that outward form
of Thine before mine eyes,
the hidden Form is shadowed forth
"in my mind," O Holy One.
In Thy visible form I see Adam,
and in Thy hidden form I see Thy Father,
who is joined with Thee. . . .
Thou art not so the Son of Man
that I should sing unto Thee a common lullaby;
for Thy Conception is new,
and Thy Birth marvelous.
Without the Spirit
who shall sing to Thee?
A new muttering of prophecy is hot within me.
How shall I call Thee a stranger to us,
Who art from us?
Should I call Thee Son?
Should I call Thee Brother?
Husband should I call Thee?
Lord should I call Thee,
O Child that didst give Thy Mother a second birth from the waters
For I am Thy sister,
of the house of David the father of us both.
Again, I am Thy Mother
because of Thy Conception
and Thy Bride am I
because of Thy sanctification,
Thy handmaid and Thy daughter,
from the Blood and Water
wherewith Thou hast purchased me
and baptized me.
The Son of the Most High came and dwelt in me,
and I became His Mother;
and as by a second birth I brought Him forth,
so did He bring me forth by the second birth
because He put His Mother's garments on,
she clothed her body with His glory. (St. Ephrem the Syrian)[394]

CHAPTER TWELVE

TRANSFORMING SOCIETY

And for anyone who is in Christ, there is a new creation; the old creation has gone, and now the new one is here. It is all God's work. It was God who reconciled us to himself through Christ and gave us the work of handing on this reconciliation. In other words, God in Christ was reconciling the world to himself, not holding men's faults against them, and he has entrusted to us the news that they are reconciled. So we are ambassadors for Christ; it is as though God were appealing through us, and the appeal that we make in Christ's name is: be reconciled to God. (2 Cor. 5:17-20)

A. Work

If work is preceded by prayer, sin will find no entrance into the soul. For when the consciousness of God is firmly established in the heart, the devices of the devil remain sterile, and matters of dispute will always be settled according to justice. Prayer prevents the farmer from committing sin, for his fruit will multiply even on a small plot of land, so that sin no longer enters together with the desire for more. It is the same with everyone; with the traveler, with somebody who prepares an expedition or a marriage. Whatever anyone may set out to do, if it is done with prayer the undertaking will prosper and he will be kept from sin, because there is nothing to oppose him and drag the soul into passion. If, on the other hand, a man leaves God out and gives his attention to nothing but his business, then he is inevitably opposed to God, because he is separated from Him. For a person who does not unite himself to God through prayer is separated from God. (St. Gregory of Nyssa)[395]

So the Christian directs every action, small and great, according to the will of God, performing the action at the same time with care and exactitude, and keeping his thoughts fixed upon the One who gave him the work to do. In this way, he fulfills the saying, "I set the Lord always in my sight; for He is at my right hand, that I be not moved" and he also observes the precept, "Whether you eat or drink or whatsoever else you do, do all to the glory of God." . . . We should perform every action as if under the eyes of the Lord and think every thought as if observed by Him . . . fulfilling the words of the Lord: "I seek not my own will but the will of Him that sent me, the Father." (St. Basil)[396]

There was a certain monk who did not do any work whatsoever with his hands, but he prayed without ceasing; and at eventide he would go into his cell and find his bread laid there for him, and he would eat it. Now another monk came to him, who had upon him materials for the labor of his hands, and wheresoever he entered in he worked, and he made the old man, into whose cell he had entered, to work with him. And when the evening had come, he wished, according to his custom, to eat, but he found nothing, and he therefore lay down in sorrow; and it was revealed unto him, saying, "Whilst thou wast occupied in converse with Me, I fed thee, but now thou has begun to work, thou must demand thy food from the labor of thy hands." (*The Wit and Wisdom of the Christian Fathers of Egypt*)[397]

However much man should do and how many justifying works he should perform, he should feel that he has accomplished nothing. And when he fasts, he should say: "I have not fasted." When he prays, let him think: "I have not prayed." Persevering in prayer, he should say: "I have not persevered. I have only begun to practice asceticism and to labor." And even if he is righteous before God, he must say: "I am not righteous. I am not working but I begin each day." (Pseudo-Macarius)[398]

A work correctly, religiously organized cannot lead to fatigue, neurasthenia or heart disease. If these symptoms exist, it is proof that a man works "in his own name"—trusting his own strength, his own charm, eloquence, kindness, and not the grace of God.

Just as there are correctly poised voices, even so, there are correctly poised souls. Caruso sang without fatigue, Pushkin would never have said that the writing of poetry was fatiguing, the nightingale sings all night, and when day breaks, its voice is untired.

If we are fatigued by our work, by our relations with other people, by conversation or prayer, this means only that our soul is incorrectly poised. There are voices naturally "poised"; others are forced to seek the same results through prolonged effort and artificial exercises. The same can be said of the soul. (Father Yelchaninov)[399]

Faith without works and works without faith will both alike be condemned, for he who has faith must offer to the Lord the faith which shows itself in actions. Our father Abraham would not have been counted righteous because of his faith had he not offered its fruit, his son (James 2:21; Rom. 4:3). (St. Diadochus of Photike)[400]

A certain old man lived in the monastery at Cuziba of whom the old men of the place told us that when he was in his own village it was his custom if he saw anyone in the village unable through poverty to sow his field, he would go by night carrying seed with him, and sow the poor man's field, the owner knowing nothing of it. And when he came to the desert and lived in the monastery of Cuziba, he did the same works of compassion. For he would go along the road that leads from the Jordan to the Holy City, carrying bread and water. And if he saw someone growing weary, he would shoulder his load and climb as far as the Holy Mount of Olives, and return again with others by the same road, carrying their burdens as far as Jericho. You might have seen the old man sometimes carrying a youngster on his shoulder; sometimes two. Sometimes he would be sitting patching the broken shoes of some man or woman; he used to carry with him whatever was needed for that task. He would give some a drink of the water that he carried, to others he would give bread, and indeed if he should come on any naked he would give him the cloak that he wore. It was sweet, to see the old man toiling day after day. And if he found one dead on the road, he would say over him the wonted psalms and prayers and give him burial. (St. John Moschus)[401]

There is no need to ask any one whether we ought to spread or propagate the Glory of God, either by writing, or by word, or by good works. This we are obliged to do according to our power and possibility. We must make use of our talents. If you think much about such a simple matter, then, perhaps, the Devil may suggest to you such foolishness as that you need only be inwardly active.

Do not only do your work when you wish to, but do it then especially, when you do not wish to. Understand that this applies to every ordinary worldly matter, as likewise and especially to the work of the salvation of your soul—to prayer, to reading God's word and other salutary books, to attending Divine service, to doing good works, whatever they may be, to preaching God's word. Do not obey the slothful, deceitful, and most sinful flesh; it is eternally ready to rest, and to lead us into overlasting destruction through temporal tranquility, and enjoyment. "In the sweat of thy face," it is said, "shalt thou eat bread." O miserable soul, "carefully cultivate the talent granted unto thee," sings the Church. "The kingdom of heaven suffers violence, and the violent bear it away," says our Lord and Savior.

Watch yourselves—your passions, especially in your home life, where they appear freely, like moles in a safe place. Outside our own home, some of our passions are usually screened by other more decorous passions, while at home there is no possibility of driving away these black moles that undermine the integrity of our soul.

Speak and do everything right undoubtingly, boldly, firmly, and decidedly. Avoid doubts, timidity, languor, and indecision. "For God has not given us the spirit of fear, but of power and of love." Our Lord is the Lord of powers. (John Cronstadt)[402]

B. Marriage

Our modern individualism creates special difficulties in married life. To overcome them a conscious effort on both sides is necessary, so that a marriage may be built which will be a "walking solution" for all problems. There is something more, something which may appear to be the simplest matter of all but is nevertheless the most difficult to achieve—the firm intention of letting each partner keep the proper place in marriage; for the wife to be humbly content with second place; for the husband to assume the burden and the responsibility of being the head. If this firm intention and desire are present, God will always help us to follow this difficult path, the path of martyrdom (the chant of the "Holy Martyrs" is sung in the course of the bridal procession), but also a way of life that yields the most intense joy. Marriage is a mysterious revelation. We see in it the complete transformation of a man, the expansion of his personality—fresh vision, a new vitality—and through it the birth of a new plenitude. (Father Yelchaninov)[403]

In marriage the festive joy of the first day should be extended to the whole of life; every day should be a feast day; every day husband and wife should appear to each other as new, extraordinary beings. The only way of achieving this: let each become more deeply spiritual, exert strong efforts in the work of self-development. . . .

Only in marriage can human beings fully know one another—the miracle of feeling, touching, seeing another's personality—and this is as wonderful and as unique as the mystic's knowledge of God. It is for this reason that before marriage man hovers above life, observes it from without; only in marriage does he plunge into it, entering it through the personality of another. This joy of real knowledge and real life gives us that feeling of achieved plenitude and satisfaction for which we are richer and wiser. (Father Yelchaninov)[404]

Neither the man, nor even less the woman possesses absolute power over the partner in marriage. Force exercised over the will of another—even in the name of love—kills love itself. Then the question arises: must one submit to this force when it threatens that which is most precious? The countless numbers of unhappy marriages result from precisely this—that each partner looks upon the loved one as an object for possession. Hence nearly all the difficulties of married life. The expression of the highest wisdom in marriage is the counterpart of marriage in heaven (Christ and the Church), where there is absolute freedom. (Father Yelchaninov)[405]

That Scripture counsels marriage, however, and never allows any release from the union, is expressly contained in the law: "You shall not divorce a wife, except for reason of immorality." And it regards as adultery the marriage of a spouse, while the one from whom a separation was made is still alive. . . . "Whoever takes a divorced woman as wife commits adultery," it says; for "if anyone divorce his wife, he debauches her," that is, he compels her to commit adultery. And not only does he that divorces her become the cause of this, but also he that takes the woman and gives her the opportunity of sinning; for if he did not take her, she would return to her husband. (Clement of Alexandria)[406]

C. Cosmic Transformation

Then man makes one earth by uniting paradise with his inhabited world through chaste conversation. His united world then becomes no longer distinct by reason of the diversity of so many parts, but rather it is brought together into a synthesis so that man no longer suffers proliferation into separated parts. Then heaven and earth are united through a virtuous life similar to that of angels. Man no longer is bound down by his bodily condition but rises through an elevation of his soul to the invisible presence of God. He thus is able to make his own way by discerning what is prior and then go back to the material creation, to the things that are secondary.

Then man unites the things known to his intellect and those known to his senses through a knowledge similar to that of the angels who see all of creation, not as separated into known and unknown, but man, become like to angels, is able to know by a knowledge that is the greatest infusion of true wisdom and given only to the worthy to know the difficult and the ineffable. Thus uniting created nature with the Uncreated through charity (O new and wonderful thing wrought in us through divine condescension) man shows all as one and the same through the power of grace. He sees all things in God first as flowing from God into existence and secondly through them, rising to God as to the end of all moved creatures and the fixed and stable ground of their being, who is the end of every rule and law, the end of every word and mind and of every nature, the infinite and unbound goal of all beings. (St. Maximus the Confessor)[407]

The pattern of our relations toward our fellowmen often appears to be the following: a person pleases us, we sincerely idealize him, we see nothing bad in him; and then, suddenly, the person in question fails us in this or that, lies or brags, or proves to be cowardly, or betrays us. So we start to re-estimate his value, we erase all that we saw in him before (and which nevertheless really was there), and throw him out of our heart. I have long understood that this is a false and sinful method of human relationship. At the basis of such an attitude toward our fellowmen lie two ideas of which we are not ourselves conscious: (1) I am above sin and (2) the person on whom I have bestowed my love is also sinless. How should we otherwise explain our severe condemnation of others and our surprise if a good, kind, pious person commits a sin? Such are my conclusions drawn from sad reflections concerning our own heart, and my conviction that we ourselves are capable of all kinds of sins.

And yet, the norm of our attitude toward our fellows is to forgive endlessly, for we are ourselves in infinite need of forgiveness. And what is essential is not to forget that the good which we valued remains; as for the sin, it was always there, but we did not notice it. (Father Yelchaninov)[408]

Our Lord Jesus Christ, then, comes from heaven; and He comes with glory at the end of this world, in the last day. For of this world there is to be an end, and this created world is to be re-made anew. . . . Would you receive the proof of this out of the words of Scripture? Listen to Isaias, saying, "And the heaven shall be rolled together as a scroll; and all the stars shall fall, as leaves from a vine, and as leaves fall from a fig-tree" (Isa. 34:4). The Gospel also says, "The sun shall be darkened and the moon shall not give her light, and the stars shall fall from heaven" (Matt. 26:29) . . . And that Lord rolls up the heavens, not that He may destroy them, but that He may raise them up again more beautiful. . . . The things then which are seen shall pass away, and there shall come the things which are looked for, things fairer than the present; but as to the time let no one be curious. For "it is not for you," He says, "to know times or seasons, which the Father has put in His own power" (Acts 1:7). And venture not thou to declare when these things shall be, nor on the other hand supinely slumber. For He says, "Watch, for in such an hour as you expect not the Son of Man comes" (Matt. 24:42, 44).

"Take heed that no man mislead you." And this word exhorts you to give heed to what is spoken; for it is not a history of things gone by, but a prophecy of things future, and which will surely come. Not that we prophesy, for we are unworthy; but that the things which are written will be set before you, and the signs declared. Observe, which of them have already come to pass, and which yet remain; and make yourself safe. (St. Cyril of Jerusalem)[409]

D. Eschatology

1. Angels

What, then, is the hierarchy of the angels and archangels, supramundane principalities and powers, virtues and dominations, divine thrones, or beings of the same rank as thrones which the word of God describes as being perpetually near God, always about Him and with Him, those being in Hebrew called cherubim and seraphim? . . . The beings and orders above us, of whom I have already made pious mention, are incorporeal, and their hierarchy is spiritual and supramundane. We observe that our own human hierarchy, conformably to our nature, abounds in a manifold variety of sensible symbols which raise us hierarchically, in proportion to our capacity, to the oneness of deification, to God and divine virtue. Since they are spirits, they know according to laws proper to them. . . . To speak truly, there is one to whom all the godlike aspire, but they do not partake of Him who is one and the same in the same manner, but as the divine ordinance assigns to each according to his merits. (Dionysius Pseudo-Areopagite)[410]

O Captains and Leaders of the armies of Heaven, unworthy as we are, we beseech you without cease to surround us with your intercessions and cover us beneath the shelter of the glory of your ethereal wings. We bend our knee and cry out with perseverance: "Deliver us from danger, O Princes of the Powers on high!" (Troparion)[411]

O Princes of the leaders of God's armies, servants of the divine glory, instructors of men and commanders of angels: ask whatever is good for us, and bountiful mercy, O Princes of the leaders of the angels! (Kontakion)[412]

2. Heaven

We can conceive then of no limitation in an infinite nature; and that which is limitless cannot by its nature be understood. And so every desire for the Beautiful which draws us on in this ascent is intensified by the soul's very progress toward it. And this is the real meaning of seeing God; never to have this desire satisfied. But fixing our eyes on those things which help us to see, we must ever keep alive in us the desire to see more and more. And so no limit can be set to our progress toward God: first of all, because no limitation can be put upon the beautiful, and secondly because the increase in our desire for the beautiful cannot be stopped by a sense of satisfaction. (St. Gregory of Nyssa)[413]

After the resurrection, when our bodies will be re-united to our souls, they will be incorruptible; and the carnal passions which disturb us now will not be present in those bodies; we shall enjoy a peaceful equilibrium in which the prudence of the flesh will not make war upon the soul; and there will no longer be that internal warfare wherein sinful passions fight against the law of the mind, conquering the soul and taking it captive by sin. Our nature then will be purified of all these tendencies, and one spirit will be in both, I mean in the flesh and in the spirit, and every corporeal affection will be banished from our nature. (St. Gregory of Nyssa)[414]

He will share in Christ's glory who, through being formed in Christ, has received renewal by the Spirit and has preserved it, and so has attained to ineffable deification. No one, there, will be one with Christ or be a member of Christ, if he has not become even here a receiver of grace and has not, thereby, become "transformed by the renewing of" his "mind" (Rom. 12:2). (St. Gregory of Sinai)[415]

The kingdom of heaven is like the tabernacle of the Lord; for in the world to come it too will have two veils, like the tabernacle of Moses. All those illumined by grace will enter past the first veil, but only the most perfect past the second. (St. Gregory of Sinai)[416]

We preach not one advent only of Christ, but a second also, far more glorious than the former. For the former gave a view of His patience; but the latter brings with it the crown of a divine kingdom. For all things, for the most part, are twofold in our Lord Jesus Christ; a twofold generation; one of God, before the ages; and one, of a Virgin, at the close of the ages; His descents twofold; one, the unobserved, like rain on a fleece (Ps. 72:6); and a second, His open coming, which is to be. (St. Cyril of Jerusalem)[417]

But let us wait and look for the Lord's coming upon the clouds from heaven. Then shall angelic trumpets sound; "the dead in Christ shall rise first" (1 Thess. 4:16); the godly persons who are alive shall be caught up in the clouds, receiving as the reward of their labors more than human honor, inasmuch as theirs was a more than human strife; according as the Apostle Paul writes, saying, "For the Lord Himself shall descend from heaven with a shout, with the voice of the Archangel, and with the trumpet of God: and the dead in Christ shall rise first. Then we which are alive and remain shall be caught up together with them in the clouds, to meet the Lord in the air; and so shall we ever be with the Lord" (1 Thess. 4:16-17). (St. Cyril of Jerusalem)[418]

3. Judgment

Terrible in good truth is the judgment, and terrible the things announced. The kingdom of heaven is set before us, and everlasting fire is prepared. How then, some one will say, are we to escape the fire? And how to enter into the kingdom? "I was hungry," He says, "and you gave Me meat." Learn hence the way; there is here no need of an allegory, but to fulfill what is said. "I was hungry, and you gave Me meat; I was thirsty, and you gave Me drink; I was a stranger, and you took Me in; naked, and you clothed Me; I was sick, and you visited Me; I was in prison, and you came unto Me" (Matt. 25:35). (St. Cyril of Jerusalem)[419]

By many mansions the Savior meant the different degrees of

existence in the other world. The kingdom is one, but within it there are many divisions, according to the difference in knowledge and virtue of those who enter therein, and to their degree of deification. For "there is one glory of the sun, and another glory of the moon, and another glory of the stars; for one star differs from another star in glory" as says the divine Apostle, though all shine alike in the firmament. (St. Gregory of Sinai)[420]

In the future life (in heaven) the saints hold inner converse with one another, the Holy Spirit speaking in them. (St. Gregory of Sinai)[421]

It is said that in the life to come the angels and saints shall never cease to progress in increasing their gifts, striving for greater and ever greater blessings. No slackening or change from virtue to sin is admitted in that life. (St. Gregory of Sinai)[422]

In the future, a man shall have the degree of deification corresponding to his present perfection in spiritual stature. (St. Gregory of Sinai)[423]

4. Hell

Also in respect of penalty, I say that all men are not equal. He that has done great wickedness is greatly tormented. And he that has offended not so much is less tormented. Some "shall go into outer darkness, where there is weeping and gnashing of teeth" (Matt. 6:12). Others shall be cast into the fire, according as they deserve; for it is not written that they shall gnash their teeth nor that there is darkness there. Some shall be cast into another place, a place where "their worm shall not die, and their fire shall not be quenched, and they shall become an astonishment to all flesh" (Isa. 66:24). In the faces of others the door shall be closed and the Judge will say to them: "I know you not" (Matt. 25:12). And consider that, as the reward for good deeds is not equal for all men, so it is also for evil deeds. Not in one fashion shall men be judged, but every man according to his works shall receive his requital, because the Judge is clothed in righteous and regards not the persons of men. (Aphrahat)[424]

Fire, darkness, worm, hell correspond to passions—lusts of all kinds, the all-embracing darkness of ignorance, the unquenchable thirst for sensual pleasures, the stench of evil-smelling sin, which, like precursors and foretastes of the torment of hell, even now being to torture sinners in whose souls they take root through long-established habit. (St. Gregory of Sinai)[425]

EPILOGUE

The introduction to this book summarized the development of the key elements in what constitutes Eastern Christian spirituality. Selections from the leading spiritual writers of this tradition followed. There remains to present a final word on the relevance of such a spirituality for Western readers.

Some Dangers

First, let me present some evident dangers or at least elements that, if not understood properly, might turn a reader away from the writings of Eastern Christian ascetics and mystics.

We have all seen in Western Christianity the abuses that come when Christians read and interpret Holy Scripture in a literal fashion. The same holds true for the reading and interpretation of the writings of the Eastern Fathers. We need to demythologize these writings by transcending the cultural history that forms the backdrop against which the ancient writers lived and wrote.

For example, a statement such as the following, written in the sixth century by St. Isaac of Nineveh, could do much damage if a person in the twentieth century tried to live by it literally: "He is a monk, who stays outside the world and is ever praying to God, so that he may gain future blessings."[1] It would encourage a spirituality of escapism from God's created world.

Gnosticism, Stoicism, and an eclectic Platonism had greatly influenced Christianity in Hellenic cultures. These non-Christian philosophies give a rather negative view toward the "world, the flesh and matter." All too often in Hellenic Christian writings the flight from the "world" represents a form of Christianity that fails to do justice to the incarnation and the true teaching of the hypostatic union of Christ, true God and true man, two complete and distinct but undivided and inseparable natures of divinity and humanity.

Such a view toward the material world tends toward *Monophysit-*

ism—the doctrine that Christ's humanity was absorbed into the divinity. Such a Monophysitic view of Christianity offers little to Christians of the twentieth century, who see the world more in terms of evolution through creative action rather than a denigration of God's material creation.

Other areas, to cite some examples of overliteral reading, are blind obedience to one's spiritual mentors, the use of psychosomatic techniques in the use of prayer, especially the traditional Eastern use of the Jesus Prayer, and the myth of the demons. Obedience to a spirit-filled, holy, and intelligent spiritual guide was one way of counteracting self-deception, but great stress was placed on discernment in the choice of such a guide before surrendering to his spiritual direction, and the freedom always remained to leave him and find another director if such direction were no longer according to God's revelation and the individual's needs for spiritual growth.

With their great stress on holistic prayer—that is, the idea that the human being, as body-soul-spirit, should pray as a whole person—the Eastern Fathers offer us many techniques in prayer. But they realized as we should that techniques are only means to the end of the entire Christian life and never should be considered as ends in themselves. If Westerners were to emphasize too exclusively the techniques that certain hesychastic writers offer in the use of the Jesus Prayer (synchronizing their breathing with the mental recitation of the prayer formula), great dangers could ensue, as we find recorded in the annals of Eastern Christianity.

In regard to their use of devils to describe the inimical forces that serious Christians face in the spiritual combat, the Desert Fathers felt they were being only scriptural in their use of devils as fallen spirits that attack from outside and can influence one's fantasies within. These desert athletes, like Jesus Christ, went into the literal desert and were tempted by demons. The essential teachings of such Fathers do not depend on whether they literally encountered fallen angels or devils. They were describing, in the symbols of the spiritual world, an adversary, an opposing force that was exercising a very negative power over them. The demons stand for all powers that oppose the work of God and his "ministering spirits" (Heb. 1:14) to divinize us into children of God. These are very real powers operating with wickedness and cunning. They stand for all enemies to one's growth as a loving human being.

The Desert Fathers used mythic language that came to them from Scripture and that described common experiences as they

entered more deeply into the hidden, dark areas of their unconscious. For those of the desert and for anyone in the twentieth
century who has had similar experiences, the mythic language is a
vehicle to describe a reality that goes far beyond a scientific, observ-
able-by-the-senses description. We must not take the devil language
too literally. Yet we must be open to the reality that such writers
were experiencing and that we too can experience in our interior
lives.

An Eastern Corrective

In a more positive vein, the common elements found in Eastern
Christianity can offer us many creative and needed elements that
can help balance the emphasis of Western Christianity. Eastern spirituality calls us to a living theology as an experience of the indwelling Trinity within the individual Christian and within the gathering of
the Christian community in liturgical prayer.

True theology for Eastern Christians is never merely speculative
and abstract but is the practical experience of living, the gift of the
Trinity as divinized Christians strive to become signs of the world's
reconciliation into a harmonious whole according to God's plan of all
things in his Word. Such living theology is therefore built on a consistent biblical anthropology that sees humanity as made by God according to his own image and likeness—Jesus Christ, the God-Man,
the Word Incarnate.

Theology, therefore, is the mystical life seen as a continued process in love relationships and self-giving between the Trinity and the
individual Christian as well as in the Christian community. Love is
always pouring itself out in activity of self-giving, and so the material
world, in all its brokenness and yet all its splendid possibilities, becomes the "place" where God is becoming incarnated and revealed
through his Son, Jesus Christ, in his spirit of love. Grace is thus not
an extrinsic "thing" that God sends down on this world from above.
Grace primarily is God in his triune, personal relationships as Father, Son, and Holy Spirit, giving himself to humanity in the context
of material existence.

Contemplation

The spiritual life of the Christian East is not conceived of as so many
steps up a ladder, climaxing in a spiritual marriage. It is, rather, a
contemplation or discovering of the unfolding, eternal love of the

triune God in the cosmos. The ascetical life is not considered as a purification and illumination that leads to some acquired or infused union with God as merit of one's efforts to storm Heaven. Instead, asceticism or *praxis* is what humanity must do in order to effect the necessary "therapy" to "see" what has always been there—God's eternal self-giving to humanity in each event of daily living. Such asceticism centers practically around two aspects: (1) the negative side, uprooting any inordinate self-love, and (2) the positive aspect, developing virtues by putting on the mind of Christ. The emphasis on self-knowledge of the inner depths of one's psyche highlights control of thoughts that eventually lead us to actions.

Modern psychologists and spiritual directors can learn much from the nuanced doctrine of the Desert Fathers concerning the sources of sinfulness in us; namely, the eight passions that are at the source of all impulses toward selfishness. This doctrine advocates the uprooting of all "worldliness," which is an obligation placed on all Christians for all generations. The stress on obeying the commandments of God's Word, found in Scripture, could helpfully call us back to a form of Christianity that unfolds in personalistic terms, and away from the heavy moralism that bombards most Western Christians in forming our conscience. Listening to the inner voice—the risen Lord Jesus speaking to us through the illumination of the Spirit—demands far more in honesty and "purity of heart" than a black and white moralism rooted in extrinsic law, and a vengeful, vindictive lawmaker God.

A Logos Mysticism

As we become purified of our self-centeredness by listening to the inner Word of God, we move into what the Desert Fathers called the contemplation of the Logos of God (*theoria physica*) in the physical or material world around us. Essential to Christian faith is the belief that all things have been created in the Logos or Word of God and are sustained by the inner, directive power of God. Contemplating each created thing in God's Logos is to discover the place it properly enjoys within the hierarchy of all things uniquely different and yet all inwardly related into a whole, the Body of Christ. Such a Logos mysticism has much to tell us in the modern world; it helps us discover our own unique personhood in Jesus Christ and, in that identity, to serve lovingly the uniqueness in each creature that we encounter in our work.

Such a Logos contemplation leads to a deepening of a oneness with the diversity of the triune God, Father, Son, and Holy Spirit. Ultimately this is true theology, the experience of the community of many people in the oneness of the Spirit of love without destroying the uniqueness of each individual.

Humanity, the Transformer of the Universe

One very beneficial element that Eastern Christian spirituality can bequeath to twentieth-century Christians is the positive vision of the entire material world as destined to enter into a spiritual transformation to form the Body of Christ, the Church. Our creative human work is to reconcile the world that sin has separated into antagonistic factions, the spiritual world over the material, man over woman, race against race, heaven over earth, and so forth. Such a positive view of the inner harmony of all things in Christ renders great value to human work as each person lovingly accepts his or her talents or charisms and brings them forth in loving service to create a better world that will become the new Heavenly Jerusalem.

The Church, then, is more than merely the institution made up of members of the hierarchy and clergy. It becomes the entire world, including the material creation, moving toward the full manifestation of the Body of Christ in glory as each human being under the Holy Spirit works to bring all things into Christ.

In such a positive context Christians are able to see trials and sufferings, not as something negative or as sent by God in punishment for our sinfulness, but as the matrix that goes into bringing forth more of the Christ-life into the world. Such Christians can strain forth in their efforts to embrace all sufferings that necessarily will come in any loving action.

Liturgical Piety

The liturgical ritual and prayer of the Eastern Christians offers us a much needed corrective in our prayer life. When Eastern Christians celebrate the death and resurrection of Jesus Christ in the context of the Divine Liturgy, or as an extension of that liturgy in their own personal or family prayer, they enter into a sense of total community, of cosmic dimension. Heavy accent on material aids in liturgical celebration, such as icons, beautiful liturgical singing, pageantry of processions, ornate architecture, vestments, and profuse use of incense and lights, all produce a microcosm of a material world that is undergoing a heavenly transformation into the glory of the risen Lord Jesus.

Thus ecclesiology in the East is tied intrinsically to the experience of the Eucharist, with the Body of Christ being formed not out of separated individuals who come to be fed, but out of the intimacy of the people of God. They are whole persons committing themselves to each other in the love received in the Eucharist. That love drives them back into their families and cities to live the Eucharist sacrament of self-giving. Thus they sacrifice selfishness, in order to fully live the Christ life, which cannot be realized unless the communicants are ready to receive each other in committed, loving service.

Devotion to Mary

The Eastern Christians have always maintained their devotion to Mary the Mother of God. This devotion is based on the perception of Mary as the archetype of what the Church and the individual Christian ought to be. She became a living experience of the *anima*, or the contemplative, listening ability that God has planted in every human being. Filial devotion to Mary has helped Eastern Christians experience life within the communion of the loving saints and angels and their powerful intercession.

By keeping alive the contemplative aspect that devotion to Mary fostered, Eastern Christians can teach us in the West how to move beyond the limitations of time and space in order to live in the eternal *now* of God's reality, where there is no separation among those who love each other in God's love. Heaven becomes a process experience of the *already now*. Resurrection is thus a participation; Mary already shares in the glory of her risen Son and Christians in this present pilgrimage already surrender to let God's Word be done in their lives.

Transfiguration

To the modern world, which is so filled with fear of impending doom and cataclysmic destruction of the universe, the ultimate message of Eastern Christianity is that of resurrectional hope, not only for individual Christians at the end of the world, but hope that the risen Lord is alive in the broken world of today. A transfiguration process is *now* going on throughout the whole cosmos, directed from the inside by the risen Lord and with the loving cooperation of each Christian. God truly loves the world he created. God's presence is sustained within all material creation by his uncreated energies of love.

The Body of Christ is being formed through the priestly ministry of each human being made according to the image and likeness that is Jesus Christ and is being shaped and fashioned by all things material. Thus, to pray we stand before God and the material world in complete self-surrender, letting the risen Jesus Christ work in and through us in a synergy of creativity between God and humanity. The pedagogic Divine Master is always instructing his children, correcting, admonishing, and exhorting even in what at times seems to be sheer negative evil for the unbeliever.

Sparks of Faith

Through contemplation, the power of Jesus Christ is discovered working in the lives not only of Christians but of all human beings, regardless of whatever culture or religion. Ghetto concepts of how God must work in his universe yield to a concept of the openness of love to embrace the whole world. To discover God inside oneself in contemplation allows us to discover God inside the entire material world of which we are a small but important part. Matter is thus sacred and becomes a point of encounter with a dynamic Trinity that out of love for all of us and a desire to share its own divine life with us is inserted "inside" of all created beings. God's material world has not been conceived by God to be destroyed but to be transfigured and brought into its fullness in and by Jesus Christ.

Presenting an anthology of selections drawn from the leading Eastern Christian writers is a very difficult task. First, it is difficult to select representative writings. Moreover, selecting writings that present Westerners—who have received a different form of Christianity through different cultural influences and different emphases due to so many particular historical events—a contrasting legitimate form of Christianity is very difficult. The uniqueness of the Eastern vision is rooted strongly in asceticism as a purification of the heart so that the individual can be open to experience God's reality, which is always present as love. The gift of contemplating God can never be truly given to others, just as the gift of loving can never be given except in the context of *experienced* gift, freely given to one who is purified of selfishness and ready to risk the death-resurrection dialectic constantly preached in Christianity.

Because of this heavy accent on a faith vision of contemplation and because of what almost amounts to scorn for "clear and distinct" ideas, such Eastern material is difficult to read or to present in an orderly synthesis. The authors' own writings were not conceived as orderly presentations of manuals of "how to do it." They were, on the contrary, conceived of as a living word given out of God's living Word in Scripture, a spark that might land on material that was inflammable and start a new fire.

Therefore I have tried to allow these authors to speak through their own works. It is a book that should be approached much as one reads Scripture. It can be instructional. It is also, I hope, a book that allows the reader to enter into a vision of faith similar to the constant experience of these Eastern holy men and women. This experience is like taking off your shoes of security in the habitual Western vision of the Christian spiritual life and coming before the Burning Bush in awe and trembling.

The important ingredient that will make this book worthwhile is a searching, hungry heart.

"If any man is thirsty, let him come to me! Let the man come and drink who believes in me! As scripture says: From his breast shall flow fountains of living water" (John 7:37-38). May the reader of this book not read the surface words so much as drink deeply from the inner presence of God's Word inside the treasures bequeathed to us by the great giants of Eastern Christianity. If you receive the Spirit of love by drinking from these fountains of living water, give God the glory!

NOTE*

1. St. Isaac the Syrian, *Directions on Spiritual Training*, in Kadloubovsky and Palmer, *Early Fathers*, p. 240.

---

* A complete reference can be found in the Bibliography.

NOTES*

1. St. Irenaeus, *Adversus Haereses*, in *ANF*, bk. 5, ch. 6, 1, pp. 531-532.
2. Clement of Alexandria, *Protrepticos*, in *ANF*, ch. 10, p. 199.
3. Origen, *De Principiis*, III, in *ANF*, ch. 6, 1, p. 344.
4. St. Athanasius, *De Incarnatione*, in *NPNF*, 11, p. 42.
5. Ibid., 14, p. 43.
6. St. Basil, *Homily on Ps. 48*, pp. 324-325.
7. St. Gregory Nazianzus, *Oratio 38*, 12, in *NPNF*, p. 349.
8. St. Gregory of Nyssa, *De Opificio Hominis*, ch. 16, in *NPNF*, 405.
9. St. Gregory Palamas, *Triades* II, 2, 12, cited by Meyendorff in *A Study of Gregory Palamas*, p. 143.
10. St. Gregory Palamas, *Triade* II, 2, 9, in Palamas, *Les Triades pour la defense des Saints Hesychastes*.
11. Pseudo-Macarius, *The Spiritual Homilies*, no. 11, p. 77.
12. St. Diadochus of Photike, *On Spiritual Knowledge*, in Palmer *et al.*, *The Philokalia: The Complete Text*, no. 4, p. 253.
13. Ibid., no. 5, p. 254.
14. St. Symeon the New Theologian, *Traites Ethiques*, 6, 217-221, pp. 134-136. Translation mine.
15. St. Cyril of Alexandria, *Glaphyria in Genesim*, in *PG*, 69, 28.
16. St. Gregory of Nyssa, *On Virginity*, in *PG*, 46, 373B.
17. St. Irenaeus, *Adversus Haereses*, III, ch. 19, 1, in *ANF*, pp. 448-449.
18. St. Athanasius, *De Synodis*, 51, in *NPNF*, p. 477.
19. St. Athanasius, *De Incarnatione et Contra Arianos*, 5, in *PG*, 23, 992.
20. St. Gregory of Nyssa, *Contra Eunomium*, III, 6, in *NPNF*, p. 149.
21. St. Cyril of Alexandria, *In Lucam*, in *PG*, 72, 488B.
22. St. Symeon the New Theologian, *Hymns of Divine Love*, Hymn 25, pp. 135-136.
23. St. Gregory of Nyssa, *De Beatitudine*, Oratio VII, in *PG*, 44, 1280B-C.
24. St. Athanasius of Mount Sinai, *Concerning the Word*, in *PG*, 89, 77B-C.
25. St. Gregory of Nyssa, *De Beatitudine*, in *PG*, 44, 38-39.
26. Ibid., 40.
27. Nicholas Cabasilas, *The Life in Christ*, p. 228.
28. St. Cyril of Alexandria, *De recta fide ad Theod.*, in *PG*, 76, 1177A.
29. Ibid., *In Joan. XIV*, 2, in *PG*, 74, 184B-D.
30. St. Basil, *Epistle to Eustathius*, cited by G. Habra in "The Patristic Sources of the Doctrine of Gregory Palamas on the Divine Energies," p. 298.

*Complete references for Notes can be found in the Bibliography.

31. St. Gregory Palamas, *Triade III, 2, 25*, in Palamas, *Les Triades.*
32. Ibid., *Triade III, 2, 29.*
33. St. Gregory Palamas, *Against Akindynos, Triade II, 9*, in Palamas, *Les Triades.*
34. Ibid. *Triade III, 8.*
35. Ibid., cited by Lossky, *Mystical Theology of the Eastern Church*, p. 172.
36. St. Mark the Ascetic, *226 Texts*, in Kadloubovsky and Palmer, *Philokalia: Early Fathers*, no. 61, p. 89.
37. St. Diadochus of Photike, in Palmer *et al., The Philokalia: The Complete Text*, no. 77, pp. 279-280.
38. Pseudo-Macarius, *The Spiritual Homilies*, Homily 40, pp. 197-198.
39. St. Diadochus of Photike, *On Spiritual Knowledge*, in Palmer *et al., The Philokalia: The Complete Text*, no. 76, p. 279.
40. Ibid., no. 89, p. 288.
41. St. Theophan the Recluse, *The Fruits of Prayer*, cited in Igumen Chariton of Valamo, *The Art of Prayer*, pp. 134-135.
42. Ibid., p. 139.
43. St. Ephrem the Syrian, *Nisibene Hymns*, in *NPNF*, vol. 13, 36, pp. 196-197.
44. St. Isaac the Syrian, *Directions on Spiritual Training*, in Kadloubovsky and Palmer, *Philokalia: Early Fathers*, no. 16, p. 186.
45. St. John Climacus, *The Ladder of Divine Ascent*, step 6, 2, p. 110.
46. Ibid., step 6, 4, p. 110.
47. Ibid., step 6, 6, p. 110.
48. Ibid., step 6, 13, p. 111.
49. Ibid., step 6, 18, p. 112.
50. Aphrahat, *Select Demonstrations, XXII: Of Death*, in *NPNF*, 1, p. 402.
51. Nilus, *Sermo Asceticus*, in *PG*, 79, 1281D.
52. Pseudo-Macarius, *The Spiritual Homilies*, no. 47, pp. 216-217.
53. Ibid., no. 2, p. 34.
54. Nicholas Cabasilas, *The Life in Christ*, pp. 200-202.
55. Aphrahat, *Select Demonstrations: Of Monks*, in *NPNF*, 2, p. 365.
56. Evagrius Ponticus, pp. 57-78 passim.
57. Pseudo-Macarius, *The Spiritual Homilies*, Homily 26, 9, p. 149.
58. St. Diadochus of Photike, *On Spiritual Knowledge*, in Palmer *et al., The Philokalia*, no. 81, p. 282.
59. St. Gregory of Sinai, *Texts on Commandments* in Kadloubovsky and Palmer, *Philokalia: Writings*, no. 71, pp. 49-50.
60. St. Irenaeus, *Adversus Haereses*, in *ANF*, bk. 4, ch. 39, 2-3, pp. 522-523.
61. St. Athanasius, *Contra Gentes*, 8, in *NPNF*, p. 8.
62. St. Theophan the Recluse, *War with Passions*, in Igumen Chariton of Valamo, *The Art of Prayer*, p. 200.
63. St. Mark the Hermit, cited in Igumen Chariton of Valamo, *The Art of Prayer*, p. 201.
64. St. Theophan the Recluse, *War with Passions*, in Igumen Chariton of Valamo, *The Art of Prayer*, pp. 205-206.
65. St. Gregory of Sinai, *Texts on Commandments*, in Kadloubovsky and Palmer, *Philokalia: Writings*, nos. 77-79, pp. 50-51.
66. Ibid., no. 131, pp. 70-71.
67. Ibid., no. 37, 45.
68. St. Maximus the Confessor, *First Century on Love*, in Kadloubovsky and Palmer, *Philokalia: Early Fathers*, 67, p. 294.
69. St. Isaac the Syrian, *Directions on Spiritual Training*, in Kadloubovsky and Palmer, *Philokalia: Early Fathers*, no. 273, etc.

70. St. John Climacus, *The Ladder of Divine Ascent,* step 23, no. 1, p. 179.
71. Ibid., step 23, no. 9, p. 180.
72. Ibid., step 23, no. 16, p. 181.
73. Ibid., step 23, no. 30, p. 182.
74. Aphrahat, *Select Demonstrations, VI: Of Monks,* in *NPNF,* 9, p. 369.
75. St. Ephrem the Syrian, *Hymns on the Nativity,* in *NPNF,* Hymn 3, pp. 232-233.
76. St. Symeon the New Theologian, *The Discourses,* (N.Y.: Paulist Press, 1980), p. 49.
77. St. Gregory Nazianzus, *Oratio 8,* 17, in *NPNF,* vol. 7, p. 294.
78. St. Tychon of Zadonsk, *Confession and Thanksgiving to Christ,* in Fedotov, *A Treasury of Russian Spirituality,* pp. 216-217.
79. Nicholas Cabasilas, *A Commentary on the Divine Liturgy,* p. 47.
80. St. Irenaeus, *Adversus Haeresus,* bk. 3, ch. 18, 7, in *ANF,* p. 448.
81. St. Athanasius, *De Incarnatione,* 14, in *NPNF,* p. 43.
82. St. Gregory of Nyssa, *De Oratione Catech. Magna,* ch. 9, in *NPNF,* pp. 484-485.
83. St. Maximus the Confessor, *Mystagogia,* in *PG,* 91, 665-668.
84. St. Maximus, *Relatio Motionis,* in *PG,* 90, 12A.
85. St. Gregory of Nyssa, *Commentary on the Canticle of Canticles,* in *PG,* 44, 947-949.
86. Ibid., Sermon 13, in *PG,* 1045D-1047D.
87. St. Maximus the Confessor, *Contemplative and Active Texts,* in Kadloubovsky and Palmer, *Philokalia: Early Fathers,* no. 67, p. 361.
88. Nicholas Cabasilas, *The Life in Christ,* pp. 110-111.
89. Ibid., pp. 60-63.
90. St. Ephrem the Syrian, *Hymn of the Baptized,* in *NPNF,* p. 283.
91. St. Cyril of Jerusalem, *First Catechetical Lecture,* in *NPNF,* vol. VII, p. 7.
92. Ibid., *Lecture III,* in *NPNF,* vol. 7, 10, p. 16.
93. Nicholas Cabasilas, *The Life in Christ,* pp. 66-67.
94. Dionysius Pseudo-Areopagite, *The Ecclesiastical Hierarchies,* pp. 31-32.
95. St. Gregory Nazianzus, *Oration XL: On Holy Baptism,* in *NPNF,* vol. 7, p. 360.
96. Dionysius Pseudo-Areopagite, *The Ecclesiastical Hierarchies,* p. 65.
97. St. Symeon the New Theologian, *The Discourses,* pp. 302-303.
98. St. John Chrysostom, *Six Books on the Priesthead,* p. 86.
99. John Cronstadt, *My Life in Christ,* in Fedotov, *A Treasury of Russian Spirituality,* pp. 376-377.
100. Ibid., pp. 377-378.
101. Ibid., pp. 383-384.
102. St. Isaac the Syrian, *Directions on Spiritual Training,* in Kadloubovsky and Palmer, *Philokalia: Early Fathers,* no. 3, p. 183.
103. Ibid., no. 8, p. 184.
104. Ibid., no. 9, pp. 184-185.
105. Ibid., no. 202, p. 242.
106. Ibid., no. 265, p. 271.
107. Origen, *On First Principles,* ch. 2, 4, p. 182.
108. Pseudo-Macarius, *The Spiritual Homilies,* Homily 39, p. 195.
109. St. Athanasius, *Ad Serapionem,* I, 25, in *PG,* 26, 589B.
110. Ibid., IV, 21, in *PG,* 26, 672C.
111. Ibid., I, 30, in *PG,* 26, 600B.
112. St. Gregory of Nazianzus, *Oratio 31,* in *NPNF,* vol. 7, p. 327.
113. Origen, *De Principiis,* I, 3, 8, in *ANF,* p. 255.

114. St. Basil, *De Spiritu Sancto,* ch. 23, in *NPNF,* vol. 8, p. 38.
115. Ibid.
116. Ibid., ch. 26, 64, in *NPNF,* p. 40.
117. St. Cyril of Alexandria, *De Trinitate,* in *PG,* 75, 1088B.
118. Ibid., 609-612.
119. St. Symeon the New Theologian, *Traites Ethiques,* 495-500, p. 294.
120. St. Symeon the New Theologian, *Catecheses,* 79-84, p. 40.
121. St. Symeon the New Theologian, *Traites Theologiques,* 1, 200-215, pp. 110-112.
122. St. Symeon the New Theologian, *Traites Ethiques,* 6, 130-134, pp. 128-130.
123. St. Symeon the New Theologian, *Hymns of Divine Love,* Hymn 44, pp. 228-232.
124. Pseudo-Macarius, *The Spiritual Homilies,* Homily 18, pp. 124-125.
125. St. Diadochus of Photike, *On Spiritual Knowledge,* in Palmer et al., *The Philokalia: The Complete Text,* nos. 28-29, pp. 260-261.
126. Ibid., no. 90, p. 289.
127. The Monks Callistus and Ignatius, *Directions to Hesychasts,* in Kadloubovsky and Palmer, *The Philokalia: Writings,* pp. 243-244.
128. St. Theophan the Recluse, *The Fruits of Prayer,* cited in Igumen Chariton of Valamo, *The Art of Prayer,* p. 128.
129. St. John Climacus, *The Ladder of Divine Ascent,* step 26, 1, p. 201.
130. Ibid., step 26, 17-18, p. 204.
131. Ibid., step 26, 22, p. 205.
132. Ibid., step 26, 58, p. 210.
133. Ibid., step 26, 67, p. 211.
134. Ibid., step 26, 91, p. 215.
135. Ibid., step 26, 111, p. 218.
136. Ibid., step 26, 137, p. 222.
137. Ibid., step 26, 156, p. 226.
138. Ibid., step 26, 117, p. 226.
139. St. Isaac the Syrian, *Directions on Spiritual Training,* in Kadloubovsky and Palmer, *Philokalia: Early Fathers,* nos. 210-215, pp. 246-249.
140. Ibid., no. 218, p. 251.
141. St. Diadochus of Photike, *On Spiritual Knowledge,* Palmer et al., in *The Philokalia: The Complete Text,* no. 30, p. 265.
142. Ibid., nos. 37-38, pp. 264-265.
143. St. Theophan the Recluse, cited in Igumen Chariton of Valamo, *The Art of Prayer,* pp. 190-191.
144. Pseudo-Macarius, *The Spiritual Homilies,* Homily 15, p. 100.
145. St. John Cassian, *Conferences,* 10, ch. 11, *NPNF,* vol. 10, p. 408.
146. Bishop Ignatius Brianchaninov, cited in Igumen Chariton of Valamos, *The Art of Prayer,* p. 190.
147. St. Isaac the Syrian, *Directions on Spiritual Training,* in Kadloubovsky and Palmer, *Philokalia: Early Fathers,* no. 57, p. 198.
148. Ibid., no. 183, p. 237.
149. Ibid., no. 120, pp. 216-217.
150. St. Maximus the Confessor, *Mystagogia,* in *PG,* 91, 665-668.
151. St. Symeon the New Theologian, *The Discourses,* pp. 68-69.
152. John Cronstadt, *My Life in Christ,* in Fedotov, *A Treasury of Russian Spirituality,* pp. 403-405.
153. St. John Climacus, *The Ladder of Divine Ascent,* step 27, 2, p. 237.

154. Ibid., step 27, 3, p. 237.
155. Ibid., step 27, 5, p. 237.
156. Ibid., step 27, 12, p. 238.
157. Ibid., step 27, 14, p. 238.
158. Ibid., step 27, 26, p. 239.
159. St. Isaac the Syrian, *Directions on Spiritual Training*, in Kadloubovsky and Palmer, *Philokalia: Early Fathers*, 21, p. 187.
160. St. Maximus the Confessor, *First Century on Love*, in Kadloubovsky and Palmer, *Philokalia: Early Fathers*, 92, p. 297.
161. Ibid., *Second Century on Love*, in Kadloubovsky and Palmer, *Philokalia: Early Fathers*, 57, p. 309.
162. St. Maximus the Confessor, *Ambigua*, in *PG*, 91, 1081D.
163. Pseudo-Macarius, *Spiritual Homilies*, Homily 40, p. 196.
164. St. Athanasius, *Vita St. Antonii*, 5, in *NPNF*, p. 197.
165. St. Isaac the Syrian, *Directions on Spiritual Training*, in Kadloubovsky and Palmer, *Philokalia: Early Fathers*, 30, pp. 188-189.
166. Ibid., step 14, no. 14, p. 142.
167. Ibid., step 14, no. 19, p. 142.
168. Ibid., step 14, no. 21, pp. 142-143.
169. Ibid., step 14, no. 27, p. 143.
170. Ibid., step 14, no. 33, p. 144.
171. St. Symeon the New Theologian, *The Discourses*, pp. 168-169.
172. St. Nil Sorsky, *Ustav*, p. 83.
173. Evagrius Ponticus, *To Anatolius: On Eight Thoughts*, in Kadloubovsky and Palmer, *Philokalia: Early Fathers*, p. 110.
174. St. Theophan the Recluse, *War with Passions*, in Igumen Chariton of Valamo, *The Art of Prayer*, p. 220.
175. St. John Cassian, *The Institutes*, in *NPNF*, vol. 10, bk. 10, p. 266.
176. St. John Climacus, *The Ladder of Divine Ascent*, step 22, no. 2, p. 174.
177. Ibid., step 22, no. 5, p. 174.
178. Ibid., step 22, no. 12, p. 175.
179. Ibid., step 22, no. 16, p. 175.
180. Ibid., step 22, no. 23, p. 176.
181. Ibid., step 22, no. 35, pp. 177-178.
182. Ibid., step 2, no. 6, p. 58.
183. St. Isaac the Syrian, *Directions on Spiritual Training*, in Kadloubovsky and Palmer, *Philokalia: Early Fathers*, 129, p. 219.
184. Ibid., 180, p. 236.
185. St. Maximus the Confessor, *First Century on Love*, in Kadloubovsky and Palmer, *Philokalia: Early Fathers*, no. 52, p. 297.
186. Origen, *On Prayer*, in *ACW*, p. 125.
187. Evagrius Ponticus, *Chapters on Prayer*, 4, p. 56.
188. Evagrius, *To Anatolius: On Eight Thoughts*, in Kadloubovsky and Palmer, *Philokalia: Early Fathers*, p. 110.
189. Hesychius of Jerusalem, *Texts on Sobriety and Prayer*, in Kadloubovsky and Palmer, *Philokalia: Writings*, 44, pp. 288-289.
190. Ibid., 45-46, p. 289.
191. Philotheus of Sinai, *Forty Texts*, in Kadloubovsky and Palmer, *Philokalia: Writings*, nos. 22-24, pp. 333-334.
192. Ibid., no. 26, pp. 334-335.
193. St. John Climacus, *The Ladder of Divine Ascent*, step 15, no. 6, p. 147.

194. Ibid., step 15, no. 10, p. 147.
195. St. John Cassian, *On the Holy Fathers of Sketis and on Discrimination*, in Palmer *et al.*, *The Philokalia: The Complete Text*, pp. 95-96.
196. St. Isaac the Syrian, *Directions on Spiritual Training*, in Kadloubovsky and Palmer, *Philokalia: Early Fathers*, p. 189.
197. St. Gregory of Nyssa, *The Lord's Prayer*, in ACW, vol. 18, pp. 24-25.
198. Ibid., pp. 28-29.
199. St. John Climacus, *The Ladder of Divine Ascent*, step 28, 1, p. 250.
200. Ibid., step 28, no. 5, p. 251.
201. Ibid., step 28, no. 6, p. 251.
202. Ibid., step 28, no. 10, p. 251.
203. Ibid., step 28, no. 17, p. 252.
204. Ibid., step 28, no. 19, p. 252.
205. Ibid., step 28, no. 31, p. 254.
206. St. Maximus the Confessor, *Second Century on Love*, in Kadloubovsky and Palmer, *Philokalia: Early Fathers*, 61, p. 309.
207. Evagrius Ponticus, *Chapters on Prayer*, pp. 56-80 passim.
208. St. John Cassian, *Conferences*, in NPNF, vol. 10, ch. 11.
209. Nicephorus, *Three Methods of Attention and Prayer*, in Kadloubovsky and Palmer, *Philokalia: Writings*, pp. 152-159. This selection is falsely attributed to Symeon the New Theologian. For true authorship, see: *Orientalia Christiana Periodica* vol. 6 (Rome: Pontifical Oriental Institute, 1927), pp. 109-210.
210. St. Isaac the Syrian, *Directions on Spiritual Training*, in Kadloubovsky and Palmer, *Philokalia: Early Fathers*, 29, p. 188.
211. Ibid., 272, p. 274.
212. St. Maximus the Confessor, *Second Century on Love*, in Kadloubovsky and Palmer, *Philokalia: Early Fathers*, 6, pp. 299-300.
213. St. Maximus the Confessor, *First Century on Love*, in Kadloubovsky and Palmer, *Philokalia: Early Fathers*, 94, p. 298.
214. St. Nil Sorsky, *Ustav*, p. 28, cited from the critical text of M. A. Borovkova-Maikova. Translation mine.
215. St. Maximus the Confessor, *Contemplative and Active Texts*, in Kadloubovsky and Palmer, *Philokalia: Early Fathers*, 77, p. 363.
216. St. Gregory Nazianzus, *Fifth Theological Oration: On the Holy Spirit*, in NPNF, p. 326.
217. St. Athanasius, *The First Letter to Serapion*, 28-30, in PG, 26, 595-599.
218. St. Maximus the Confessor, *Second Century on Love*, in Kadloubovsky and Palmer, *Philokalia: Early Fathers*, 29, pp. 303-304.
219. St. Symeon the New Theologian, *Hymns of Divine Love*, Hymn 12, pp. 39-40.
220. St. Gregory of Sinai, *Texts*, in Kadloubovsky and Palmer, *Philokalia: Writings*, nos. 29-32, pp. 43-44.
221. St. Didymus of Alexandria, *De Spiritu Sancto*, n. 25, in PG, 39, 1055-1056.
222. St. Cyril of Alexandria, *Commentary on the Gospel of St. John*, in PG, 74, 293.
223. Ibid., 553-561.
224. St. Isaac the Syrian, *Directions on Spiritual Training*, in Kadloubovsky and Palmer, *Philokalia: Early Fathers*, 42-45, pp. 192-194.
225. Dionysius Pseudo-Areopagite, *Mystical Theology*, p. 130.
226. Ibid., p. 132.
227. St. Gregory of Nyssa, *Canticle of Canticles*, in PG, 44, 1000D, quoted and translated by Musurillo, *From Glory to Glory*, p. 247.
228. St. Gregory of Nyssa, *Commentary on the Canticle of Canticles*, in PG, 44, 1001B.

229. St. Gregory of Nyssa, *Commentary on Ecclesiastes, Sermon 7,* in *PG,* 44, 724D-723D, quoted in Musurillo, *From Glory to Glory,* p. 128.

230. St. Gregory of Nyssa, *Life of Moses,* in *PG,* 44, 376C-377A, cited in Musurillo, *From Glory to Glory,* p. 118.

231. Dionysius Pseudo-Areopagite, *Mystical Theology,* p. 131.

232. St. Gregory Palamas, *Triade* II, 3, 26, in Palamas, *Les Triades.*

233. St. Diadochus of Photike, *On Spiritual Knowledge,* in Palmer *et al., The Philokalia: The Complete Text,* nos. 68-72, pp. 275-277.

234. St. Maximus the Confessor, *Contemplative and Active Texts,* in Kadloubovsky and Palmer, *Philokalia: Early Fathers,* p. 348, no. 8.

235. *The Pilgrim,* in Fedotov, *A Treasury of Russian Spirituality,* pp. 309-310.

236. *A Conversation of St. Seraphim of Sarov with Motovilov,* in Fedotov, *A Treasury of Russian Spirituality,* pp. 274-275.

237. The Monks Callistus and Ignatius, *Directions to Hesychasts,* in Kadloubovsky and Palmer, *Philokalia: Writings,* p. 173.

238. Hesychius of Jerusalem, *Texts on Sobriety and Prayer,* in Kadloubovsky and Palmer, *Philokalia: Writings,* p. 279.

239. The Monks Callistus and Ignatius, *Directions to Hesychasts,* in Kadloubovsky and Palmer, *Philokalia: Writings,* pp. 253-254.

240. St. Gregory of Sinai, *Instructions to Hesychasts,* in Kadloubovsky and Palmer, *Philokalia: Writings,* pp. 74-75.

241. The Monks Callistus and Ignatius, *Directions to Hesychasts,* in Kadloubovsky and Palmer, *Philokalia: Writings,* pp. 192-193.

242. Ibid., pp. 193-194.

243. Ignatius Brianchaninov, *On the Prayer of Jesus,* p. 18.

244. St. Theophan the Recluse, cited in Igumen Chariton of Valamo, *The Art of Prayer,* p. 270.

245. Ignatius Brianchaninov, *On the Prayer of Jesus,* p. 95.

246. *The Pilgrim,* in Fedotov, *A Treasury of Russian Spirituality,* pp. 309-310.

247. St. Theophan the Recluse, cited in Igumen Chariton of Valamo, *The Art of Prayer,* p. 92.

248. Evagrius Ponticus, *On Prayer,* nos. 5, 6, and 7, in Palmer *et al., The Philokalia: The Complete Text,* vol. 1, p. 58.

249. Abba Poemen, cited in Budge, *The Wit and Wisdom of the Christian Fathers of Egypt,* no. 154, p. 44.

250. St. John Climacus, *The Ladder of Divine Ascent,* step 7, 6, p. 114.

251. Ibid, step 7, 23, p. 116.

252. St. Isaac the Syrian, *Directions on Spiritual Training,* in Kadloubovsky and Palmer, *Philokalia: Early Fathers,* pp. 251-252.

253. St. Symeon the New Theologian, in *PG,* 120, 640D.

254. St. Symeon the New Theologian, *Practical and Theological Precepts,* in Kadloubovsky and Palmer, *Philokalia: Writings,* p. 113.

255. St. Symeon the New Theologian, *Chapitres Théologiques, Gnostiques et Pratiques,* 3, 23, 1-7, p. 87.

256. St. Isaac the Syrian, *Logos 91,* "Concerning the Distinctions of Virtues," in Spanos, *Apanta,* p. 306. Translation mine.

257. Ibid., p. 308.

258. Nicholas Cabasilas, *A Commentary on the Divine Liturgy,* p. 47.

259. St. John Chrysostom, *Homily 15,* 6, in *PG,* 60, 547-548.

260. St. John Climacus, *The Ladder of Divine Ascent,* step 5, 1, p. 98.

261. Ibid., step 5, 30, p. 108.

262. Ibid., step 5, 38, p. 109.

263. St. Symeon the New Theologian, *The Discourses*, pp. 90-91.
264. St. Theophan the Recluse, cited in Igumen Chariton of Valamo, *The Art of Prayer*, pp. 124.
265. The Monks Callistus and Ignatius, *Directions to Hesychasts*, in Kadloubovsky and Palmer, *Philokalia: Writings*, p. 250.
266. Ibid., p. 195.
267. Nicephorus the Solitary, *Profitable Discourse on Sobriety*, in Kadloubovsky and Palmer, *Philokalia: Writings*, p. 32.
268. St. Symeon the New Theologian, *Traites Ethiques*, 11, 167, 177, pp. 340-342.
269. St. Symeon the New Theologian, *Hymns of Divine Love*, no. 15, pp. 288-292.
270. John Cronstadt, *My Life in Christ*, in Fedotov, *A Treasury of Russian Spirituality*, pp. 405-406.
271. St. Maximus the Confessor, *Contemplative and Active Texts*, in Kadloubovsky and Palmer, *Philokalia: Early Fathers*, no. 66, p. 361.
272. *Byzantine Liturgy of St. John Chrysostom*, tr. and ed. by Russian Center, pp. 57-58.
273. Prayer attributed to St. Simeon Metaphrastes, found in the *Prayers after Communion* of the Russian Center's *Byzantine Liturgy of St. John Chrysostom*, pp. 80-81.
274. Nicholas Cabasilas, *The Life in Christ*, p. 193.
275. St. Ignatius of Antioch, *Letter to the Romans*, in Jurgens, *The Faith of the Early Fathers*, 4, 1, pp. 21-22.
276. Ibid., 7, 3, p. 22.
277. St. John Chrysostom, *Commentary on St. John the Evangelist*, Homilies 1-47, Homily 46, pp. 468-469.
278. St. Symeon the New Theologian, *Hymns of Divine Love*, Hymn 30, pp. 169-170.
279. St. Cyril of Alexandria, *In Ioannem*, in *PG*, 74, 11, 560.
280. St. Cyril of Alexandria, *In Mattheum*, 26, 27, in *PG*, 72, 452C.
281. St. Cyril of Alexandria, *In Ioannem*, in *PG*, 73, 4, 2, 577.
282. Nazarus of Valaam, in S. Tyszkiewiez, S. J., *Ascetes Russes*, p. 54.
283. St. Symeon the New Theologian, *The Discourses*, p. 56.
284. Ibid., pp. 195-196.
285. Ibid., pp. 200-201.
286. *Phos Hilaron*, an ancient hymn sung daily in Byzantine Vespers.
287. St. Seraphim of Sarov, cited by M. Behr-Sigel in *La Prière à Jesus*, p. 87.
288. Pseudo-Macarius, Homily 44, *The Spiritual Homilies*, p. 205.
289. Nicholas Cabasilas, *Vita in Christo*, 7, in *PG*, 150, 685.
290. St. Maximus the Confessor, *Ambigua*, in *PG*, 91, 1305C-1308C.
291. St. Gregory Palamas, cited by Basil Krivoshein, in "The Ascetical and Theological Teaching of Gregory Palamas," p. 15.
292. St. Gregory Nazianzus, *Oratio 38*, 12, in *NPNF*, vol. 7, p. 348.
293. Metropolitan Philaret of Moscow in *Choix de Sermons et Discours de S. Em. Mgr. Philarete*, translated from Russian by A. Serpinet, 1 (Paris, 1886), pp. 3-4; cited by John Meyendorff in *St. Gregory Palamas and Orthodox Spirituality*, p. 127.
294. Budge, *The Wit and Wisdom of the Christian Fathers of Egypt*, no. 303, p. 88.
295. Nicholas Cabasilas, *The Life in Christ*, pp. 146-147.
296. Aphrahat, *Select Demonstrations, VIII: Of the Resurrection of the Dead*, in *NPNF*, 25, p. 383.
297. St. John Chrysostom, *On the Pasch*, in *PG*, 50, 437.

298. St. Proclus, Patriarch of Constantinople, *On the Holy Pasch*, in *PG*, 57, 795.
299. Hirmos of the Easter Service of the Byzantine Rite, attributed to St. John Damascene, cited from *Byzantine Daily Worship*, p. 855.
300. St. Symeon the New Theologian, *The Discourses*, pp. 183-184.
301. Dionysius Pseudo-Areopagite, *The Ecclesiastical Hierarchies*, p. 74.
302. Aphrahat, *Select Demonstrations VI: Of Monks*, in *NPNF*, pp. 363-365.
303. St. Symeon the New Theologian, *The Discourses*, pp. 63-64.
304. St. Nil Sorsky, *The Monastic Rule*, in Fedotov, *A Treasury of Russian Spirituality*, p. 131.
305. *Letter to Diognetus*, in Jurgens, *The Faith of the Early Fathers*, in Kadloubovsky and Palmer, *Philokalia: Early Fathers*, 5, 1, pp. 40-41.
306. St. Isaac the Syrian, *Directions on Spiritual Training*, nos. 22-23, p. 187.
307. Pseudo-Macarius, *The Spiritual Homilies*, Homily 5, 1, 11, pp. 51, 61.
308. St. Symeon the New Theologian, *The Discourses*, pp. 57-58.
309. Ibid., pp. 109-110.
310. Aphrahat, *Select Demonstrations, XXI: Of Persecution*, in *NPNF*, 23, pp. 401-402.
311. Origen, *Exhortation to Martyrdom*, pp. 172, 174, 176, 177.
312. St. Gregory Nazianzus, *Oratio 39: On the Holy Lights*, p. 358.
313. St. John Climacus, *The Ladder of Divine Ascent*, step 1, 7, p. 51.
314. Ibid., step 4, 6, pp. 67-68.
315. Ibid., step 4, 74, p. 87.
316. St. Symeon the New Theologian, *The Discourses*, pp. 232-233.
317. Ibid., p. 283.
318. St. Isaac the Syrian, *Directions on Spiritual Training* in Kadloubovsky and Palmer, *Philokalia: Early Fathers*, no. 67, p. 201.
319. Ibid., no. 70, p. 202.
320. Ibid., no. 71, pp. 202-203.
321. Ibid., no. 248, p. 264.
322. Ibid., no. 236, pp. 258-259.
323. St. Diadochus of Photike, *On Spiritual Knowledge* in Palmer et al., *The Philokalia: The Complete Text*, no. 94, pp. 291-292.
324. St. Isaac the Syrian, *Directions on Spiritual Training*, in Kadloubovsky and Palmer, *Philokalia: Early Fathers*, 225, p. 255.
325. St. John Climacus, *The Ladder of Divine Ascent*, step 4, 3, pp. 66-67.
326. Ibid., step 4, 7, p. 68.
327. Ibid., step 4, 61, p. 85.
328. Ibid., step 4, 105, pp. 91-92.
329. St. Gregory of Nyssa, *The Lord's Prayer*, in *ACW*, pp. 58-59.
330. St. Isaac the Syrian, in Kadloubovsky and Palmer, *Philokalia: Early Fathers, Directions on Spiritual Training*, 136, pp. 221-222.
331. St. Philotheus of Sinai, *Forty Texts on Sobriety*, in Kadloubovsky and Palmer, *Philokalia: Writings*, 16, pp. 329-330.
332. St. Isaac the Syrian, *Directions on Spiritual Training*, in Kadloubovsky and Palmer, *Philokalia: Early Fathers*, no. 100, pp. 210-211.
333. Ibid., no. 106, p. 212.
334. Ibid., no. 115, p. 215.
335. Ibid., no. 131, p. 220.
336. Ibid., no. 133, p. 221.
337. Ibid., no. 164, p. 232.
338. St. John Climacus, *The Ladder of Divine Ascent*, step 25, 3, pp. 190-191.

339. Ibid., step 25, no. 10, p. 193.
340. Ibid., step 25, no. 14, p. 193.
341. Ibid., step 25, no. 16, pp. 193–194.
342. Ibid., step 25, no. 19, p. 194.
343. Ibid., step 25, no. 30, p. 195.
344. Philotheus of Sinai, *Forty Texts*, in Kadloubovsky and Palmer, *Philokalia: Writings*, no. 13, p. 327.
345. Aphrahat, *Selected Demonstrations: On Faith*, in *NPNF*, vol. 13, pp. 345–346.
346. Ibid., no. 3, p. 346.
347. Ibid., no. 18, pp. 351–352.
348. St. Gregory of Sinai, in Kadloubovsky and Palmer, *Philokalia: Writings, Texts on Commandments*, no. 119, p. 65.
349. Clement of Alexandria, *Stromateis or Miscellanies*, cited by Jurgens in *The Faith of the Early Fathers*, p. 182.
350. Ibid., p. 182.
351. St. Isaac the Syrian, *Directions on Spiritual Training*, in Kadloubovsky and Palmer, *Philokalia: Early Fathers*, no. 281, p. 277.
352. St. Maximus the Confessor, *Contemplative and Active Texts*, in Kadloubovsky and Palmer, *Philokalia: Early Fathers*, p. 368.
353. St. Cyril of Jerusalem, *Lecture XV*, in *NPNF*, no. 1, p. 104.
354. John Cronstadt, *My Life in Christ*, in Fedotov, *A Treasury of Russian Spirituality*, pp. 405–406.
355. St. Maximus the Confessor, *Centuries on Love*, in Kadloubovsky and Palmer, *Philokalia: Early Fathers*, nos. 1, 10, pp. 287–288.
356. Ibid., no. 13, p. 288.
357. Ibid., no. 23, p. 289.
358. Ibid., no. 40, p. 290.
359. Ibid., no. 71, p. 294.
360. Ibid., no. 1, p. 300.
361. Ibid., no. 9, p. 300.
362. Ibid., no. 10, p. 300.
363. Ibid., no. 30, p. 304.
364. Ibid., no. 48, p. 307.
365. Ibid., no. 100, p. 332.
366. Ibid., no. 40, p. 338.
367. Ibid., no. 100, p. 346.
368. St. Isaac the Syrian, *Directions on Spiritual Training*, in Kadloubovsky and Palmer, *Philokalia: Early Fathers*, no. 53, p. 197.
369. Ibid., no. 149, pp. 227–228.
370. Ibid., no. 234, p. 258.
371. St. Symeon the New Theologian, *The Discourses*, p. 45.
372. Bar Hebraeus, *Book of the Dove*, pp. 100–102.
373. St. Maximus the Confessor, *First Century on Love*, in Kadloubovsky and Palmer, *Philokalia: Early Fathers*, 24, 26, p. 289.
374. St. Diadochus of Photike, *On Spiritual Knowledge*, in Palmer et al., *The Philokalia*, no. 66, pp. 274–275.
375. John Cronstadt, *My Life*, in *A Treasury*, pp. 403–405.
376. St. Isaac the Syrian, *Directions on Spiritual Training*, in Kadloubovsky and Palmer, *Philokalia: Early Fathers*, no. 7, p. 184.
377. St. Maximus the Confessor, *First Century on Love*, in Kadloubovsky and Palmer, *Philokalia: Early Fathers*, no. 45, p. 291.
378. St. John Climacus, *The Ladder of Divine Ascent*, step 15, 60, p. 155.

379. Ibid., step 15, 3, p. 146.
380. Ibid., step 2, 1, pp. 56-57.
381. Ibid., step 2, 1, pp. 58-59.
382. Ibid., step 2, 9, p. 59.
383. *Didache*, in Jurgens, *The Faith of the Early Fathers*, no. 14, 1, 3, p. 4.
384. The Priest's Prayer before the Great Entrance of St. John, The Russian Center's *The Byzantine Liturgy of St. John Chrysostom*, pp. 36-37.
385. John Cronstadt, *My Life in Christ*, in Fedotov, *A Treasury of Russian Spirituality*, pp. 353-354.
386. Ibid., p. 378.
387. Leontius of Neapolis, *Veneration of Icons*, in *PG*, 94, 1384D.
388. St. John Damascene, *On Icons*, 1, 16, in *PG*, 94, 1245A.
389. Ibid.
390. *Evkholohion ily Terbnyk (Book of Blessings and Rituals)*, pp. 436-438. My translation.
391. The Homilies of *The Annunciation*, in Mango, *The Homilies of Photius, Patriarch of Constantinople*, pp. 120-121.
392. Ibid., Homily IX: *The Birth of the Virgin*, pp. 174-176.
393. St. Maximus the Confessor, in Kadloubovsky and Palmer, *Philokalia: Early Fathers, Contemplative and Active Texts*, 79, pp. 363-364.
394. St. Ephrem the Syrian, *Hymns on the Nativity*, Hymn XI to the Virgin Mary, in *NPNF*, p. 245.
395. St. Gregory of Nyssa, *The Lord's Prayer*, in *ACW*, vol. 18, p. 23.
396. St. Basil, *Regulae Fusius*, in *PG*, 31, Regula 5, 920C-921B.
397. Budge, *The Wit and Wisdom of the Christian Fathers of Egypt*, no. 130, p. 38.
398. Pseudo-Macarius, *The Spiritual Homilies*, Homily 26, p. 150.
399. Father Yelchaninov, in Fedotov, *A Treasury of Russian Spirituality*, p. 463.
400. St. Diadochus of Photike, *On Spiritual Knowledge*, in Palmer et al., *The Philokalia: The Complete Text*, no. 20, p. 258.
401. St. John Moschus, *Pratum Spirituale (The Spiritual Meadow)*, in *Vitae Patrum*, X, as cited by Waddell, *The Desert Fathers*, pp. 168-169.
402. John Cronstadt, *My Life in Christ*, in Fedotov, *A Treasury of Russian Spirituality*, p. 393.
403. Father Yelchaninov, *Fragments of a Diary*, in Fedotov, *A Treasury of Russian Spirituality*, pp. 429-430.
404. Ibid., p. 446.
405. Ibid., p. 476.
406. Clement of Alexandria, *Stromata*, cited in Jurgens, *The Faith of the Early Fathers*, p. 182.
407. St. Maximus the Confessor, *Ambigua*, in *PG*, 91, 1305C-1308C.
408. Father Yelchaninov, *Fragments of a Diary*, in Fedotov, *A Treasury of Russian Spirituality*, p. 464.
409. St. Cyril of Jerusalem, Lecture XV, in *NPNF*, nos. 3-4, p. 105.
410. Dionysius Pseudo-Areopagite, *The Ecclesiastical Hierarchy*, pp. 18-19.
411. *Troparion* for Mondays, dedicated to the holy angels.
412. *Kontakion* for Mondays, in Raya, *Byzantine Daily Worship*, pp. 405-406.
413. St. Gregory of Nyssa, *The Life of Moses*, in *PG*, 44, 405A.
414. St. Gregory of Nyssa, *Commentary on the Canticle of Canticles*, in *PG*, 44, 776A-777C.
415. St. Gregory of Sinai, *Texts*, in Kadloubovsky and Palmer, *Philokalia: Writings*, no. 42, pp. 45-46.
416. Ibid., no. 43, p. 46.

417. St. Cyril of Jerusalem, *Lecture XV,* in *NPNF,* no. 1, p. 104.
418. Ibid., p. 110, no. 19.
419. Ibid., p. 112, no. 26.
420. St. Gregory of Sinai, *Texts,* in Kadloubovsky and Palmer, *Philokalia: Writings,* no. 29-32, pp. 43-44.
421. Ibid., no. 49, p. 47.
422. Ibid., no. 54, p. 47.
423. Ibid., no. 56, p. 47.
424. Aphrahat, *Select Demonstrations, XXII: On Death and the Latter Times,* in *NPNF,* 22, p. 409.
425. St. Gregory of Sinai, *Texts,* in Kadloubovsky and Palmer, *Philokalia: Writings,* no. 34, p. 44.

BIBLIOGRAPHY

*Ancient Christian Writers [ACW].** Westminster, Md.: Newman Press.
  a. Vol. 18. St. Gregory of Nyssa. *The Lord's Prayer; The Beatitudes.* Translated by H. Graef. 1954.
  b. Vol. 19. Origen. *Prayer; Exhortation to Martyrdom.* Translated by John J. O'Meara. 1954.
  c. Vol. 21. St. Maximus the Confessor. *Four Centuries on Charity.* 1955.

Aumann, Jordan, O.P., ed. *Christian Spirituality East and West.* Chicago: Priory Press, 1968.

Bar Hebraeus. *Book of the Dove.* Translated by A. J. Wensinck. Leyden: Brill, 1919.

St. Basil. *Homily on Ps. 48.* Fathers of the Church series, vol. 46. Washington, D.C.: Catholic University of America, 1963.

Behr-Sigel, M. *La Prière à Jesus.* Dieu Vivant series, no. 8. Paris: Seuil, 1948.

Borovkova-Maikova, M. A. *Nila Sorskago Predanie i Ustav s vsupital' noi stat'ei.* In *Pamiatniki drevai mennosti* 179. St. Petersburg, 1912.

Bouyer, Louis. *The Spirituality of the New Testament and the Fathers.* New York: Desclée, 1963.

*Brianchaninov, Bishop Ignatius. *On the Prayer of Jesus.* Translated by Father Lazarus Moore. London: Watkins, 1952.

Budge, E. A. Wallis, comp. and trans. *The Wit and Wisdom of the Christian Fathers of Egypt.* London: Oxford University Press, 1934.

Cabasilas, Nicholas. *A Commentary on the Divine Liturgy.* Translated by J. M. Hussey and P. A. McNulty. London: S.P.C.K., 1960.

Cabasilas, Nicholas. *The Life in Christ.* Translated by C. J. de Catanzaro. Crestwood, N.Y.: St. Vladimir's Seminary Press, 1974.

St. John Chrysostom. *Commentary on St. John the Evangelist,* Homilies 1–47. Translated by Sr. Thomas Aquinas Coggin, S.C.H. Fathers of the Church series. New York: Fathers of the Church, 1957.

St. John Chrysostom. *Six Books on the Priesthood.* Translated by Graham Neville. London: S.P.C.K., 1964.

St. John Climacus. *The Ladder of Divine Ascent.* Translated by Archimandrite Lazarus Moore. London: Faber & Faber, 1959.

Danielou, J. and Herbert Musurillo, S.J., eds. *From Glory to Glory: Texts*

---

*Titles that are provided with acronyms (e.g., *ACW*) are referred to by those acronyms in the Notes.

   from Gregory of Nyssa's Mystical Writings. New York: Scribner's, 1961.

Dictionnaire de Spiritualité. Paris: Beauchesne, 1960.

Oeuvres spirituelles: Cent Chapitres Gnostiques. Diadochus of Photike. Edited and translated by E. des Places, S.J. In Sources Chrétiénnes, vol. 5. Paris: Cerf, 1955.

Dorr, F. Diadochus von Photike und die Messalianer, Ein Kampf Zwischen wahrer und falschen Mystik im funften Jahrhundert. In Freiburger Theologische Studien 47. Fribourg-en-Brisgau, 1937.

Evagrius Ponticus. The Praktikos/Chapters on Prayer. Translated by John Eudes Bamberger, O.C.S.O. Cistercian Studies series, no. 4. Spencer, Mass: Cistercian Publications, 1970.

Evkholohion ily Terbnyk (Book of Blessings and Rituals). Translated by G. A. Maloney, S.J. N.P.: Khovkva, Ukraine, 1926.

Fedotov, G. P., ed. A Treasury of Russian Spirituality. New York: Sheed & Ward, 1948.

Festugiere, A. Contemplation et vie contemplative chez Platon. Paris: Cerf, 1958.

Gardet, M. L. "La mention du nom divin en mystique musulmane." In Revue Thomiste 3 (1952).

Gouillard, J. Petite Philocalie de la Prière du Couer. In Documents Spirituels, vol. 5. Paris: Cerf, 1953.

Habra, G. "The Patristic Sources of the Doctrine of Gregory Palamas on the Divine Energies." In Eastern Churches Quarterly 12 (1957-1958).

Hausherr, I., S.J. "La Methode d'oraison hesychastes." In Orientalia Christiana Periodica 9, no. 36 (1927).

Hausherr, I., S.J. "L'erreur fondamentale et la logique du Messalinisme." In Orientalia Christiana Periodica 17, no. 1 (1935).

Igumen Chariton of Valamo, compiler. The Art of Prayer: An Orthodox Anthology. Translated by E. Kadloubovsky and G. E. H. Palmer. London: Faber & Faber, 1966.

Jaeger, Werner. Early Christianity and Greek Paideia. Cambridge, England: Cambridge University Press, 1961.

Jurgens, W. A., ed. and trans. The Faith of the Early Fathers. Collegeville, Minn.: Liturgical Press, 1970.

Kadloubovsky, E., and G. E. H. Palmer, trans. Philokalia: Early Fathers from the Philokalia. London: Faber & Faber, 1954.

Kadloubovsky, E., and G. E. H. Palmer, trans. Philokalia: Writings from the Philokalia on Prayer of the Heart. London: Faber & Faber, 1951.

Krivoshein, Basil. "The Ascetical and Theological Teaching of Gregory Palamas." In Eastern Churches Quarterly 3 (1938-1939).

Lossky, Vladimir. Mystical Theology of the Eastern Church. Naperville, Ill.: Allenson, 1957.

Maloney, George A., S.J. The Mystic of Fire and Light. Denville, N.J.: Dimension Books, 1975.

Maloney, G. A., S.J. *Russian Hesychasm*. The Hague: Mouton, 1973.

Mango, Cyril, trans. *The Homilies of Photius, Patriarch of Constantinople*. Cambridge, Mass.: Harvard University Press, 1958.

Meyendorff, John. *A Study of Gregory Palamas*. Translated by G. Lawrence. Aylesbury, Bucks: Faith Press, 1964.

Meyendorff, John. *St. Gregory Palamas and Orthodox Spirituality*. Translated by Adele Fiske. Crestwood, N.Y.: St. Vladimir's Seminary Press, 1974.

Migne, J. P., ed. *Patrologia Graeca (PG)*. Paris, 1844.

Migne, J. P., ed. *Patrologia Latina (PL)*. Paris, 1857–1866.

Miguel, P. "La Conscience de la grace selon Symeon le Nouveau Théologian." In *Irenikon* 42 (1969).

St. John Moschus. "Pratum Spirituale (The Spiritual Meadow)." In *Vitae Patrum*, X, as cited by Helen Waddell in *The Desert Fathers*. Ann Arbor: Ann Arbor Paperbacks, University of Michigan Press, 1936.

O'Brien, Elmer, S.J. *Varieties of Mystic Experience*. New York: Holt, Rinehart & Winston, 1964.

Origen. *Exhortation to Martyrdom; Prayer, First Principles*. Translated by Rowan A. Greer. The Classics of Western Spirituality series. New York: Paulist Press, 1979.

St. Gregory Palamas. *Les Triades pour la defense des Saints Hesychastes*. Edited by John Meyendorff. 3 vols. Louvain: Spicilegium Sacrum Lovaniense, 1959.

Palmer, G. E. H., Philip Sherrard, Kallistos Ware, *et al.*, eds. and trans. *The Philokalia: The Complete Text,* vol. 1. London: Faber & Faber, 1979.

St. Philotheus. *Forty Texts on Sobriety*. In *Dobrotoliubie,* T.3. Moscow, 1888. (Translated by G. A. Maloney, S.J.)

Pseudo-Areopagite, Dionysius. *The Ecclesiastical Hierarchies*. Translated by Thomas L. Campbell. Washington, D.C.: University Press of America, 1981.

Pseudo-Areopagite, Dionysius. *Mystical Theology*. In *The Works of Dionysius the Areopagite,* by John Parker. New York: Richmond, 1976.

Pseudo-Macarius. *The Spiritual Homilies*. Translated by G. A. Maloney, S.J. as *Intoxicated with God: The Spiritual Homilies of Pseudo-Macarius*. Denville, N.J.: Dimension Books, 1978.

Raya, Archbishop Joseph, and Jose de Vinck, eds. *Byzantine Daily Worship*. Allendale, N.J.: Alleluia Press, 1969.

Roberts, A., and J. Donaldson, eds. *The Ante-Nicene Fathers (ANF)*. Grand Rapids, Mich.: Eerdmans, n.d.
  a. Vol. 1: *Writings of St. Irenaeus.*
  b. Vol. 2: *Writings of Clement and Origen.*

Russian Center, ed. and trans. *The Byzantine Liturgy of St. John Chrysostom*. New York: Fordham University, 1955.

Schaff, Philip, and Henry Wace, trans. *The Nicene and Post-Nicene Fathers (NPNF)*. 2nd series. Grand Rapids, Mich.: Eerdmans, n.d.

a. Vol. 4. *Writings of St. Athanasius: Select Works and Letters.*
b. Vol. 5. *Dogmatic Treatises, etc. of St. Gregory of Nyssa.*
c. Vol. 7. *St. Cyril of Jerusalem and St. Gregory Nazianzus.*
d. Vol. 8. *St. Basil.*
e. Vol. 10. *St. John Cassian.*
f. Vol. 13. *Ephrem the Syrian and Aphrahat.*

Schmemann, Rev. Alexander. *Sacraments and Orthodoxy.* New York: Herder & Herder, 1965.

Spanos, ed. *Apanta.* Athens: Spanos, 1955.

Spidlik, J., S.J. *Joseph de Volokolamsk: Un Chapitre de la spiritualité russe.* Rome: Pontifical Oriental Institute, 1956.

St. Nil Sorsky. *Ustav (Rule).* Cited and translated by G. A. Maloney, S.J., in *Russian Hesychasm.* The Hague: Mouton, 1973.

St. Symeon the New Theologian. *Catecheses.* Translated by Archbishop Basile Krivocheine. *Sources Chrétiénnes* series, vol. 104. Paris: Cerf, 1964.

St. Symeon the New Theologian. *Chapitres Théologiques, Gnostiques et Pratiques.* Translated by Jean Darrouzes, A.A. *Sources Chrétiénnes* series, vol. 51. Paris: Cerf, 1960.

St. Symeon the New Theologian. *The Discourses.* Translated by C. J. Catanzaro. New York: Paulist Press, 1980.

St. Symeon the New Theologian. *Hymns of Divine Love.* Translated by G. A. Maloney, S.J. Denville, N.J.: Dimension Books, 1973.

St. Symeon the New Theologian. *Traites Ethiques.* Translated by Jean Darrouzes, A.A. *Sources Chrétiénnes* series, vol. 129. Paris: Cerf, 1967.

St. Symeon the New Theologian. *Traites Théologiques. (TT).* Translated by Jean Darrouzes, A.A. *Sources Chrétiénnes* series, vol. 122. Paris: Cerf, 1966.

Tyszkiewiez, S., S.J., ed. and trans. *Ascetes Russes.* Namur, Belgium: Les Editions du Soleil Levant, 1957.

Vanneste, J., S.J., *Le Mystere de Dieu: Essai sur la structure rationelle de la doctrine mystique du Pseudo-Denys l'Areopagite.* Paris: Cerf, 1959.